AF361575

Aquinas on Prophecy

Aquinas on Prophecy

Wisdom and Charism in the
Summa Theologiae

Paul M. Rogers

The Catholic University of America Press
Washington, D.C.

Cataloging-in-Publication Data available from the Library of Congress

ISBN: 978-0-8132-3679-7

eISBN: 978-0-8132-3680-3

For my mother and father

Contents

Acknowledgments

Inspiration for this book stems from doctoral research supervised by Dr. Anna Williams and Prof. Janet Soskice at the University of Cambridge; I am indebted to them for their guidance and encouragement when it came to developing my thinking on prophecy further. Another major stimulus for this study came from a year-long *Summa theologiae* Seminar taught by Prof. Thomas D'Andrea. I am most grateful to him for this formative introduction to Thomistic thought and for many conversations since, as well as for the invitation to join as a Research Associate the Centre for the Study of Philosophy, Politics, and Religion (CSPPR) in Cambridge which he founded. Prof. Catherine Pickstock generously commented on earlier drafts of this manuscript and offered some very useful advice. I thank Profs. Simon Oliver, Brian FitzGerald, Anna Bonta Moreland, William McCormick, SJ, and the two anonymous readers at CUA Press for their generous comments on previous versions. Whatever shortcomings found in this book are in no way attributable to them.

As a Visiting Fellow at Cambridge's Faculty of Divinity I found helpful stimulus for writing from conversations with members of the D Society, particularly Profs. Andrew Davison, Jacob Sherman, and Dr. Daniel Weiss. In the last stages of writing, I benefited from regular discussions with the members of the Against Modernity without Restraint Project at CSPPR: Prof. Harald Wydra, Mr. Nicholas McBride, and Dr. Mark Retter.

I would also like to express my gratitude to the Department of Classics at Williams College and to Emmanuel College, Cambridge for their past assistance in funding my research. Emmanuel College has provided an especially warm, stimulating environment for academic work, and I thank in particular its dean, Jeremy Caddick, for practical assistance at various stages.

Finally, my family—my father and mother above all—have shown limitless good humor and support throughout the work that went into this book; I cannot thank them enough.

Abbreviations

De ver.	*Quaestiones disputatae de veritate*
In Ioan.	*Super Evangelium S. Ioannis lectura*
In Post.	*Expositio libri Posteriorum*
In Sent.	*Scriptum super libros Sententiarum*
SCG	*Summa contra Gentiles*
ST	*Summa theologiae*
a.	article
aa.	articles
ad	answer to objection
c.	chapter
co.	corpus / article's response
d.	distinction
l.	*lectio* / reading subdivision in a commentary
obj.	objection
q.	question
qq.	questions
sc.	sed contra

Introduction

Certain background assumptions centered around prophecy shape and inform what Thomas Aquinas calls "sacred doctrine," the central focus of his greatest work the *Summa theologiae*. In its much commented on Question One, he introduces the nature of this doctrine and its reliance on a divinely revealed teaching, stating that "our [Christian] faith is founded on a revelation made to apostles and prophets who wrote the canonical books"—an indication that some notion of prophecy informs his project from the outset.[1] He highlights in the same question the crucial role played by those individuals "through whom divine revelation came to us," namely, apostles and prophets, in making possible the very existence of sacred doctrine as a locus for divinely revealed saving wisdom and knowledge.[2] It is "through those to whom revelation was made" that others are instructed about the things pertaining to salvation.[3] This book's central claim is that Thomas's accounts of sacred doctrine and prophecy, when read together, reveal striking parallels between the prophet and "the teacher

---

1. Thomas Aquinas, *Summa theologiae* (hereafter ST), I, q. 1, a. 8, ad 2: "innititur enim fides nostra revelationi apostolis et prophetis factae, qui canonicos libros scripserunt." Citations to the Latin text of ST are to *Summa theologiae*, Leonine Edition, vols. 4–12 (Rome: Ex Typographia Polyglotta S. C. de Propaganda Fide, 1888–1906). All English translations of Thomas's texts are mine, unless noted otherwise. My translations were made at times with the help of the English and French translations cited in the bibliography.

2. ST, I, q. 1, a. 2, ad 2: "singularia traduntur in sacra doctrina, non quia de eis principaliter tractetur, sed introducuntur … ad declarandum auctoritatem virorum *per quos ad nos revelatio divina processit*, super quam fundatur sacra scriptura seu doctrina" (emphasis mine).

3. ST, I, q. 1, a. 9, ad 2: "per eos quibus revelatio facta est, alii etiam circa haec instruantur."

of catholic truth" named in the *Summa*'s prologue.[4] The activity of instructing according to divine revelation is profoundly shaped by the gift of prophecy, a topic that the *Summa* devotes four rich questions to in its Second Part (qq. 171–74). To bring into relief these background assumptions, I undertake a close reading centered on the *Summa theologiae* that sketches out the links between his treatment of sacred doctrine in Question One and these later questions on prophecy. Throughout this sketching exercise, the structural setting of certain question clusters or treatises will serve as a roadmap that will help accentuate prophecy's hitherto underrealized ability to shed light on sacred doctrine, one of the foundational concepts in Thomas's thought.

Setting Out a Structural Reading and Earlier Scholarly Approaches to Prophecy in Thomas

A perceived need to situate prophecy in relation to Thomas's notion of sacred doctrine comes as a response to the dominant way scholars have read his questions on prophecy for the past two hundred years, which has been isolationist. Scholarship on his notion of prophecy has been pursued chiefly along two lines. The first focused primarily on studying the history of medieval, scholastic theories of prophecy and Thomas's place in it. These inquiries usually had multiple motivations and were often occasioned by questions that arose from broader discussions in the academic disciplines of the history of Christian doctrine or the history of philosophy; emphasis was placed overwhelmingly on identifying and analyzing the sources of Thomas's thinking on prophecy, both Christian and non-Christian (Islamic, Jewish, and classical pagan philosophers).

The second major line of scholarship took a different tack and focused largely on how Thomas's account of prophecy could be utilized within modern theological debates on scriptural inspiration and inerrancy. While not entirely disinterested in his thirteenth-century historical context, this second group of studies tended to adopt an approach determined more by the perceived needs of dogmatic and systematic theology; Thomas's treatment of prophecy was mined so as to identify theological principles that could effectively address certain developments in nineteenth- and twentieth-century historical biblical scholarship and the questions these raised for dogmatic theology, such as in

---

4. ST, prologue. The "teacher of catholic truth" (*catholicae veritatis doctor*) certainly includes Thomas himself, but also likely his audience as future teachers.

the doctrine of the dual authorship of biblical texts. Separate developments in modern psychology had simultaneously called for renewed attempts to describe the relationship between the Bible's various human authors and its divine author with more precision. This second line of scholarship, while initially embedded in contemporaneous systematic theology, gradually came to utilize many of the results of the historical research of the first line; the application of this material, however, remained localized largely to the topics of scriptural inspiration and inerrancy, thus limiting itself to the boundaries of the problematics initially set out by scriptural and systematic theologians.

Within the first line, the late nineteenth century saw a number of scholars begin to draw attention to Thomas's treatment of prophecy for his use and awareness of medieval Jewish and Arabic sources.[5] One of the earliest of these was the German Protestant theologian and semiticist Adalbert Merx whose 1879 book, a historico-exegetical study of the prophet Joel, devoted a short excursus to exploring how Thomas's thinking on prophecy related to the medieval Jewish thinker Moses Maimonides.[6] Merx concluded that the medieval friar's notion of prophecy was almost entirely dependent on Maimonides's *The Guide of the Perplexed*, whose Latin translation Thomas had read and engaged with from early on his career and notably in his disputed question *De veritate* on prophecy (q. 12).[7] This account was challenged twenty years later by the Catholic professor of moral theology at Münster, Joseph Mausbach, who thought Merx's portrayal significantly overestimated Maimonides's

---

5. For an overview, see Jean-Pierre Torrell, introduction to *Somme théologique, la prophétie: 2a-2ae, Questions 171–178*, by Thomas Aquinas (Paris: Cerf, 2005), 11*–133*, at *15–*19. See also José María Casciaro, *El diálogo teológico de santo Tomás con musulmanes y judíos: El tema de la profecía y la revelación* (Madrid: Consejo Superior de Investigaciones Científicas, 1969); José María Casciaro, "Santo Tomás ante sus fuentes (Estudio sobre la II-II, q. 173, a. 3)," *Scripta Theologica* 6 (1974): 11–65.

6. Adalbert Merx, *Die Prophetie des Joel und ihre Ausleger von den ältesten Zeiten bis zu den Reformatoren: Eine exegetisch-kritische und hermeneutisch-dogmengeschichtliche Studie* (Halle: Verlag der Buchhandlung des Waisenhauses, 1879), 341–67.

7. Moses Maimonides, *The Guide of the Perplexed*, trans. Shlomo Pines, 2 vols. (Chicago: University of Chicago Press, 1963); the main sections treating prophecy are Book II, c. 27, 32–48; Book III, c. 24, 27. See also Leo Elders, "Les rapports entre la doctrine de la prophétie de saint Thomas et 'le Guide des égarés' de Maïmonide," *Divus Thomas* 78 (1975): 449–56; Alexander Altmann, "Maimonides and Thomas Aquinas: Natural or Divine Prophecy?" *Association for Jewish Studies Review* 3 (1978): 1–19. Citations to the Latin text of *De veritate* (hereafter *De ver.*) are to *Quaestiones disputatae de veritate*, ed. A. Dondaine, Leonine Edition, vol. 22 (Rome: Editori di San Tommaso, 1970–76).

influence.[8] At the material level, Mausbach pointed out that Thomas cited Christian patristic authorities just as much as Maimonides in his writings on prophecy, and when it came to writing his *Summa theologiae*, citations of the Jewish thinker drop out altogether in his treatise on prophecy; I will say more about this shortly. In general, the studies of Merx and Mausbach tended to hinge almost exclusively on the history of the influence of Judeo-Arabic sources on Thomas's theory of prophecy.[9] They were less interested in exploring how his writings on prophecy related to other areas of his thought, and paradoxically, these scholars, devoted to uncovering the sources alive in the thirteenth century, occasioned a somewhat stagnant debate that failed to engage either Thomas's thinking as a whole or its potential relationship to living theological questions.

Despite this, another sub-group of historical research was stimulated in the early twentieth century thanks in part to these earlier studies. These scholars followed up especially Mausbach's central claim and set out to identify and analyze the Christian (and especially Latin) patristic sources of Thomas's thinking on prophecy. Serafino Zarb identified St. Augustine as the most critical patristic source and through a close textual analysis of the twelfth book of the bishop of Hippo's *The Literal Meaning of Genesis* traced out the prominence in Thomas's thought of the threefold classification scheme for biblical prophecy presented there. This Augustinian scheme associated three distinct "types" of prophecy with three categories of human vision: bodily, imaginative, and intellectual.[10] Thomas relies on this threefold scheme of prophetic vision at critical moments in his own analysis of prophecy in the *Summa*. To what extent the Augustinian scheme was completely (or exclusively) operational in Thomas's thought, however, was not fully explored by Zarb.

As other scholars quickly noted, there was a rich confluence of sources in addition to scripture and the Latin patristic (and predominantly Augustinian) theories of prophetic vision available to Thomas; the broader thirteenth-century intellectual culture of his day was also engaging with and at times appropriating elements of Aristotelian gnoseology and of Judeo-Arabic prophetology.[11] Several

---

8. Joseph Mausbach, "Die Stellung des hl. Thomas von Aquin zu Maimonides in der Lehre von der Prophetie," *Theologische Quartalschrift* 81 (1899): 533–79.

9. Torrell, *Somme théologique, la prophétie*, 16*.

10. Serafino M. Zarb, "Le fonti agostiniane del trattato sulla profezia di S. Tommaso d'Aquino," *Angelicum* 15 (1938): 169–200.

11. See Anna Rodolfi, *Cognitio obumbrata. Lo statuto epistemologico della profezia nel secolo XIII*, Micrologus' Library 74 (Florence: SISMEL-Edizioni del Galluzzo, 2016),

historical studies by Bruno Decker,[12] Hans Urs von Balthasar,[13] Jean-Pierre Torrell,[14] and Marianne Schlosser[15] ensued, each of them offering a more refined and nuanced analysis of the medieval scholastic context where Thomas's thought took shape.[16] The chief accomplishment of these four scholars was to illustrate

---

which gives a succinct overview of this intellectual environment in the medieval universities (especially Paris) and of the main debates on the process or "mechanism" of prophetic knowledge. As a philosopher, Rodolfi's methodology is set largely by topics of interest to historians of philosophy.

12. Bruno Decker, "Die Analyse des Offenbarungsvorganges beim hl. Thomas im Lichte vorthomistischer Prophetietraktate: Ein historischer Kommentar zu *S. theol.* II-II q. 173 a. 2 (*De ver.*, q. 12 a. 7)," *Angelicum* 16 (1939): 195–244; Bruno Decker, *Die Entwicklung der Lehre von der prophetischen Offenbarung von Wilhelm von Auxerre bis zum Thomas von Aquin* (Breslau: Müller & Seiffert, 1940).

13. Hans Urs von Balthasar, *Thomas und die Charismatik: Thomas von Aquin, Kommentar zu Summa theologica quaestiones II-II 171–182, Besondere Gnadengaben und die zwei Wege menschlichen Lebens* (Freiburg: Johannes Verlag Einsiedeln, 1996), first published as vol. 23 of *Die Deutsche Thomas-Ausgabe*, ed. Heinrich M. Christmann (Graz: Anton Pustet, 1954); citations refer to the Johannes Verlag edition. Von Balthasar's commentary on ST, II-II, qq. 171–82 includes detailed analysis of the scholastic background. On the background of this commentary (intriguing in its own right) and for an overview, see Aidan Nichols, *Balthasar for Thomists* (San Francisco: Ignatius Press, 2020), 172–89.

14. Jean-Pierre Torrell, *Théorie de la prophétie et philosophie de la connaissance aux environs de 1230: La contribution d'Hugues de Saint-Cher (Ms. Douai 434, Question 481)* (Louvain: Spicilegium sacrum Lovaniense, 1977); Jean-Pierre Torrell, *Recherches sur la théorie de la prophétie au Moyen Âge, XIIe-XIVe siècles: Études et textes* (Fribourg: Éditions universitaires, 1992).

15. Marianne Schlosser, *Lucerna in caliginoso loco: Aspekte des Prophetie-Begriffes in der scholastischen Theologie* (Paderborn: Ferdinand Schöningh, 2000).

16. See also Brian FitzGerald, *Inspiration and Authority in the Middle Ages: Prophets and Their Critics from Scholasticism to Humanism* (Oxford: Oxford University Press, 2017), which gives a detailed historical survey on the political, cultural, and literary influence of prophecy and claims to prophetic inspiration in European medieval society from 1120–1320. Fitzgerald identifies important strands of evidence surrounding claims to prophecy and their importance for medieval understandings of history and political/ecclesiastical authority. While my study does not look directly at claims of prophecy in the thirteenth century, his book helpfully situates how such claims during this period often aroused ecclesiastical interest, but also controversy. Awareness of such cases may perhaps account for why Thomas shies away from drawing an overly explicit link between the work of the theologian and the prophet in his own texts, but not without leaving enough indications to conclude that he clearly thought the teacher or theologian held a function analogous to that of the prophet. On this point, see also Schlosser, *Aspekte des Prophetie-Begriffes*, 203–24. Also still worth consulting is Marjorie Reeves, *The Influence of Prophecy in the Later Middle Ages: A Study in Joachimism* (Oxford: Oxford University Press, 1969).

just how much his thinking on prophecy was informed by the already complex environment of twelfth- and thirteenth-century theological debates. Among the scholastics, the gift of prophecy was primarily analyzed along the lines of its function as a communication of the divine revelation that was needed for supernatural faith. Schlosser and Torrell in particular have highlighted this concern for prophecy's relationship to faith in Thomas's own writings, and they have situated their respective studies on prophecy within their own broader and more theologically oriented reading of his corpus as a whole, emphasizing his role first and foremost as a theologian and "teacher of catholic truth" and of spirituality. Their emphasis on him as a resourceful, but not slavishly source-bound, theologian has made apparent certain inherent tensions in the earlier historical approach of scholars like Merx who tended to depict Thomas as a theologically unimaginative inheritor of Maimonides. In place of this, the picture that emerges from this last group of studies is Thomas's creative appropriation of aspects of Arabo-Aristotelian gnoseology in the service of clarifying difficulties that had arisen in the thirteenth century surrounding the reception of a patristic (and strongly Augustinian) tradition of prophetic vision and illumination. In his hands, the traditional Augustinian theory of prophetic illumination gets re-envisioned and reinvigorated, which in turn allowed Thomas to reassert confidently prophecy's status as certain "knowledge" (*scientia*) that required its own distinct prophetic "light" to illuminate the prophet's mind, comparable to the light of natural reason and the supernatural lights of faith and glory.

The second main line of scholarship into Thomas's treatment of prophecy arose during the first half of the twentieth century around a series of debates over scriptural inspiration and inerrancy undertaken predominantly by Roman Catholic theologians.[17] These debates intensified largely as a result of the promulgation of Pope Pius XII's 1943 encyclical on the study of scripture,

---

17. For an overview of these Catholic debates on scriptural inspiration stretching back to the early nineteenth century, see James Tunstead Burtchaell, *Catholic Theories of Biblical Inspiration since 1810: A Review and Critique* (Cambridge: Cambridge University Press, 1969), 8–278. A study that incorporates an analysis of the simultaneous Protestant debates and interlocutors over scriptural inspiration is Bruce Vawter, *Biblical Inspiration* (Philadelphia: Westminster, 1972), 43–94. Following a hiatus after the Second Vatican Council, scholarly interest in these debates on scriptural inspiration has recently remerged; see Denis Farkasfalvy, *Inspiration and Interpretation: A Theological Introduction to Sacred Scripture* (Washington, DC: The Catholic University of America Press, 2010); Denis Farkasfalvy, *A Theology of the Christian Bible: Revelation, Inspiration, Canon* (Washington, DC: The Catholic University of America Press, 2018), and their respective bibliographies.

Divino Afflante Spiritu. Scholars who weighed in tended to interpret Thomas's questions on prophecy in a somewhat *ad hoc* manner; they were more interested in the implications his account of prophecy might have for dogmatic theology on the neuralgic issue of scriptural inspiration.[18] A 1947 French translation and commentary of the *Summa theologiae* II-II, qq. 171–78 compiled by Dominican priests Paul Synave and Pierre Benoit is a prime example; it devotes more than half of its commentary space to an extended essay on scriptural inspiration.[19] Benoit, a scriptural exegete working at the time at the École Biblique de Jerusalem, considered these *Summa* questions with an eye toward applying certain principles derived from Thomas's thinking on prophecy to the ongoing debates over scriptural inspiration, while being less concerned to situate the questions on prophecy within the structure of the *Summa* as a whole.[20] Other articles followed where Benoit continued to look to Thomas's account of prophecy to resolve problems in the theology of inspiration and biblical inerrancy, although his later work was already becoming more methodologically aware of the limitations he was facing when trying to transpose certain aspects of Thomas's thought into modern problematics.[21]

---

18. See Peter Paul Zerafa, "The Limits of Biblical Inerrancy," *Angelicum* 39 (1962): 92–119; Brian McCarthy, "El modo del conocimiento profético y escriturístico según Santo Tomás de Aquino," *Scripta Theologica* 9 (1977): 425–84.

19. Paul Synave and Pierre Benoit, *Saint Thomas d'Aquin: Somme théologique, la prophétie: 2a-2ae, Questions 171–178*, Éditions de la Revue des Jeunes (Paris: Desclée, 1947), 269–376; Synave, who is listed as the volume's co-editor, died prematurely in 1937. Benoit, one of his former pupils at Le Saulchoir, completed the commentary and composed this large appendix on his own. Most of the accompanying explanatory notes, Benoit reports, were Synave's along with the French translation. An English translation appeared as *Prophecy and Inspiration: A Commentary on the Summa Theologica II-II, Questions 171–178*, trans. Avery R. Dulles and Thomas L. Sheridan (New York: Desclée, 1961), 84–168, which includes a number of significant additions and corrections made by Benoit (noted at 13–14).

20. This was one of the main criticisms raised in an essay reviewing *La prophétie*'s commentary material by M.-M. Labourdette, "Théologie morale," *Revue Thomiste* 50 (1950): 396–421. Benoit acknowledged the validity of Labourdette's criticisms on this front in the revised 1961 English edition, notably in frequent footnotes; see *Prophecy and Inspiration*, 75n2, 76n1, 80n3, 94n2, 118n1, 165n2.

21. Pierre Benoit, *Inspiration and the Bible*, trans. J. Murphy-O'Connor and M. Keverne (London: Sheed and Ward, 1965); Pierre Benoit, "Saint Thomas et l'inspiration des écritures," in *Atti del Congresso internazionale (Roma–Napoli, 17–24 aprile 1974): Tommaso d'Aquino nel suo settimo centenario*, vol. 3, *Dio e l'economia della salvezza* (Naples: Edizioni domenicane italiane, 1976), 19–30. Benoit's late work on scriptural inspiration recentered itself around a Thomistic-inspired engagement with the Second Vatican Council's teaching on

Without oversimplifying the content and occasion of these intricate mid-century debates, it seems that many of these studies into biblical inspiration were driven by deeper questions concerning the role of historical scholarship, and especially of historical biblical criticism (or criticisms), in Christian theology. At the heart was the question of the relationship between philosophy and theology and whether Thomas's understanding of this relationship could be constructively appropriated given modern developments in theological method and historical research. As scholars reflected on these issues in the light of Thomas's notion of prophecy, they had a tendency to read his texts somewhat anachronistically. They also tended to approach his questions on prophecy as if they existed as an isolated treatise in his work, neglecting to consider at times how prophecy related to his understanding of sacred doctrine as a whole. This led to strained readings and interpretations where Thomas's texts on prophecy were deployed in an *ad hoc* and limited manner and not always with convincing and lasting results. Prophecy was analyzed on minor points, but it remained difficult to integrate these minor points into larger claims about the theological categories of scriptural inspiration and inerrancy, categories which Thomas himself did not explicitly treat in great detail.

A different and perhaps more fruitfully approach lies in situating theological concepts such as inspiration and inerrancy within the broader context of Thomas's account of faith and reason—as treated largely in his writings on sacred doctrine—and not primarily within the context of Thomas's theory of prophecy. Once prophecy is understood in the context of sacred doctrine as whole, one is in a stronger position to evaluate the possible positive and lasting contributions Thomas's notion of prophecy might bring to contemporary theological problems. The central task of this book, thus, is not to identify specific areas of Thomas's thinking on prophecy that could contribute positively to contemporary theological problems as such. This task would be too premature; instead, it adopts an integrative approach to reading prophecy and sacred doctrine in Thomas.

Our main task then will be to situate his major texts on prophecy within his concept of sacred doctrine as a whole, a whole which is articulated most maturely in his *Summa theologiae*, and which accounts for our decision to

---

divine revelation in *Dei Verbum*; see Paul M. Rogers, "Pierre Benoit's 'Ecclesial Inspiration': A Thomistic Notion at the Heart of Twentieth-Century Debates on Biblical Inspiration," *The Thomist* 80, no. 4 (2016): 521–62, at 553–59.

prioritize the *Summa*'s questions on prophecy in our analysis, drawing on his other writings that treat the prophetic gift as needed. Only after prophecy is integrated into the whole of sacred doctrine—an integration that will coincide with a discovery of its foundational importance—can one begin to discern areas where it could potentially be useful in contemporary theology.[22]

Judeo-Arabic Prophetology in Thomas

In the first historical line of scholarship, we have already seen that interest in the Judeo-Arabic sources for Thomas's thinking on prophecy goes back at least two centuries. This raises the larger question of how certain aspects of the medieval Jewish and Islamic intellectual traditions interacted within the thirteenth-century Latin scholastic milieu and how this would have influenced Thomas's thought. In order to adequately appreciate this interaction, an intensive study of medieval Judeo-Arabic prophetology would be necessary, which our study cannot undertake for various reasons. Since our scope must be limited, what is presented now is merely the briefest of sketches of what can be drawn from existing scholarship about how Thomas's thinking on prophecy most noticeably diverges from medieval Judeo-Arabic philosophers.[23]

In addition to infeasibility, there is another reason to restrict our scope, and this stems from our decision to try to situate prophecy within Thomas's own notion of sacred doctrine. While sacred doctrine does indeed draw on non-Christian sources in the service of expounding Christian faith, it does so treating them only as "extrinsic authorities" that are meant principally to help shed light on the truths of the faith.[24] In this context of Thomas's own stated method, we can consider again the fact observed already that in his *Summa* questions on prophecy explicit citations to Maimonides are absent. Thomas liberally cites the Jewish thinker in his earlier writings on prophecy alongside other Muslim philosophers (especially Avicenna and Averroes), and the earlier disputed question *De veritate* (q. 12) on prophecy shows much more direct engagement with this tradition of Judeo-Arabic prophetology. When

---

22. For a study exemplifying some of the contemporary interest among systematic theologians in prophecy, see Niels Christian Hvidt, *Christian Prophecy: The Post-Biblical Tradition* (Oxford: Oxford University Press, 2007).

23. See Altmann, "Maimonides and Thomas Aquinas"; Elders, "Les rapports entre Thomas et Maïmonide."

24. ST, I, q. 1, a. 8, ad 2.

commenting on this disputed question, Jean-Pierre Torrell has even mused that identifying its title as "On Prophecy" runs the risk of overlooking the fact that Thomas understands his subject to extend beyond simply biblical prophecy, which many of his readers today might assume is the limit of his interest in the subject as a Christian. In fact, he shows a keen awareness of the non-biblical, philosophical traditions of prophecy and the intellectual problems that these raise for sacred doctrine. Prophecy, thus, for Thomas is not something exclusively found in scripture, in the first instance. Other thinkers have grappled with it in other intellectual traditions, and Thomas was of the view that addressing the reflections of these non-Christian philosophers was warranted, even needed, especially when they potentially threatened the integrity of the faith; indeed, this protective role of sacred doctrine is itself outlined in Question One (a. 8). Engaging such reflections was also clearly useful to Thomas, and the speculation he encountered in Maimonides, Averroes, and Avicenna regarding how prophets know appears to have been for him, alongside scripture and the Fathers, an early exploration ground. The evidence of Judeo-Arabic influence can still be seen by comparing some of his earlier texts on prophecy with the *Summa* treatise, despite the fact most explicit citations to these Judeo-Arabic sources are absent in the latter given its narrower purpose—to summarize sacred doctrine pedagogically.

While Thomas's citation and knowledge of these Judeo-Arabic texts (at times to varying degrees) are present in his earlier disputed question on prophecy, even there his appropriation of them is far from uncritical. The areas that most strikingly highlight the radical differences between Judeo-Arabic prophetology and Thomas's approach are his denial of "natural prophecy" and his rejection of prophecy being "a steady disposition" or *habitus*.[25] Many of the differences revolve around the psychology of prophetic knowledge and the way the respective epistemic-cognitive accounts underpin it. Adopting in part a certain type of Avicennian-Aristotelian epistemology that saw an "external" agent intellect capable of illuminating the individual human's mind in the act of knowing, someone like Maimonides developed a view of prophecy according to which it could potentially be a natural capacity within certain individuals. While for Maimonides scripture still indicates that prophets are chosen by God, their

---

25. Given the difficulty of finding a suitable translation for *habitus*—"habit" is too unhelpful because of the automatic, unconsidered aspect it implies—I have chosen in most cases to leave it untranslated.

minds can only reach this heightened state of illumination if their own body and imagination are free from certain defects or cognitive hindrances. Without these "natural" dispositions, the heightened illumination of the intellect that is required for prophecy cannot occur.

Thomas was familiar with Maimonides's naturalistic account of prophecy that stemmed from his broadly Avicennian-Aristotelian gnoseology, where prophecy ultimately looks more like a natural capacity, albeit a rare one; according to this gnoseology, only great individuals with exceptional intellectual potential and the correct disposition are able to join their minds to the agent intellect in the heighten prophetic state. Although Thomas ultimately rejects Avicenna's account of prophetic illumination, an unresolved remanent, one might say, of his engagement with it can still be seen even in his mature thought in the *Summa*. There he acknowledges that there may be reason to consider that prophets, having once received the light of prophecy, might acquire "a certain susceptibility" (*habilitas*) to undergo an illumination of prophetic light again in the future—an unresolved aspect of Avicenna's view that prophets could at times prophesy at will.[26] Thomas explicitly rejects this view as part of his denial that prophecy is a *habitus*; this marks a clear break with Avicenna and a view of prophecy as potentially natural. In contrast, prophecy for Thomas will be a transient light that illuminates the intellect only when it is given by God. Thus, calling someone a "prophet" does not result from the fact there is a continuous illumination of the prophet's mind, which in many biblical cases like Jeremiah's was not actually continuously illuminated, but rather it comes from there being a divine calling and bestowal of the prophetic gift.[27] Thomas's insistence on the essentially supernatural character of prophecy (and all that entails) is what sets Thomas most apart from the major streams of medieval Judeo-Arabic prophetology.

One final divergence from Maimonides worth noting for our discussion is seen in Thomas's clear rejection of the political role of the prophet, a notable theme in *The Guide to the Perplexed*.[28] Maimonides there developed a view of the prophet based on Moses whom scripture singles out among all prophets

---

26. ST, II-II, q. 171, a. 2, ad 2. See Jean-Pierre Torrell, notes to *Questions disputées sur la vérité, Question XII: La prophétie* (*De prophetia*), by Thomas Aquinas (Paris: Vrin, 2006), 191–240, at 194.

27. ST, II-II, q. 171, a. 2, ad 2.

28. Torrell, *Question XII: La prophétie*, 198, 239–40. See *De ver.*, q. 12, a. 3, ad 11.

(Dt 34:10). In Moses he sees especially the prophet as lawgiver and later in the other biblical prophets, as political actors *par excellence* who possess knowledge of the divinely revealed law and the certitude of its application in particular socio-political circumstances. Moreover, being publicly recognized as having the prophetic gift, they are seen as offering the most perfect form of government due to their ability to embody and unite political and prophetic authority by a single appeal to God's command. Thomas shows some awareness of these considerations in his earlier disputed question on prophecy, and certain remnants of them continue even in his *Summa* article, most strikingly in its article on whether Moses was the greatest prophet (Q. 174, a. 4).[29] However, as already seen, Thomas resists situating prophecy within the natural order and excludes prophets from being directly necessary for civil government.[30] He prefers instead to situate prophesying firstly in the supernatural life of grace and of the Church. This reflects his thinking that prophecy and the gratuitous graces in general are meant principally to serve the ecclesial community as a whole in its specific mission, which is not essentially political. Thus, prophecy's ecclesial setting is not only indicated structurally in the *Summa theologiae*, as will be spelled out more clearly later on, but also it is what proves to be decisive in his rejection of Maimonides's view of political prophecy. While Thomas was working in the line of Judeo-Arabic prophetology by considering the structure of the human mind and its interaction with higher intelligences (angels or demons), gnoseology, and the imagination, his engagement with and appropriation of its sources were complex, not always direct, and seldom uncritical.[31]

---

29. Compare the parallel article *De ver.*, q. 12, a. 14.

30. *De ver.*, q. 12, a. 3, ad 11; ST, II-II, q. 174, a. 6, co.

31. On a more contemporary line of inquiry, see Anna Bonta Moreland, *Mohammad Reconsidered: A Christian Perspective on Islamic Prophecy* (Notre Dame: Notre Dame University Press, 2020), which indicates a growing interest in Thomas's interaction with medieval Judeo-Arabic prophetology among scholars engaging in comparative interreligious theology or dialogue. Moreland looks to Thomas's account of prophecy with an eye toward addressing current, neuralgic questions about Muhammed as a prophet within Christian-Muslim interreligious dialogue. Her study gives evidence that direct attention to these intellectual exchanges surrounding the nature of prophecy between medieval Christians and Judeo-Arabic thinkers could unearth models (albeit ones historically deployed at times in interreligious polemics and, thus, requiring some transposition) for interreligious debate and discussion. Implicit in these "dialogues" (both medieval and modern) is the fact that interreligious dialogue itself presumes a type of testimony communicated by members of belief-communities. While not adopting her interfaith approach, this study indirectly

A Structural and Synthetic Reading
of the *Summa theologiae*

Our proposed structural reading of prophecy in relation to sacred doctrine will proceed in two stages. The first three chapters provide the needed background through an examination of Thomas's questions from the *Summa theologiae* on sacred doctrine, happiness or the final end, and faith. Once this spadework is done, the foreground we are aiming at will come into view: the structural location of his questions on prophecy and the foundational role prophecy plays in his account of sacred doctrine. Chapter one focuses in on the *Summa*'s prologue and Question One in particular and illustrates how Thomas's notion of sacred doctrine is centrally concerned with wisdom and knowledge (*scientia*). Three aspects of knowledge are identified as important for our later discussion of prophecy: (1) the knowledge that humans can have about God (whether natural or supernatural), (2) the role this knowledge has in divine governance, and (3) its orientation to salvation and happiness, mankind's final end.

At the same time, knowledge gives only a partial picture, for Thomas calls sacred doctrine both knowledge and wisdom. As wisdom, it pertains to sacred doctrine to treat the highest principle, God, as self-revealed and self-known, and to judge things in light of the highest truth. When discussing things other than this highest principle, sacred doctrine, under the aspect of wisdom, relates those things to God as their beginning and end. Within the *Summa*, Question One serves to clarify what things fall under sacred doctrine's subject and how they do so. In this capacity, the question defines the scope of sacred doctrine and, by extension, of the entire work. Things that are treated later in the *Summa* relate back to and remain dependent on this initial laying out of the purview and principles of sacred doctrine for the intelligibility of their place within the whole. Our proposed reading of the later set of questions on prophecy in light of earlier ones would seem then not only to be warranted but demanded by sacred doctrine's sapiential character.

This discussion of Question One will also make apparent that sacred doctrine as wisdom and knowledge has an inherent goal, which is not knowledge itself, but "salvation" (*salus*). The themes of human happiness or the final end and the "need" for human salvation through faith come to be seen as the *raison*

---

indicates how Thomas's notion of prophecy and his analogous usage of the term as it emerged from his intellectual milieu uniquely motivated such interfaith engagement to take place and still potentially fosters it today.

d'être of Thomas's accounts of both sacred doctrine and prophecy. Because of this, any discussion of sacred doctrine and prophecy must be further situated in relation to his questions on happiness and the final end (I-II, qq. 1–5) and on the theological virtue of faith (II-II, qq. 1–16), which orients the human person to that end in the order of grace.

Chapter two turns to Thomas's treatment of happiness or the final end at the start of the Second Part (the moral part of the *Summa*). The questions on happiness and the final end shape his entire account of human morals and structure the later sections on the gratuitous graces, of which prophecy is the chief one. Such special graces will be concerned with instructing humans about their ordination to God as the cause of their ultimate happiness. Attending to happiness as the human final end will enable us to see the central role prophecy plays in orienting human persons, especially in moral matters, through the virtue of faith toward God as their final supernatural end.

The third chapter examines the questions on faith, the opening questions of the *Secunda secundae* (the same part of the *Summa* that also contains the subsection including his questions on prophecy). Thomas situates faith as the definitive ordering of humans to their supernatural end within the framework of a participation in God's own knowledge; faith is made concrete for individual persons when, in their personal act of faith, an implicit appeal to prophetic testimony is made, and this appeal helps us to see that every personal act of faith simultaneously has social and historical aspects. Faith also bestows the principal light under which sacred doctrine is learned and taught. When sacred doctrine's and prophecy's respective ordinations to theological faith are perceived, a common function of both is discovered; both are meant to communicate to others supernatural knowledge received through divine revelation—offered initially to prophets and apostles and "internalized" for each person in faith— that serves to orient humans continually toward God as their highest good and the final source of all knowledge. Reading the questions on faith with prophecy and the final end in the background will help us to see especially why Thomas thinks only certain things that have been divinely revealed about God make up the things that ought to be believed—faith's *credenda*. The *credenda* are ultimately rooted in God's testimony that has been revealed to prophets and apostles. It is this divine testimony that serves as the principle of faith and, by extension, of sacred doctrine.

During our analysis of the gift of faith, we will explore the fact that a believer does not fully understand what is believed in theological faith. Faith's incompleteness (if we can call it that) indicates for Thomas that the intellect is not fully satisfied with the assent of faith, at least from the intellect's perspective. Something remains unseen in faith:

> Insofar as it depends on itself alone, the understanding is not satisfied [by the assent of faith] and is not limited to one thing; instead, its action is terminated only from without. Because of this the understanding of the believer is said to be *held captive* (2 Cor 10:5), since, in place of its own proper determinations, those of something else are imposed on it.[32]

We will see how this restlessness of the intellect in faith—so much a feature of sacred doctrine—and its accompanying "captivity" is structured by prophetic revelation. When it is believed, prophetic testimony "captivates" the believer's mind and mediates a kind of "determination" of what the understanding should assent to. Simultaneously, prophecy mirrors faith's structure as it is oriented to communicating goodness to others through sharing God's testimony. The basis for these parallels between faith and prophecy emerges from their mutual ordering to God as final end. That God's testimony is mediated through others—angels in the first instance and subsequently by prophets and apostles—indicates also that it is given with the good of a community in mind. This reveals that faith's underlying structure is social, and this social structuring is thrown into stark relief when its dependence on prophetic revelation is adequately appreciated. Faith's social orientation also helps us to situate more satisfactorily Thomas's classification (following St. Paul in 1 Corinthians 12) of prophecy as a "gratuitous grace" that is meant primarily for the good of a community rather than for the good of the individual recipient.

With this background in place, the last two chapters explore how prophecy functions in Thomas's thought as a whole through looking closely at his *Summa* questions on prophecy. Chapter four argues that his full definition of prophecy relies on a double-appeal to its formal object—the prophetic light—and its function. Prophetic light causes supernatural knowledge that is conducive to inducing others to faith. Prophecy thus manifests both an individual and a social dimension—its intrinsic openness to sharing. Openness will be seen to be a prominent feature of prophecy both functionally (its openness to sharing)

---

32. *De ver.*, q. 14, a. 1, co. (English translation from *Truth*, trans. Robert W. Mulligan, James V. McGlynn, and Robert W. Schmidt, 3 vols. [Indianapolis: Hackett, 1994]).

and notionally (its conceptual open-endedness) for Thomas. On the latter, since prophecy is determined only by what God wills to reveal, the concept resists any attempt by human reason to overdetermine it; a rationalistic or naturalistic view of prophecy is ruled out. Such resistance to closed conceptualization is also a general structural feature of both faith and sacred doctrine, given their dependence on revelation. From this we conclude that prophecy is best understood according to Thomas not as something determined and possessed exclusively by one prophet's mind, but as something shared.[33] This will help us to see the decisive nature of his characterization of prophecy as a gratuitous grace whose goodness is meant to be shared for the building-up of the ecclesial community. This structural feature of his notion of prophecy—its "openness to sharing"— will suggest that prophecy should also be regarded as reflecting God's goodness since it manifests His desire for communion.[34]

Chapter five identifies the act of judgment as the key locus where prophetic light interacts with human knowing. In the act of prophetic judgment, the structural interdependence of Thomas's accounts of wisdom and sacred doctrine come to the fore, thus confirming the latter's prophetic foundation in its ability to testify to divinely revealed truth and attract others to the good offered by God in theological faith. Sacred doctrine thus has not only the aspect of knowledge but also the correlative purpose of sharing this truth as a good with others, which is an ecclesial function of its sapiential character. Prophecy also shares this dual aspect of knowing and sharing, and in prophetic judgments we will encounter it again in the way they are structured to point beyond themselves back to the root

---

33. See Rudi te Velde, *Aquinas on God: The "Divine Science" of the* Summa theologiae (Farnham: Ashgate, 2006), which highlights how Thomas saw the theologian's central task as integrating salvific knowledge with God's knowledge by emphasizing the presence of a rich metaphysics of participation in his thought. Less attention in te Velde's study is devoted to exploring the particular and concrete ways Thomas sees the theologian imitating divine knowledge with a view to testifying to God through the task of teaching and writing. Prophecy—with its emphasis on knowledge—helps to develop this theme along such lines by highlighting Thomas's understanding of theology as *witness-bearing* knowledge. For a discussion of testimonial knowledge as central to revelation, see Mats Wahlberg, *Revelation as Testimony: A Philosophical-Theological Study* (Grand Rapids: Eerdmans, 2014).

34. This also mirrors how faith in Thomas's account is ordered to charity, which is the communion of friendship; see ST, II-II, q. 23, a. 1. See also Jean-Pierre Torrell, "Charity as Friendship in St. Thomas Aquinas," in *Christ and Spirituality in St. Thomas Aquinas*, trans. Bernhard Blankenhorn (Washington, DC: The Catholic University of America Press, 2011), 45–64.

of their own truth and diffusiveness: God's own light and diffusive goodness. This will invite an extended comparison between prophetic judgments and wisdom as a gift of the Holy Spirit that will point to the integrative aspect of both. Prophecy attempts to lead others and the Church to happiness in God, which is accomplished in prophetic judgments. Wisdom when it judges as a gift of the Spirit judges with a God's-eye perspective and sees the truth in a way that is far closer to the way God beholds Himself as truth. Sacred doctrine through the light of faith undertakes this task of integrating all truth with a view to sharing truth's goodness with others in the Church governed by the Holy Spirit. In the end the ecclesial setting of both prophecy and sacred doctrine comes to the fore, ensuring equally their rooting in wisdom.

While it is one thing to say that sacred doctrine is true or good, it is still another thing to show how and why it is so. It seems that the specific issue of sacred doctrine's "goodness" was not a prominent enough question for Thomas to raise explicitly himself or feel the need to address it in a *quaestio*; at least, this appears to be the case in the *Summa theologiae*. Thomas lived in a different time, and unsurprisingly, he was responding to the different needs and questions of that time. While today there is still a pressing need to account for why sacred doctrine constitutes a true knowledge that has an effective influence over the course of a person's life, there also seems today to be a pressing need to help others appreciate this truth as a good, not only for the individual who comes to believe, but also as a good that can be shared freely with others in a community. When prophecy is situated within sacred doctrine, its goodness shines forth, and this is a deeper reflection of its status as redeeming wisdom. The aspect of possessing this saving wisdom with its openness to being shared with others in faith is what I identify as sacred doctrine's "prophetic aspect" or character, an aspect that is embedded in the overall purpose of the *Summa theologiae* and that is particularly visible at its outset.

1

Sacred Doctrine and Its First Principles

The interdependence of Thomas's accounts of sacred doctrine and prophecy is witnessed from the outset of the *Summa theologiae* in Question One. What this chapter attempts to do is introduce this presentation of sacred doctrine as knowledge or "science" (following the word's Latin etymology *scientia*) and wisdom. We will pay special attention to how Thomas envisions it resting on and proceeding from principles that are materially known through prophetic revelation and formally known in the light of the higher *scientia* of God and the blessed through faith.

None of the articles of Question One explicitly emphasize a connection between sacred doctrine and prophecy or develop one to any great extent, but Thomas does draw our attention to it in key places—albeit briefly—and from time to time elsewhere. This will indicate a structural link between the two that will be developed in the chapters that follow. By looking closely at his treatment of sacred doctrine in this chapter, we want to lay the groundwork needed to see how sacred doctrine's status as science and highest wisdom hinges on the theological virtue of faith and, by extension, on the fact of revelation being made to certain individuals—prophets and apostles.

Sacra doctrina as "Science"

Thomas treats the subject of sacred doctrine at several key moments over the course of his career. The prologue to his commentary on the *Sentences* of Peter Lombard—the *Scriptum super libros Sententiarum* (composed between

1252/3–1254/56)—marks his first exposition of sacred doctrine; he treats the subject again in the *Super Boetium de Trinitate* (1257–58) and one last time in Question One of the *Summa theologiae* (1265–67).[1] For our purposes, this last treatment is the most important; not only does Question One of the *Summa* mark the final time Thomas explicitly wrote on the subject, but it also marks the beginning of his vast project to conceive of sacred doctrine as that which integrates divine revelation and human knowledge into a unified "science" (*scientia*) directed toward human salvation and existing "as a kind of impression of divine science, which is one and simple, but about everything."[2]

When employing the word *scientia*, Thomas unsurprisingly does not intend to connote the exact same thing as what we today call "science." Contemporary usage of the word "science" is almost exclusively restricted to signifying empirical or experimental fields of study—physics, chemistry, biology and the like. While Thomas would certainly consider these empirical sciences *scientiae*, his own usage of *scientia* is not quite as restricted as our term "science." For instance, he thinks one can talk about two types of *scientia*, where each type is distinguished by the different way its principles are held by the person who is said "to know."[3] The first type of *scientia* proceeds "from principles known by the natural light of the intellect" and includes subjects like arithmetic and geometry. The second type proceeds "from principles known by a higher *scientia*, just as the study of perspective proceeds from principles that are learned through geometry, and music from principles known through arithmetic."[4] Of these two types of *scientiae*, Thomas thinks *sacra doctrina* belongs to the second type, since it proceeds:

> From principles known by the light of a higher *scientia*, namely, the *scientia* of God and the blessed. Hence, just as music believes the principles handed over to it by arithmetic, so too does *sacra doctrina* believe the principles revealed to it by God.[5]

---

1. On the dating of these works, see Jean-Pierre Torrell, *Initiation à saint Thomas d'Aquin: Sa personne et son oeuvre*, new ed. (Paris: Cerf, 2015), 65–77, 101–3, 192–206, 432–37, 459; the English translation of which is *Saint Thomas Aquinas*, vol. 1, *The Person and His Work*, trans. Matthew K. Minerd and Robert Royal, 3rd ed. (Washington, DC: The Catholic University of America Press, 2022).

2. ST, I, q. 1, a. 3, ad 2: "sacra doctrina [potest] … considerare [ea] sub una ratione, inquantum scilicet sunt divinitus revelabilia, ut sic sacra doctrina sit velut quaedam impressio divinae scientiae, quae est una et simplex omnium."

3. ST, I, q. 1, a. 2, co.: "sciendum est quod duplex est scientiarum genus."

4. ST, I, q. 1, a. 2, co.

5. ST, I, q. 1, a. 2, co.: "Et hoc modo sacra doctrina est scientia, quia procedit ex

A critical feature of this second type of subalternated *scientia* is that its principles are believed and dependent on someone else knowing them.

It is because of this second type of *scientia* that it remains somewhat unhelpful to translate *scientia* as "science." In its usual sense, the English word "science" tends to be taken to refer to a body of knowledge; the person who is said to know a given "science," say biology, either knows or is at least capable of knowing everything that falls in that science through the dint of human effort. This would include the possibility of knowing the science's conclusions and principles through the natural light of the human intellect. This description of "science," however, is just not what Thomas presents to his reader when explaining the second type of *scientia*.

What Thomas means here in Question One by this second type of subalternated *scientia* is less "science" taken in our modern-day, restrictive sense of the term (as in natural, experimental science), and more "knowledge" in the sense of something certain or fixed. It is this latter sense of *scientia* that Thomas has in mind when he asks whether *sacra doctrina* is a *scientia*.[6] Despite the fact that the principles of *sacra doctrina* are only believed and impossible to discover by the light of reason, Thomas still thinks they are appropriately called principles of a *scientia* because they are most certain. Their certitude does not derive exclusively from the believer's act of faith, but also from God's own knowledge and the knowledge shared by the blessed in heaven, neither of which can be uncertain or false. In this way, Thomas calls sacred doctrine a *scientia* primarily because its principles are revealed by God and consequently believed, and not primarily because the human believer can discover some intrinsic intelligibility among the divinely revealed principles irrespective of them being believed or not.[7] This last point bears keeping in mind because we will soon see that, while it so happens that humans can and do discover an intelligibility in divine revelation through the use of their reason, this in itself is not the primary reason why Thomas calls *sacra doctrina* a *scientia*.

There is thus no quick and easy translation for what Thomas means by *scientia* or *sacra doctrina*. Because the term *scientia* for him embraces not only empirical sciences, but also other bodies of knowledge, it seems inappropriate to

principiis notis lumine superioris scientiae, quae scilicet est scientia Dei et beatorum. Unde sicut musica credit principia tradita sibi ab arithmetico, ita doctrina sacra credit principia revelata sibi a Deo."

6. ST, I, q. 1, a. 2.

7. When these principles are "believed" under the light of faith, they are believed precisely to have been revealed by God.

translate *scientia* as "science" at every occasion. At the same time, a danger also lies in translating it exclusively by "knowledge." Thomas employs several words that can potentially be translated by the English verb "to know." *Cognoscere* and *scire* are the two most prominent, and these two verbs are used in subtly different ways. In addition to "to know," *cognoscere* can sometimes refer to any act of reasoning: considering, deducing, or becoming acquainted with. *Scire* tends to be used more restrictively, referring more to a fixed type of knowing: "to know with certitude." It is from *scire* that *scientia* is derived, and this explains why *scientia* is sometimes appropriately translated by "knowledge." There are reasons, then, for resisting slavishly literal translations of the word *scientia*. I have chosen to adapt my translations of it to the given context in which Thomas employs it; sometimes it is appropriate to translate it as "science" in the sense of *a body of conclusions* or *a habit of the mind about conclusions*, but at other times Thomas means something more like *fixed knowledge*.

As regards translations for *sacra doctrina*, "holy teaching" remains a very good one advocated by Victor White, since it conveys an active sense of a teacher instructing students.[8] This, White thinks, captures an essential dimension of *sacra doctrina*: it is God who is actively teaching humanity. This translation also possesses an appropriate passive sense that can refer to the content of what is being taught. While coming closest to the actual Latin phrase and conveying well the passive sense that refers to the content taught, "sacred doctrine" poorly conveys any active sense implied in "holy teaching." In common English usage "doctrine" usually refers to the "thing" or "subject" taught to students; it refers more to the content than to the act of teaching itself. Thomas's usage of *doctrina* embraces both active and passive senses, referring potentially either to the act of teaching or content taught, or to both.[9]

---

8. Victor White, *Holy Teaching: The Idea of Theology according to St. Thomas Aquinas*, Aquinas Papers 33 (London: Blackfriars, 1958). See also Brian Davies, "Is *Sacra doctrina* theology?" *New Blackfriars* 71, no. 836 (1990): 141–47, who largely reiterates White's view.

9. See *Expositio libri Posteriorum*, ed. R.-A. Gauthier, Leonine Edition, vol. 1*/2 (Rome: Commissio Leonina, 1989), I, l. 1: "doctrina est actio eius qui aliquid cognoscere facit." See further treatment in Gerald F. Van Ackeren, *Sacra doctrina: The Subject of the First Question of the* Summa theologica *of St. Thomas Aquinas* (Rome: Catholic Book Agency, 1952), 53–77; Yves Congar, "Tradition et *sacra doctrina* chez saint Thomas d'Aquin," in *Église et Tradition*, ed. Johannes Betz and Heinrich Fries (Le Puy: Xavier Mappus, 1963), 157–94, at 161–63. For a general treatment of Thomas's approach to education, see T. C. O'Brien, "'Sacra doctrina' Revisited: The Context of Medieval Education," *The Thomist* 41, no. 4 (1977): 475–509; Leo Elders, "St. Thomas Aquinas on Education and Instruction," *Nova et Vetera* 7, no. 1 (2009): 107–24.

Within the context of Question One of the *Summa theologiae*, the sense of *scientia* as "fixed knowledge" seems to predominate. One sees this especially in the question's second article where Thomas asks: *utrum sacra doctrina sit scientia*—"whether sacred doctrinc is knowledge." Later on in Question One, Thomas will go on to consider sacred doctrine as an intellectual *habitus*[10] and a body of conclusions argued from given first principles.[11] Nevertheless, the primary sense of *scientia* employed in the second article is that of "fixed knowledge." Sacred doctrine is "fixed knowledge" because it proceeds from principles known by the light of a higher knowledge, that is, God's knowledge and the knowledge of the blessed. The emphasis in this article falls on *sacra doctrina* as a sharing in God's knowledge and that of the blessed.

In most ordinary human circumstances, to believe something or someone indicates a degree of uncertainty on the part of the person believing. People believe things because they do not know for certain themselves. Strictly speaking, Thomas calls this an example of "opinion." An opinion occurs when a person gravitates to one side of an affirmative or negative proposition but still entertains the possibility of being wrong.[12] Opinions and beliefs are less certain than knowledge (*scientia*) from the perspective of the person as a knower. However, from the perspective of what, or more properly, of who, is believed in faith—that is, faith's object—Thomas highlights a radical asymmetry with regards to certitude. In faith, God is the one who is believed, and what God says or reveals can never contradict God's own knowledge. It is this asymmetry that explains why Thomas thinks belief, even if it is less certain from the perspective of the believer, can still be the basis for fixed knowledge. God's knowledge is the reference point to be kept in mind, and from it, sacred doctrine receives the characteristic of being "a kind of impression of divine knowledge, which is one and simple, but about everything."[13]

There are other scholars who, while accepting a fairly similar sketch to the one outlined above, also stress that Thomas frames Question One in such way that his notion of *scientia* is presented along a broadly Aristotelian model of *epistēmē*.[14] This claim that Thomas's presentation of knowledge (*scientia*) in

---

10. ST, I, q. 1, a. 6, ad 3.

11. ST, I, q. 1, a. 8.

12. ST, II-II, q. 1, a. 4, co.

13. ST, I, q. 1, a. 3, co.

14. See James A. Weisheipl, "The Meaning of Sacred Doctrine in the *Summa theologiae* I, q. 1," *The Thomist* 38, no. 1 (1974): 49–80, at 79: "for Thomas, *sacra doctrina* as explained in question one is necessary for salvation. This doctrine is not incoherent and absurd but has an

Question One is broadly indebted to Aristotle's account of *epistēmē* I take to be, for the most part, uncontroversial and representative of a current scholarly consensus.[15] Most scholars agree that Thomas is roughly following a method outlined in Aristotle's *Posterior Analytics* that first tries to establish whether the thing intended to be studied actually exists (*an est*);[16] if it is found to exist, one can then inquire into its nature by asking "what it is" (*quid est*) and how ought one to go about inquiring (*de modo*). Both Weisheipl and Torrell, for instance, are in agreement about the general breakdown of Question One according to this model: a. 1 (*an est*), aa. 2–7 (*quid est*), and aa. 8–10 (*de modo*).[17]

intrinsic rationale wherein one truth of faith is the reason for another truth, also accepted on faith; *this intrinsic rationale renders this doctrine 'scientific' even in Aristotle's sense of the term*" (emphasis mine). Weisheipl argues consistently that Thomas is closely modelling his notion of *sacra doctrina* on Aristotle's *epistēmē* as outlined in the *Posterior Analytics*; Weisheipl claims he is basing his own argument on our knowledge of Thomas in his historical context and of the common methods used there (64). He reports with some dissatisfaction "the net conclusion" among Question One commentators that sees the meaning of *sacra doctrina* shift subtlety from article to article so that sometimes *sacra doctrina* means "Christian faith," sometimes "theology," and sometimes "sacred scripture." This alleged "oscillation of meaning" in the term *sacra doctrina* he finds so dissatisfying because it does not come close enough to the "canon of method outlined in Aristotle's *Posterior Analytics*" and is, on top of this, "contrary to common sense" (55). Weisheipl also retraces the main positions of earlier Thomistic commentators on Question One from the sixteenth to the early twentieth century.

   15. See Marie-Dominique Chenu, *La théologie comme science au XIIIe siècle*, 3rd ed. (Paris: Vrin, 1969); Weisheipl, "The Meaning of Sacred Doctrine"; Adriano Oliva, *Les débuts de l'enseignement de Thomas d'Aquin et sa conception de la* sacra doctrina (Paris: Vrin, 2006). Oliva helpfully distinguishes the different purposes between Question One's treatment of sacred doctrine and that of the early *Scriptum super libros Sententiarum*; see also his correction of Weisheipl, who erred principally by reading the earlier *Scriptum* too much into the later *Summa theologiae*'s account of sacred doctrine (272–79).

   16. See White, *Holy Teaching*, 8; Chenu, *La théologie comme science au XIIIe siècle*; Weisheipl, "The Meaning of Sacred Doctine"; John I. Jenkins, *Knowledge and Faith in Thomas Aquinas* (Cambridge: Cambridge University Press, 1997); Oliva, *Les débuts de l'enseignement*, 274, who shows that Thomas in the earlier *Scriptum* is following more closely the order of Boethius's four questions from his second commentary on the *Isagoge* of Porphyry.

   17. Weisheipl, "The Meaning of Sacred Doctrine," 65; Jean-Pierre Torrell, "Le savoir théologique chez Saint Thomas," *Revue Thomiste* 96 (1996): 355–96, at 365–66; reprinted in *Recherches thomasiennes* (Paris: Vrin, 2000), 130–31. Torrell opines that almost all the studies on Thomas's notion of *sacra doctrina* in the second half of the twentieth century tend either to offer only modest clarifications or to modify or accentuate one particular aspect over another from Yves Congar's earlier work (131n2); most of these later studies are essentially working in the shadow of Congar's "foundational" studies on the nature of theology. See especially

The consensus, however, starts to dissolve when one asks to what extent Aristotle's notion of *epistēmē* is determinative in Question One as a whole. Here, as Weisheipl's survey points out, there has been frequent disagreement among Thomas's readers with regards to the exact sense of *sacra doctrina* at different points within the articles of Question One. While Thomas does begin with an article (a. 1) that seems to resemble an Aristotelian inquiry into whether there is something actually to know (*an est*), the text itself really asks whether another discipline "beyond the philosophical disciplines" is "necessary for salvation." If Thomas were following a strict Aristotelian method in Question One, one might expect him to subdivide his introduction more clearly into the three divisions of *an est*, *quid est*, and *de modo*.[18] The fact remains that Thomas's text does not follow this strict division. There seems to be a potential danger in identifying too strictly Thomas's aims in Question One with the aims of outlining and introducing an Aristotelian science.

Here, the work of Victor White has proven a helpful corrective by highlighting the places within Question One where Thomas does not immediately equate sacred doctrine with a habit of conclusions demonstrated by discursive reasoning and following necessarily from given first principles; rather, White points out that in the question's second article the "basic meaning" of sacred doctrine "is that of sure and thorough knowledge as against opinion or sentiment, of *epistēmē* as against *doxa*, rather than that of methodical, discursive science (however defined) as against haphazard science."[19] According to White, sacred doctrine can be called "knowledge" not on account of any human act of

---

Yves Congar, "Le sens de l'économie salutaire dans la 'theologie' de saint Thomas d'Aquin," in *Festgabe Joseph Lortz*, vol. 2, *Glaube und Geschichte*, ed. Erwin Iserloh and Peter Manns (Baden-Baden: Bruno Grimm, 1958), 73–122; Congar, "Tradition et *sacra doctrina*"; Yves Congar, "Le moment 'économique' et le moment 'ontologique' dans la sacra doctrina (Révélation, théologie, Somme théologique)," in *Mélanges offres à M.-D. Chenu, maître en théologie* (Paris: Vrin, 1967), 135–87; Yves Congar, *A History of Theology*, trans. Hunter Guthrie (Garden City, NY: Doubleday, 1968). More recently see Thomas Michelet, *Sacra doctrina: Mystère et sacramentalité de la parole dans* la Somme de théologie *de S. Thomas d'Aquin* (Paris: Parole et Silence, 2019). Michelet offers a pregnant analysis of Question One as an exercise rooting one in the "logic" of the transcendentals (aa. 1–6) under sacred doctrine and in its subject and formal object by which the subject is known (i.e., God) under theology (*theologia*). He maintains both are best understood as the same reality, the Word of God (270–71). I became aware of Michelet's study at too late a stage to be able to address its rich findings.

18. Weisheipl, "The Meaning of Sacred Doctrine," 80.

19. White, *Holy Teaching*, 13.

reasoning, but because people believe and take to be true the divinely revealed testimony that derives from the absolutely sure "knowledge of God and the blessed." In calling sacred doctrine a *scientia*, then, the emphasis is placed on the one believing the divinely revealed testimony and the knowledge of the person who testifies. Human beings ultimately believe the divine teacher, God, not as one who possesses knowledge discursively or habitually, but as one whose knowledge is identical with His substance.[20] The fact that prophetic revelation is also not the product of discursive reasoning, but is nonetheless certain knowledge and not opinion, suggests that it functions as an appropriate medium between theological faith and God's knowledge. This appropriateness comes from the fact that prophetic revelation preserves the characteristic of being non-discursive and immediate; this, I claim, allows prophets to effectively point beyond their own discrete, individual knowledge toward the ultimate source of their prophetic knowledge: God.

Precedents for Considering Sacred Doctrine a Science in the 13th Century

Thomas was one of the first prominent Christian thinkers to defend rigorously the claim that sacred doctrine could possess the character of a subalternate science. He was not, however, the first person to ask whether sacred doctrine could classify as a *scientia*. William of Auxerre in the 1220s offered one of the earliest reflections on this issue of sacred doctrine's relationship to fixed knowledge.[21] Ultimately, William thought that sacred doctrine could not properly be defined as a science without compromising the nature of Christian faith. Faith, he explained, was about things that were not self-evident to human understanding, and hence, they needed to be believed. While these "objects" of faith were not, strictly speaking, provable by human reason, William did speak about the Christian's ability to know and express them as "articles of faith." He drew an analogy between these articles of faith, known through the light of faith, and the first principles of a human science, which are seen in the light of natural reason as self-evident or *per se nota*.[22] Employing an Aristotelian notion of first

---

20. ST, I, q. 14, a. 1, ad 1: "scientia non est qualitas in Deo vel habitus, sed substantia et actus purus."

21. See Chenu, *La théologie comme science au XIIIe siècle*, 31–37, 58–60.

22. See Guy Mansini, "Are the Principles of *Sacra doctrina Per Se Nota*?" *The Thomist* 74, no. 3 (2010): 407–35.

principles that act as the cause of all subsequent knowledge within a science, William set up a comparative relationship between the articles of faith and the first principles of a science. Even having argued for this parallel between the articles of faith and the first principles of a science, William still hesitated to ascribe to the articles of faith any power to cause a science; instead, he focused on how the articles of faith were knowable because their cause could be traced back to God as First Truth.[23] The analogy William set up was concerned to show that "the knowledge of God which is faith" was like the knowledge of first principles, because first principles precisely cannot be resolved any further beyond themselves. In this way, faith's divine cause was ensured and affirmed. In this respect, it seems fair to say that William was more concerned to show how faith and the objects of faith as expressed in the articles were caused by God than to give an argument for how the articles of faith could be said to have their own integral capacity to cause further knowledge. It also appears that Chenu is right when he concludes that William's point of comparison lies "not in the role of first principles in the construction of discrete knowledge [*d'un savoir*], but in the character of immediate and immediately evident knowledge that these principles have."[24] While the trajectory of William's thought seemed to be pointing toward the possibility of a science being developed from faith under an Aristotelian model starting from first principles,[25] he never fully arrived at the assertion that sacred doctrine was a science, nor did he ever go on to equate theology (*theologia*) with such a science, if one were to be developed from faith.[26]

---

23. *Summa aurea*, III, tr. 8, cap. de sapientia, q. 1: "fides enim innititur prime veritati super omnia et propter se; unde cognitio Dei que est fides est quasi cognitio principiorum; sicut enim in hoc principio: omne totum est majus sua parte, invenitur cause sue cognitionis nec alia causa queritur, ita anima fidelis in ipsa veritate que creditur invenit causam fidei, nec aliam causam querit" (cited by Chenu, *La théologie comme science au XIIIe siècle*, 59).

24. Chenu, *La théologie comme science au XIIIe siècle*, 60.

25. Evidence of this trajectory is seen at *Summa aurea*, III, tr. 3, c. I, q. 1: "si in theologia non essent principia, non esset ars vel scientia" (cited by Chenu *La théologie comme science au XIIIe siècle*, 59).

26. On this latter point, see Henry Donneaud, *Théologie et intelligence de la foi au XIIIème siècle* (Paris: Parole et Silence, 2006), 28–29. Donneaud has also provided some important correctives to Chenu's general historical method in Henry Donneaud, "Histoire d'une histoire: M.-D. Chenu et *La théologie comme science au XIIIe siècle*," *Mémoire Dominicaine* 4 (1994): 139–75; Henry Donneaud, "Note sur le *revelabile* selon Étienne Gilson," *Revue Thomiste* 96, no. 4 (1996): 633–52; Henry Donneaud, "M.-D. Chenu et l'exégèse de *sacra doctrina*," *Revue des sciences philosophiques et théologiques* 81 (1997): 415–37.

Even if William of Auxerre never went as far as Aquinas in concluding that sacred doctrine could be called a "science," he nevertheless held that one could direct "argumentative" statements toward the things believed in faith, that is, its objects.[27] When arguing from the objects of faith, William advocated that there should be a certain method of argumentation that was distinct from the other philosophical sciences. The basis for this distinction in method, according to William, came down to the different objects of inquiry held respectively by sacred doctrine and the other philosophical sciences. The order of argument in philosophy, he observed, was to start with things that one could know by reason and to move through argumentation or dialectic to more probable conclusions about things that were previously unknown. In contrast, for sacred doctrine a seemingly inverse method was characteristic; theologians began not with objects known, but with objects believed in the light of Christian faith. They then proceeded to apply rational arguments to these objects of faith in an attempt not to demonstrate them, but to understand them more fully in the light of the other articles of faith. By following this order of argument, William thought theologians were safely preserving faith's motive. The motive for believing the objects of faith came from the fact that they had been revealed by God, and once one recognized that they were divinely revealed, a person was moved to believe them as true. The status of these objects as being divinely revealed was the key motive for theological faith. In applying rational arguments to the objects of faith, theologians were not aiming to prove the objects by rendering them more probable to those individuals without faith; instead, they were attempting to render the objects of faith more readily intelligible in the light of their divinely revealed status.

William summarized three main reasons for why one would apply rational argumentation to the articles of faith.[28] First and foremost, rational arguments helped to "increase and confirm" the faith of believers and their love of God; second, they could help in defending the faith against heretics; and third, they supported and encouraged the *simplices* to hold to true faith—the *simplices* being those individuals who, for various reasons, were unable to devote time to the advanced study of the faith. A common element can be discerned among William's three reasons: rational arguments are meant principally to preserve and deepen faith's merit among believers.

---

27. See Chenu, *La théologie comme science au XIIIe siècle,* 34–37.

28. *Summa aurea,* prologue (cited by Chenu, *La théologie comme science au XIIIe siècle,* 35).

In his definition of faith as "an assenting to the first truth on account of [the first truth] before everything else," William emphasized that Christian faith stemmed directly from a relationship with God as First Truth, to whom the believer "assents" (*acquiescere*).[29] Because God as First Truth is the unique object and motive of assent in theological faith, William thought argumentation about Christian faith could not proceed along the same exact lines of argument in philosophy. For him to assert that sacred doctrine was a science would be in some way to ignore the unique character of faith's more basic assent. Reasoning about faith required its own unique methods to correspond to faith's unique object— God as First Truth. The theologian, while free to employ rational arguments, always needed to regard the prior relationship established in theological faith between God and the human person as the controlling point of reference. William worried that if theological methods were confused with philosophy, the motive of faith would be brought down to an object knowable by reason; this would potentially diminish or destroy altogether the merit of faith, since William insisted along with much of the tradition before him that "faith has no merit where human reason has supplied a proof."[30] Such a conflation of faith and reason would be untenable for any Christian, since the resulting conflation would remove the primacy and immediacy of the believer's supernatural assent to God as First Truth in theological faith. In the last analysis, William's own approach to the issue of the scientific character of sacred doctrine was marked by a stronger desire to preserve and deepen the motive and merit of Christian faith than by a desire to establish or extend a body of theological knowledge.

In his own treatment of the problem, Thomas builds on the analogy offered by William of Auxerre between the articles of faith and the first principles of a science. However, where William saw the need to assert a contrast between faith's motive and the possibility of developing the articles of faith into a sacred science, Aquinas envisions a possible harmonization; faith's motive can be preserved by admitting that the science of sacred doctrine is a subalternate science, whose principles are given and established only in Christian faith. This attempted harmonization enables Thomas to extend to sacred doctrine the character not only of a science, but also of wisdom, the grasping of the highest

---

29. *Summa aurea*, prologue: fides "est acquiescere primae veritati propter se super omnia" (cited by Chenu, *La théologie comme science au XIIIe siècle*, 59).

30. *Summa aurea*, prologue (quoting St. Gregory the Great): "fides non habet meritum ubi humana ratio prebet experimentum" (cited by Chenu, *La théologie comme science au XIIIe siècle*, 34n1).

principle and the judging of all things in light of it. Most of Thomas's predecessors in the twelfth and thirteenth centuries were much more inclined to call the task they were engaged in Christian "wisdom" (*sapientia*) than "science" (*scientia*).[31] One of Thomas's key achievements was to explain why sacred doctrine understood as a science "is among all human wisdoms, supremely wisdom, not only in some class as such, but absolutely."[32]

Sacred Doctrine, Subalternation, and Revelation

Aquinas draws on the distinction between subalternate and non-subalternate sciences and applies it to sacred doctrine. To explain this distinction, he sets up a comparison based on the two ways first principles are knowable within philosophy. In some philosophical sciences, principles are discoverable directly by the light of human reason; Thomas calls these principles *per se nota*. In others, their principles are not directly discoverable by reason, but must be given and mediated through some other science. For this latter type, he gives the example of music deriving some of its principles from arithmetic. In this pair, music is a subalternate science since its principles are taken from another science. Like music, the principles of sacred doctrine are not discovered directly; instead, they derive from another science—"the science of God and the blessed."[33] From this Aquinas concludes that:

> just as the musician believes the principles handed over to him by the arithmetician, so also does sacred doctrine believe principles revealed to it by God (*principia revelata sibi a Deo*).[34]

The principles of the "science of God and the blessed" are things that are divinely revealed. Thus, sacred doctrine is a subalternate science whose principles come through divine revelation—"a kind of teaching according to divine revelation."[35]

---

31. See Chenu, *La théologie comme science au XIIIe siècle*, 93–96.

32. ST, I, q. 1, a. 6, co.: "haec doctrina maxime sapientia est inter omnes sapientias humanas, non quidem in aliquo genere tantum, sed simpliciter." See also Mark F. Johnson, "The Sapiential Character of the First Article of the *Summa theologiae*," in *Philosophy and the God of Abraham: Essays in Memory of James A. Weisheipl, OP*, ed. R. J. Long (Toronto: Pontifical Institute of Mediaeval Studies, 1991), 85–98.

33. ST, I, q. 1, a. 2, co.

34. ST, I, q. 1. a. 2, co.

35. ST, I, q. 1, a. 1, co.: "doctrinam quandam secundum revelationem divinam."

If God's revelation to humanity is required for sacred doctrine's scientific structure according to Aquinas, it would be advantageous to probe more deeply what he understands by this revelation. Throughout his account of sacred doctrine in the *Summa theologiae*, one rarely encounters revelation as something problematized or studied directly by Thomas. Something similar can be said to happen in metaphysics with reference to the theory of knowledge or epistemology. Metaphysics offers a rational inquiry into first causes, and as an inquiry into first causes, it begins with an assumption that one can know something about causes; otherwise, an inquiry would never get started. This implies that some theory of knowledge must be functionally in place in order for any metaphysical inquiry to occur, even though at the outset of such an inquiry one may not be able to give a full account of what it means to know. It is more likely that someone at the outset has an intuitive but unarticulated grasp of what it is "to know," and when pressed to give an account of knowing by being asked "how do you know that you know?" such a person would find the task challenging. It is understandable that difficulties should arise when one is asked to provide an account of knowing, given the degree of separation such an account requires one to have from some of the more familiar and easily knowable things, such as sensible things. In sacred doctrine a similar difficulty arises when one begins to ask for an account of revelation. Just as in metaphysics, in one sense, sacred doctrine must assume that there is something to inquire into (an object) and a motive for inquiring into such an object (a desire to know it). In sacred doctrine the fact that revelation has occurred and exists precedes any investigation of it. Just as any theory of knowledge will depend on contributions from metaphysics (and will, in the final analysis, remain subject to metaphysics within the hierarchy of philosophical disciplines), so too an account of revelation will come as a part of sacred doctrine, which itself depends on revelation already having been given.

Revelation and Scripture

There seem to be many possible reasons why Thomas or any theologian of the thirteenth century never wrote a disputed question *de revelatione*. Belief in revelation and in its transmission (at least partially) through sacred scripture was the common starting point nurtured and assumed by the Christian faith that permeated the thirteenth-century world. It did this in a way that is difficult for us in the twenty-first century to reconstruct completely. The fact that divine revelation was not extensively problematized either by Thomas or by his contemporaries is hardly surprising.[36] Even if his historical context gave him little reason for seeing the fact of revelation as something needing explanation in itself, one still finds that almost all of his thinking bears the marks of being in constant dialogue with the divinely revealed mysteries of his Christian faith. Nowhere is this more prominent than in the role scripture plays as root and foundation of almost all of Thomas's theological reflections.

In the recent scholarship there has been a "re-discovery" of the scriptural focus of his thought, which has unsurprisingly centered around Thomas, the biblical commentator.[37] Without wishing to downplay the importance of these biblical commentaries for his theological method, one can discern underlying his approach to the Bible a more basic and, in the final analysis, more primary structure: it is found in faith's orientation to human salvation. Here one sees the crux of Thomas's notion of revelation operative as a continual and progressive human encounter with God that only reaches fulfilment in the beatific vision. Such an encounter is mediated in various ways, and scripture is certainly one of the most important ways Thomas thinks humans encounter God. Nevertheless, he thinks that profitable reading of the Bible is itself mediated through the theological virtue of faith. In the heart of the believer, faith initiates an immediate and direct encounter with God; this same faith also is normally mediated socially. Throughout his career, Thomas devoted careful attention to the ways divine revelation comes and has come to human beings. He tended

---

36. At the same time, questions about the historical status of revelation were not altogether foreign to this period; for the example of Herbert of Bosham, contemporary of Thomas Becket, see Congar, "Le moment 'économique' et le moment 'ontologique' dans la *Sacra doctrina*," 171. On historicity in the medieval universities and in Thomas, see also Étienne Gilson, *The Spirit of Mediaeval Philosophy*, trans. A. H. C. Downes (New York: Scribner, 1936), 383–402; Armand A. Maurer, *St. Thomas and Historicity* (Milwaukee: Marquette University Press, 1979); Jean-Pierre Torrell, "Saint Thomas et l'histoire: État de la question et pistes de recherches," *Revue Thomiste* 105, no. 3 (2005): 355–409; reprinted in *Nouvelles recherches thomasiennes* (Paris: Vrin, 2008), 131–75.

37. See Thomas G. Weinandy, Daniel A. Keating, and John P. Yocum, eds., *Aquinas on Scripture: An Introduction to his Biblical Commentaries* (London: T & T Clark, 2005); Michael Dauphinais and Matthew Levering, eds., *Reading John with St. Thomas Aquinas: Theological Exegesis and Speculative Theology* (Washington, DC: The Catholic University of America Press, 2005); Matthew Levering and Michael Dauphinais, eds., *Reading Romans with St. Thomas Aquinas* (Washington, DC: The Catholic University of America Press, 2012).

to approach these different ways under three main rubrics: God's revealed self-knowledge (1) in sacred doctrine, (2) in faith, and (3) in prophecy—a unique and special case of God communicating His self-knowledge directly to select individuals.

The Prologue and Intention of the *Summa theologiae*

This brief aside about how Thomas's practice of reading scripture fits into his thought in general now sets the stage for turning to his most mature discussion of theological method in the *Summa theologiae*. The occasion for this work, as Aquinas himself reports, arose in part from his dissatisfaction with current pedagogical methods practiced most likely within his own Dominican order.[38] In the *Summa*'s general prologue, he states: "our proposed intention in this work is to treat the things that pertain to Christian religion in a way that is suitable for the education of beginners."[39] The "teacher of catholic truth" (*catholicae veritatis doctor*), he explains, while having the duty "to build up" (*instruere*) those who are already advanced, must also be prepared "to educate beginners" (*incipientes erudire*). In this task, foremost in his mind as a model is St. Paul, whom he cites directly as someone who knew to give only milk to those "infants in Christ" (*parvulis in Christo*) and not solid food.[40] Since the "teacher of catholic truth" must also consider "those who are new" (*novitios*), Thomas justifies to himself and to his reader an assessment of current pedagogical practice. His report is somewhat grim: the instruction of "beginners" has become overly complicated and aimless; teachers no longer taught "according to the order of the discipline"

---

38. For an overview of the historical evidence and scholarship that situate the ST within contemporaneous Dominican education, see Mark F. Johnson, "Aquinas's *Summa theologiae* as Pedagogy," in *Medieval Education*, ed. Ronald B. Begley and Joseph W. Koterski (New York: Fordham University Press, 2005), 133–42. On some of the precursors, see Romanus Cessario, "Toward Understanding Aquinas' Theological Method: The Early Twelfth-Century Experience," in *Studies in Thomistic Theology*, ed. Paul Lockey (Houston: Center for Thomistic Studies, 1995), 17–89.

39. ST, prologue: "Quia catholicae veritatis doctor non solum provectos debet instruere, sed ad eum pertinet etiam incipientes erudire, secundum illud apostoli I ad Corinth. III, 'tanquam parvulis in Christo, lac vobis potum dedi, non escam;' *propositum nostrae intentionis in hoc opere est, ea quae ad Christianam religionem pertinent, eo modo tradere, secundum quod congruit ad eruditionem incipientium*" (emphasis mine).

40. See Anthony Keaty, "The Demands of Sacred Doctrine on 'Beginners,'" *New Blackfriars* 84 (2003): 500–509.

(*secundum ordinem disciplinae*), but, in its place, offered their own commentaries on other books or simply rehashed older academic disputations; students were getting bogged down in repetitions that were putting them off (*fastidium*) and causing them to become confused "in their souls" (*in animis*).[41] The criticisms are stark; and if the last one is any indication, Thomas may have even been concerned that these pedagogical hindrances were potentially harming the spiritual and moral formation of novices. So direct and vivid are these criticisms that one is inclined to think that Aquinas observed much of this firsthand. To address the current state of pedagogy in his order, he thus set out to compose "this work," which we now call the *Summa theologiae*,[42] as a reformed pedagogy: "thus, eager to avoid these [hindrances] and others like them, we will endeavor, with a reliance on divine help, to describe in detail those things which pertain to sacred doctrine briefly and clearly, following what the material will allow."[43]

If a reformed pedagogy is what Thomas had in mind, the question of the intended audience of the work soon arises. On this point, scholars have held various opinions. Weisheipl characterizes the *Summa theologiae* as "a handbook suitable for novices."[44] Leonard Boyle tends, in general, to agree with Weisheipl that the *Summa* is meant for "beginners"—the *incipientes* mentioned in the prologue—and has even presented a cunningly-crafted argument that identifies these "beginners" as Thomas's own students at the Dominican Convent of Santa Sabina in Rome around 1265, who would have been under his sole care and direction.[45] However, other scholars have sometimes found it hard to believe

---

41. ST, prologue: "Consideravimus namque huius doctrinae novitios, in his quae a diversis conscripta sunt, plurimum impediri, partim quidem propter multiplicationem inutilium quaestionum, articulorum et argumentorum; partim etiam quia ea quae sunt necessaria talibus ad sciendum, non traduntur secundum ordinem disciplinae, sed secundum quod requirebat librorum expositio, vel secundum quod se praebebat occasio disputandi; partim quidem quia eorundem frequens repetitio et fastidium et confusionem generabat in animis auditorium."

42. It is still unclear whether Thomas himself ever gave the name *Summa theologiae* to "this work." For the various early testimonies of the work's name, see Angelus Walz, "De genuino titulo *Summae theologiae*," *Angelicum* 18 (1941): 142–51; see also Mark D. Jordan, *Rewritten Theology: Aquinas after His Readers* (Oxford: Blackwell, 2006), 118n5.

43. ST, prologue: "haec igitur et alia huiusmodi evitare studentes, tentabimus, cum confidentia divini auxilii, ea quae ad sacram doctrinam pertinent, breviter ac dilucide prosequi, secundum quod materia patietur."

44. Weisheipl, "The Meaning of Sacred Doctrine," 54.

45. Leonard E. Boyle, "The Setting of the *Summa theologiae* of St. Thomas—Revisited," in *The Ethics of Aquinas*, ed. Stephen J. Pope (Washington, DC: Georgetown University Press, 2002), 1–16, at 6–9. Compare Torrell, *Initiation*, 192–94, who (following Oliva, *Les débuts*

that Aquinas would have intended the *Summa theologiae* to be meant for absolute beginners. Basing his arguments largely on the philosophical aspects and difficulty of the work as a whole, John Jenkins is critical of Boyle's thesis and argues that the intended audience could not have been absolute beginners but were more likely students already somewhat familiar with sacred doctrine.[46] When one considers the attention Thomas pays to pedagogical issues in the prologue, it seems probable that the intended audience of the new *Summa* would have already been studying for some time and likely would have been familiar with (and perhaps even sympathetic to) some of Thomas's criticisms.

The question of the identity of Thomas's intended audience may not seem to be the most relevant for a discussion of sacred doctrine. However, when one examines the different ways that scholars have treated the question, one begins to see just how often they appeal to the larger theme of *sacra doctrina* to make their arguments. Jenkins, for instance, seems to base the main thrust of his argument for why the intended audience could not be absolute beginners on Thomas's explicit identification of sacred doctrine as a *scientia*. In general, Jenkins tends to read this identification strongly in terms of Aristotle's notion of *epistēmē* from his account in the *Posterior Analytics*. In Aristotle's account as outlined by Jenkins, *epistēmē* is concerned with demonstrations from first principles. The person who sets out to acquire a new *epistēmē* must first be acquainted with first principles, which are only introduced and identified

---

de l'enseignement) admits the possibility of Thomas teaching portions of the First Part of the ST at a so-called *studium personale* in Rome, but is more tentative than Boyle on this point. Torrell tends to downplay the significance of the scholarly debate about whether the *incipientes* were absolute beginners or more advanced students and refrains from taking a decisive stand on either side, being more eager to point out how the ST's prologue manifests "the concerns of a pedagogue" (193). In this last respect, Torrell seems to come quite close to the opinion held by Mark Jordan that the ST represents "an ideal pedagogy" that was never taught "verbatim" by Thomas; see Jordan, *Rewritten Theology*, 119–20. Jordan argues creatively for this position by pointing to certain textual parallels between the First Part and the earlier *Summa contra Gentiles*, rather than between the First Part and the so-called *Lectura romana* discovered and attributed to Thomas by Boyle. *Lectura romana in primum Sententiarum Petri Lombardi*, ed. Leonard E. Boyle and John F. Boyle (Toronto: Pontifical Institute of Mediaeval Studies, 2006). On the latter text, see the corrective assessment of Torrell, *Initiation*, 73–77.

    46. Jenkins, *Knowledge and Faith*, 79–85, at 83: "the content of the ST is not that of a work gauged for neophytes in a field." Compare James A. Weisheipl, *Friar Thomas d'Aquino: His Life, Thought, and Works* (Oxford: Basil Blackwell, 1975), 362, whose view that only the First Part is truly for "beginners" is less than satisfactory.

through "first-level pedagogy."[47] Only after this "first-level pedagogy," where one has become acquainted with the "fundamental concepts" and principles of the field, can a person then proceed to "second-level" pedagogy, which is aimed at developing an *epistēmē*. Jenkins thinks Aristotle's account from the *Posterior Analytics* is the predominant controlling account for Thomas's own notion of a *scientia*, and from this, he concludes that the intended audience of the *Summa theologiae* could not have been absolute beginners; they would already need to have been instructed in "first-level pedagogy" and be acquainted with the first principles of sacred doctrine before they could ever proceed to study and acquire it as a *scientia*.

Mark Jordan, while materially sharing Jenkins's conclusion that the *Summa* was never intended for absolute beginners, remains critical of how he comes to this conclusion. He thinks that Jenkins relies "too much on contemporary evaluations of the work's scope or difficulty" and over-reads the importance of "Aristotelian paradigms of *scientia*" in the *Summa theologiae*.[48] For Jordan the *Summa* represents Thomas's "ideal pedagogy" or "ideal curriculum" designed "for middle learners in a vowed community of Christian pastors."[49] Given that both Jordan and Jenkins are in material agreement that the *Summa* was not intended to be read by absolute neophytes, it is all the more striking that each advances his own argument by appealing differently to broader notions of *scientia* and sacred doctrine. These debates surrounding the identity of the intended audience are best understood not as ends in themselves, but as entry-points into a series of broader considerations about Thomas's purpose in the *Summa theologiae*. Such considerations represent the fruits of some of the more minute research carried out in the twentieth century on Thomas's historical context. Once these broader considerations come into view the controversy over any strict identification of the intended audience becomes somewhat secondary; baring the discovery of any additional manuscript evidence, any identification must remain somewhat tentative and ought to be based on a detailed analysis of what Thomas means to accomplish by "treating" or, more literally, by "handing over (*tradere*) the things that pertain to Christian religion." This phrase just-mentioned—*ea quae ad Christianam religionem pertinent ... tradere*—is

---

47. Jenkins, *Knowledge and Faith*, 80; here Jenkins clarifies what he means by a "first-level" pedagogy.

48. Jordan, *Rewritten Theology*, 117n4.

49. Jordan, *Rewritten Theology*, 120.

Thomas's first expression of the scope and definition of what he will explicitly call in Question One *sacra doctrina*.

Yet, before turning to Question One itself, an additional observation regarding this phrase may be pertinent. Thomas here associates his intent "to treat the things pertaining to Christian religion" with the task of "the teacher of catholic truth." In this juxtaposition, he is not opposing the two or strictly subordinating one to the other. On the one hand, it seems at first the treatment of the things of Christian religion is a specification of the role of the teacher of catholic truth—the sense of "catholic" here meaning "universal" as based on the word's Greek etymology.[50] On the other, the juxtaposition could also be seen to work in the opposite direction; Christian religion is a point of reference for the "teacher of catholic truth." Far from subordinating one to the other, Thomas proposes an ordered relationship between universal truth and Christian religion.[51] This ordered relationship allows us a first glimpse at a deep chord sounding throughout the work concerning the relationship between reason and faith and between nature and grace. While the dominant emphasis in the *Summa theologiae* will be to hand over the things divinely revealed as relating to Christian religion, this will be accomplished with the help of "the teacher of catholic truth." From the outset it is important to observe that Thomas does not conflate here the "teacher of catholic truth" to a *doctor christianiae religionis*, nor does he conflate "Christian religion" to *vera religio*.[52] By "Christian religion," he means here the life of Christian faith—belief in a divinely revealed truth that is orderable to the teaching of universal truth. Deep within this Christian faith there is a dimension that seeks to communicate knowledge of the truth and the truths of faith to others, and to announce that this truth is mankind's ultimate end and good. This inner dimension of the life of faith, which attempts to communicate truth to others, is also a key component of *sacra doctrina*;

---

50. As Thomas is well aware, the term "catholic" is not necessarily limited to a Christian application; see *Super Boetium de Trinitate*, ed. P.-M. Gils, Leonine Edition, vol. 50 (Rome: Commissio Leonina, 1992), II, prologue: "catholicum enim Graece Latine universale dicitur." In fact, Thomas is implicitly reminding his reader of this broader scope of the word by having it modify *veritatis* as opposed to *fidei* or *doctrinae*.

51. Compare *Summa contra Gentiles* (hereafter *SCG*), ed. P. Marc, C. Pera, and P. Carmello. 3 vols. (Turin: Marietti, 1961–1967), I, 2, 5: "quomodo demonstrativa veritas, fidei Christianae religionis concordet."

52. See Erich Heck, *Der Begriff* religio *bei Thomas von Aquin: Seine Bedeutung für unser heutiges Verständnis von Religion* (Paderborn: Ferdinand Schöningh, 1971), 105.

this aspect is brought out more clearly, I maintain, when one sees it in light of Thomas's notion of prophecy. Prophecy starkly reminds one that the source of any truth, whether divinely revealed or not, lies beyond the individual person, and that any communication of truth is orderable toward a common good. From prophecy too, sacred doctrine receives the character of being oriented toward a common good.

The Intention of Question One

Having introduced the work's intention in the prologue, Aquinas goes on to delimit this intention further in Question One by proposing to investigate "this sacred doctrine" (*de ipsa sacra doctrina*): "what kind" (*qualis sit*) of doctrine is it and "to what does it extend" (*ad quae se extendat*).[53] The investigation of Question One aims to allow the reader to comprehend the work's intention "under some fixed boundaries" (*sub aliquibus certis limitibus*). The entirety of this intention is what he calls "sacred doctrine." It is, therefore, essential to observe what he says about these intentional boundaries.

A medieval author's intention is closely related to what today we would call a work's "subject."[54] An intention orients something toward a particular end or purpose. In grasping the intention of an author, one grasps what the author through the work is trying to say. A medieval work's intention should also be understood in a macroscopic sense. In introducing the intention, an author allows the entirety of the work to be seen, but the individual parts are not yet fully distinguished. At the same time, the intention of the work is the starting point. These starting points are called principles when one starts to consider how other things relate to them. This task of seeing what things follow (logically, for instance) from given principles and the subsequent comparison back to the principles by means of a judgment is central to Thomas's account of the acts of

---

53. The Latin may be helpful here; ST, I, q. 1, prologue: "et ut intentio nostra sub aliquibus certis limitibus comprehendatur, necessarium est primo investigare de ipsa sacra doctrina, qualis sit, et ad quae se extendat."

54. On Thomas's notion of the *intentio auctoris* and its larger place in medieval hermeneutics, see Torrell, *The Person and His Work*, 275–76 (*Initiation*, 305–6), who deviates little from the earlier observations of Marie-Dominique Chenu, *Toward Understanding Saint Thomas*, trans. A.-M. Landry and D. Hughes (Chicago: Regnery, 1964), 153–54. In other works, Aquinas presents his intention elaborating on the work's purpose and method; see *SCG*, I, 9. For a general discussion of the place of the *intentio* in medieval prologues, see the bibliography cited by Oliva, *Les débuts de l'enseignement*, 256–57, 269n68.

knowledge (*scientia*) and understanding (*intellectus*). Each of these acts corresponds to sacred doctrine's respective identifications as knowledge (*scientia*) and the understanding of the highest principle, or wisdom.

In order for a whole to "be comprehended" (*comprehendatur*), there must also be boundaries; something limitless cannot be grasped. That the boundaries are "fixed" also suggests that they do not or cannot change and that they are capable of being discerned.[55] The whole exists before any of the individual parts are discerned or treated, and any part can only be identified *qua* part through its relationship to a whole. Question One, as Thomas explains in its prologue, allows one to see what sacred doctrine is in its entirety before he begins to treat the individual parts. Because the question approaches sacred doctrine in the round, its articles do not emphasize the different parts of sacred doctrine, but its unity—a unity that ultimately derives not from the human mind, but from God's own knowledge, which is absolutely simple and extends to everything.[56]

These fixed boundaries by which Thomas wishes to reach his intended end are divinely revealed. As boundaries, they permit one to see the whole of sacred doctrine as one, unified divine teaching. This one divine teaching simultaneously embraces both the orders of nature and grace, which Thomas carefully distinguishes but without ever isolating them from their prior unity in God's unified knowledge. The unity and certitude of God's knowledge ensures that sacred doctrine is of unshakable certitude.[57] Moreover, not every boundary can be discerned in the course of Question One; after all, Thomas speaks of *aliquibus limitibus*. The *aliquibus* here expresses an indefiniteness when juxtaposed with *certis*, but this indefiniteness is not with regard to the certitude of the boundaries, which being revealed by God are unshakably certain; instead, the indefiniteness is with regard to the number and extensiveness of the boundaries that can be comprehended by human beings. This suggests that Thomas does not intend his discernment of the boundaries here in Question One to be an exhaustive or complete delimiting of sacred doctrine.[58]

---

55. The phrase is also evoked in discussions concerning the limiting of a creature to its nature; compare this to a passage from St. Ambrose cited by Thomas that observes that every creature "is circumscribed by the fixed boundaries of its nature" (*certis suae naturae circumscripta est limitibus*); see ST, I, q. 50, a. 1, obj. 3. Compare also *De ver.*, q. 20, a. 4, obj. 13.

56. See ST, I, q. 1, a. 3, ad 2.

57. Sacred doctrine's unity is a closer approximation to God's unity than that of any other human science.

58. Thomas's reluctance to present an exhaustive account of sacred doctrine has rightfully drawn the attention of scholars in recent times; see Jordan, *Rewritten Theology*, 119 and

Intention Explored through Thomas's Fifth Way

Having introduced his intention, Thomas immediately expresses a need to set "fixed limits." In what sense does Thomas mean these limits are "fixed" (*certis*)? Who or what fixes these limits? In one sense, Thomas as the work's author fixes the limits himself so that his discrete intention may be comprehended by his reader; this is the task of Question One. However, the matter is not quite so straightforward, because in that same question Thomas confesses that he is not the ultimate person who fixes these limits. The limits again refer to sacred doctrine, which he thinks allows his intention to be comprehended by the reader. But sacred doctrine is "according to a divine revelation" that goes beyond the reach of human reason.[59] To recall, the intention stated in the general prologue is "to treat the things that pertain to Christian religion" in a fashion suitable to the education of beginners. The boundaries thus are also fixed in part

---

123n23. On the one hand, the sheer length and breadth of the ST have led some to think that Thomas meant to give a complete overview or encyclopaedic account of theology that was exhaustive; often this observation has been made either as a kind of criticism or as a point of admiration. The latter often came to justify (in the minds of some) Thomas's canonization as an unshakably orthodox theological authority. Is either of these a fair assessment? Without intending to resolve the debate concerning the merits or demerits of complete and closed accounts of theology, it seems fair to say there has been confusion among some of Thomas's readers who appear to have conflated his intention to present the whole of sacred doctrine intact, so to speak, and an intention to offer a complete and closed account of sacred doctrine. Thomas does the former, but I highly doubt he intended the latter. Some of these worries about whether Thomas is being overly confident in human reason's ability to approximate divine truths are not trivial, and many of them seem to stem in part from a renewed appreciation for the apophatic dimension of Christian theology; indeed, there likely is a deeper connection here between Thomas not claiming to offer a complete account of sacred doctrine and his acute awareness of the limitations of human thought and language about God. On the other hand, perhaps this renewed interest in apophaticism has led some scholars to be critical of those interpreters of Thomas who see in his work a complete or quasi-closed system of theology. At the same time, closer attention to the "cataphatic dependencies" (as Mark Johnson puts it) of apophatic theology may help to resolve the tension between the two and explain why one would want to talk about "the things that pertain to Christian religion" in the first place; for more on these "cataphatic dependencies," see Mark F. Johnson, "Apophatic Theology's Cataphatic Dependencies," *The Thomist* 62, no. 4 (1998): 519–31. Victor Preller's overemphasis of the apophatic dimension in Thomas leads one to have reservations about his analysis in *Divine Science and the Science of God: A Reformulation of Thomas Aquinas* (Princeton, NJ: Princeton University Press, 1967).

    59. ST, I, q. 1, a. 1, co.

by the divinely revealed "Christian religion," which earlier we suggested means the entire life of Christian faith.

The gift of faith is foundational for the Christian life, and as a prelude to our later discussion of his questions on faith in the *Summa theologiae*, Thomas notably defines it there as "a habit of the mind by which eternal life begins in us."[60] He also takes important note of how the author of Heb 11:1 describes faith as "the substance of things hoped for, the evidence of things unseen." Thomas takes the first half of the Hebrews definition to be identifying faith as a "likeness" to God's own eternal substance and knowledge.[61] Within its act, faith entails an intellectual grasping of God as one's own final end, a divinely-assisted first motion of the will toward God, and a stabilization of the will's orientation to that end as an object of hope, the virtue that subsequently perfects the will along with charity.[62] While a full analysis of theological faith will come later in the third chapter, enough of the elements of Thomas's notion of faith have already been introduced to draw out some of its parallels with our discussion of intention. From the part of the individual human person, the act of faith is the initial grasping of God as highest truth and final end (final end here also = highest good) accompanied by a corresponding, divinely-assisted act of the will that moves the intellect to assent to that end. In this way, faith orients the intention of an entire human life toward God. From God's perspective, faith is a beginning (of sorts) of God realizing the divinely-willed intention for each human person that imitates (and echoes) the realization of God's intentional act of creation.

The doctrine of creation, thus, for Thomas is the constant reference point for explaining faith on the level of intention, because like creation, faith is, in the end, a freely given outpouring of divine goodness. Because creation is God's free decision, this means that we can also say that his act of creation is *intentional* in the qualified sense that it is the product of God's own practical knowledge.[63]

Turning back now to the question of the *Summa theologiae*'s intention, one can see that in being limited by divine revelation Thomas's intention is not shaped by his mind or will alone, but Thomas himself thinks it reflects God's

---

60. ST, II-II, q. 4, a. 1, co.: "fides est habitus mentis, qua inchoatur vita aeterna in nobis."

61. ST, II-II, q. 4, a. 1, ad 1: "substantia non sumitur hic secundum quod est genus generalissimum contra alia genera divisum, sed secundum quod in quolibet genere invenitur *quaedam similitudo substantiae*" (emphasis mine).

62. See ST, II-II, q. 4, a. 1, ad 2

63. See David Burrell, *Knowing the Unknowable God: Ibn-Sina, Maimonides, Aquinas* (Notre Dame: University of Notre Dame Press, 1986), 90.

own practical knowledge, which desires to lead all things back to God through divine governance. Admittedly, what we have outlined above represents a very condensed account of how his stated intention in writing the *Summa* relates to his larger understanding of faith and sacred doctrine as the intended instruments of divine governance. In order to bring out more clearly this relationship between intention and knowledge and between divine intention and divine governance, it may be helpful to situate this discussion in the context of Thomas's Fifth Way in Question Two.[64]

The Fifth Way begins "from the government of things" (*ex gubernatione rerum*). Aside from suggesting guidance and direction, the term "government" already implies some type of intention by which other things are directed (or governed) to some end. Thomas notes that we see things that lack knowledge, like plants, acting for some end (*propter finem*). These things appear to be acting for an end because they always or very frequently act in the same way; plants, for instance, almost always tend to grow toward sunlight. This "tending toward," as suggested etymologically, gets behind one sense of what Thomas means by "intention"—*in aliquid tendere*.[65] Plants tend to act this way "so that they will reach that which is best" (*ut consequantur id quod est optimum*). Thomas's use of the neuter here (*id quod est optimum*) suggests that the good he has in mind is not exclusively the good of the individual plant (or of any other *corpus naturale*), but the good of a whole. Individual plants, thus, do not seem to be acting randomly, but rather "they arrive at an end by intention" (*ex intentione perveniunt ad finem*).

Do things like plants possess this intention themselves? Thomas thinks, no. While things like trees do tend to an end by growing toward sunlight, Thomas denies that they possess their own intention. An intention strictly speaking requires a will being directed toward an end by some ordering of reason.[66] Since trees lack reason, they cannot possess wills and, thus, do not have intentions. Thomas's example of an arrow being shot by an archer reinforces the point; an arrow, being inanimate, also lacks its own intention and remains entirely dependent on the archer for its direction in flight. The arrow itself does not

---

64. ST, I, q. 2, a. 3, co.

65. ST, I-II, q. 12, a. 1, co.: "intentio, sicut ipsum nomen sonat, significat in aliquid tendere."

66. ST, I-II, q. 12, a. 1, ad 3: "nomen intentio nominat actum voluntatis, praesupposita ordinatione rationis ordinantis aliquid in finem."

intend to hit the target. It is the archer who intends to hit it. Once the target "is seen"—or perceived as an end[67]—the archer orders the arrow so that it will hit the target by adjusting the height of the bow or the bowstring's tension. The arrow itself only tends to the target depending on how well the archer has aimed and executed the shot. The archer, and the archer alone, can be said to intend the arrow to hit its target. From this example, Thomas concludes that there must be "some intelligence" (*aliquid intelligens*) ordering all natural things to an end, and "this we call God" (*hoc dicimus Deum*).

Without entering into the larger debates about Thomas's Five Ways, their general purpose and probative value, we can still take from this outline of the Fifth Way several insights into how Thomas conceives of divine intention as an act of divine governance. In a very basic sense, an intention belongs to something that moves itself or others voluntarily toward some end.[68] In creatures that possess a will, so-called voluntary creatures, the will is the power that moves them and the other things they act upon toward some end. This voluntary movement is not random, but is ordered and directed by reason to an end. In creatures that lack wills, like rocks, an intention is not ascribed directly to them as such. Yet, because rocks move in very regular ways falling almost always to the ground (Thomas thinks), it "appears" that rocks do act with an intention. If we cannot ascribe an intention to rocks, there has to be some other intelligent agent that accounts for the intended motion. When Thomas, at the end of the Fifth Way, invokes God as the intelligence that orders everything to its end, he describes "everything" as "all natural things" (*omnes res naturales*). By this phrase, Thomas means now to include under God's ordering intelligence not only involuntary and inanimate creatures, but also voluntary and rational ones—in short, all of creation. The entire created universe comes under the intention of God's intelligence, and this intention includes God's governance of all natural things.

Would sacred doctrine classify as a *res naturalis* given that it is divinely revealed? Within the strict context of the Fifth Way it seems unlikely. Like all the other ways, the Fifth Way is a demonstration that begins "from effects

---

67. Thomas perspicuously remarks that "sight" is said metaphorically in intention-language and refers primarily to something previously known and "presupposed" as an end; see ST, I-II, q. 12, a. 1, ad 1: "intentio nominatur oculus metaphorice, non quia ad cognitionem pertineat; sed quia cognitionem praesupponit, per quam proponitur voluntati finis ad quem movet; sicut oculo praevidemus quo tendere corporaliter debeamus."

68. See ST, I-II, q. 12, a. 1, co.

that are known to us."[69] I suggest that what is meant here in the context of the Fifth Way by "effects known to us" are "effects" that are *naturally* known to us. This reading is supported by Thomas's explicit example of *corpora naturalia* at the beginning of the way and his mention of *res naturales* at the end.[70] Sacred doctrine, in contrast, begins from a supernatural revelation, and cannot be called "natural." Does this mean that sacred doctrine lacks an intention? The answer to this depends on the perspective one considers. From God's perspective, sacred doctrine receives its intention from Him and is a part of divine governance. How can we be sure that it is a part of divine governance? Paradoxically, that God intended something to be divinely revealed to us, Thomas thinks, can only be known to us through divine revelation itself. For this reason, sacred doctrine is "knowable" as a part of divine governance not as something demonstrable from its effects, but from it being perceived through the *eyes of faith* as being ordered to the same end as all *res naturalia*: the *bonum optimum*. It is taken "on faith" and "in faith" that God intends in divine revelation our ultimate happiness and the greatest good for the universe, that is, that divine revelation is part of divine governance. Faith reveals that the basis for this hope is God.

This unity of God's intention is what enables, in part, Thomas to see the continuity between the created order (*omnes res naturales*) and the supernatural order of grace. Our knowledge of God's intention in divine revelation does not come from "natural things" (*naturalia*) as such, but from the human encounter with God in the light of faith, where one begins to see God's intention with His own "eyes." In more specific terms, in faith one begins to see one's own life as ultimately ordered to God—as someone intended for God; through faith one begins to know things according to God's knowledge of them and is called to try to live and to act how God intended.

---

69. See ST, I, q. 2, a. 2, co.

70. That said, the phrase *ex gubernatione rerum*—the real starting point of the Fifth Way—complicates the matter. One cannot exclude the possibility of supernatural revelation (*supernaturalia*) being included under "the governance of things" and thus being taken as an effect from which a causal demonstration can begin. An earlier passage from Question One leaves this possibility open; see ST, I, q. 1, a. 7, ad 1: "licet de Deo non possimus scire quid est, utimur tamen *eius effectu*, in hac doctrina, vel *naturae vel gratiae*, loco definitionis, ad ea quae de Deo in hac doctrina considerantur, sicut et in aliquibus scientiis philosophicis demonstratur aliquid de causa per effectum, accipiendo effectum loco definitionis causae" (emphasis mine). The *eius effectu gratiae* (a possible reading) would imply anything divinely revealed.

This discussion with the help of the Fifth Way now allows us to make better sense of Thomas's restatement of the intention of the *Summa* at the beginning of Question Two:

> the principal intention of this sacred doctrine is to hand over knowledge of God, not only as He is in Himself, but also as He is the beginning of things and their end, and especially of the rational creature.[71]

This statement is not primarily a definition transposed from metaphysics—whose own object is the highest principle and everything else in relation to it—over to sacred doctrine with the aim of intelligibly expressing the contents of divine revelation. While the statement does have the effect of making divine revelation intelligible to the human mind by proposing an order of learning (*ordo disciplinae*), the statement first and foremost follows the order of God's own knowledge; in knowing Himself (*in se*), God knows everything else as a product of divine practical knowledge.[72] All things outside of God are products of God's practical intellect because they are intended, which means they are freely willed and caused by His knowledge.[73]

Returning now to the question of the intention of sacred doctrine, it can be seen more clearly how knowledge of God (*Dei cognitio*) is that which sets the boundaries of sacred doctrine. The only reason why we have knowledge of these boundaries is because they have been divinely revealed. Beyond setting boundaries, knowledge of God remains the ultimate aim of sacred doctrine. This means not just knowledge of God, but also a closer approximation of God's mode of knowing. This also includes knowledge of divine governance and, crucially, for rational creatures, a participation in this governance.

---

71. ST, I, q. 2, prologue: "principalis intentio huius sacrae doctrinae est Dei cognitionem tradere, et non solum secundum quod in se est, sed etiam secundum quod est principium rerum et finis earum, et specialiter rationalis creaturae."

72. ST, I, q. 14, a. 16, ad 2: Deus "in speculativa sui ipsius scientia, habet cognitionem et speculativam et practicam omnium aliorum."

73. ST, I, q. 14, a. 16, ad 1: "scientia Dei est causa, non quidem sui ipsius, sed aliorum." This does not mean that in knowing all creatures God causes everything in the divine mind to come to be. Thomas clearly thinks that outside of creatures God also possesses a speculative and non-practical knowledge of uncreated things that could have been created but never will be; on both categories, see ST, I, q. 14, a. 16, co. In and of themselves, humans cannot know these "virtual" realities ("virtual" because they remain solely in God's power to create) other than their logical possibility or impossibility, unless God decides to reveal them.

Intention as an Entry Point for Sacred Doctrine's Subject

A quick comparison with the first major theological work of Thomas's career, his *Scriptum super libros Sententiarum*, reveals how he initially hesitated to identify God as the subject of sacred doctrine. He was afraid that by calling God its "subject" he would be implying that some kind of total comprehension of God was possible. Yet, the divine essence, he thought, could never be fully comprehended by any created intellect.[74] In explaining this hesitation, he acknowledges that there is a qualified sense in which God can be said to be a "subject" in sacred doctrine: "God is not a subject, except inasmuch as He is that which is principally intended; and it is under this aspect [of being that which is principally intended] that everything in the science [of sacred doctrine] is considered."[75] When revisiting the issue in the *Summa theologiae* later in his career, Thomas no longer hesitates to identify God as the subject of sacred doctrine, devoting an entire article to the topic.[76] Nonetheless, this earlier passage from the *Scriptum* remains illuminating, because it highlights the aspects of intention and final causality within Thomas's notion of a "subject," which one might quickly gloss over if reading the *Summa* article alone. This later article does not contradict the *Scriptum*'s earlier qualified sense of sacred doctrine's "subject" as "that which is principally intended" and under which everything else is considered as tending toward:

> All things are held together in sacred doctrine under the aspect of God, either because they are identical with God or because they possess an ordering toward God, as toward beginning and end. Hence, it follows that God truly is the subject of this science.[77]

---

74. See ST, I, q. 12, a. 7, co.

75. *Scriptum super libros Sententiarum magistri Petri Lombardi episcopi Parisiensis*, ed. Pierre Mandonnet and M. F. Moos, 4 vols. (Paris: P. Lethielleux, 1929–47), I, prologue, q. 1, a. 4, ad 1: "Deus non est subiectum nisi sicut principaliter intentum et sub cuius ratione omnia que sunt in scientia considerantur." The Latin text of *In I Sent.*, prologue and q. 1 is taken from the critical edition of Oliva, *Les débuts de l'enseignement*, 303–40.

76. ST, I, q. 1, a. 7.

77. ST, I, q. 1, a. 7, co.: "Omnia autem pertractantur in sacra doctrina sub ratione Dei, vel quia sunt ipse Deus; vel quia habent ordinem ad Deum, ut ad principium et finem. Unde sequitur quod Deus vere sit subiectum huius scientiae."

Another text from the same article reveals a similar emphasis on ordination to God as the unifying aspect: "all the other things that are determined in sacred doctrine are comprehended under God, not as parts, species, or accidents, but as things in some way ordered to Him."[78] This aspect regards everything in sacred doctrine as how it is intended by God. Divine intentions are acts of God's practical reason, and divine practical reason is itself causative; it creates. This is why the other things determined in sacred doctrine cannot be said to be parts, species, or accidents; they are created by God and, thus, are ontologically distinct from God. They are not in the same genus and, therefore, cannot be species; nor since they are substances can they be accidents. In considering things as they are ordered to God—as they are intended by God for God—Thomas presents an *ordo disciplinae* that mirrors God's order of causation.

Because Thomas stresses "that which something is tending toward" as the focal meaning of God as "subject" of sacred doctrine, he explicitly rules out identifying the subject of sacred doctrine with the alternative models of other theologians—the works of reparation, the *totus Christus*. Certainly, these alternative theological schemas are treatable in sacred doctrine, but Thomas thinks that they are treatable only "according to their ordination to God."[79] He ultimately rejects these other ways of framing sacred doctrine because they are not founded on the order of divine intention and divine causation.

The following five points summarize our findings so far: (1) by examining sacred doctrine's intention, we observe that Thomas identifies sacred doctrine's end with God's own knowledge; (2) it is from God's own order of knowing that sacred doctrine receives its order of knowledge, which, in turn, gives it its unique *ordo disciplinae*; (3) in knowing Himself, God's knowledge is the cause of what He knows *ad extra*; (4) since God's knowledge is causative, sacred doctrine's *ordo disciplinae* mirrors the order of causation (as things are caused and intended by God); (5) this leads Thomas to conclude that the "order of discipline" in sacred doctrine is determined by God's intention. Sacred doctrine treats principally God and everything else in relation to Him as beginning and end, that is, as caused by God.

---

78. ST, I, q. 1, a. 7, ad 2: "omnia alia quae determinantur in sacra doctrina, comprehenduntur sub Deo, non ut partes vel species vel accidentia, sed ut ordinata aliqualiter ad ipsum."

79. ST, I, q. 1, a. 7, co.: "de omnibus enim istis tractatur in ista scientia, sed secundum ordinem ad Deum."

Article One: Sacred Doctrine's Existence and the "Need" for Another Doctrine

The first article of Question One asks whether "another doctrine" (*aliam doctrinam*) beyond the philosophical disciplines "is necessary to be held." Two characteristics of this article are worth highlighting for our discussion: first, there is its emphasis on "the need" (*necessarium*) for another doctrine that is according to divine revelation; second, there is its identification of the guiding aim or intention of this doctrine with human salvation (*salus*). This latter point makes it clear that Article One functions as Thomas's attempt to discern the boundaries of sacred doctrine by using divine intention as its focal point. In this article, God's intention is described and explored under the aspect of something "necessary" for the human creature.

While Thomas may think philosophy is ordered almost entirely to God, he makes it clear in other works that this ordination is only realized during the last stages of philosophy when one studies metaphysics.[80] This fact about philosophy's order of discipline seems to limit knowledge about God only to those who are able to persevere through a difficult and prolonged course of studies. Philosophy's limited accessibility, however, is only part of the problem. Thomas sees philosophy's inadequacy extending much deeper; it stops short of fulfilling the need for human salvation.

Aquinas addresses philosophy's inadequacy somewhat obliquely at first in the article's *sed contra*. There he notes the existence of sacred scripture, which properly cannot be called a part of philosophy because it is divinely revealed. The implications of this appeal to scripture are not fully defined at first, and Thomas probably does this intentionally. Given that scripture exists, he says that it is "useful" (*utile*) that there is another doctrine beyond the philosophical disciplines that is divinely inspired. "Usefulness," strictly speaking, does not answer the question of whether another doctrine is "necessary" (*necessarium*). Nevertheless, this *sed contra* does orient the reader toward the key point of the remainder of the article and highlights another aspect of sacred doctrine's intention: its usefulness for salvation. In the article's body, Thomas will draw further attention to the existence of a deeper need in the human person that philosophy does not sufficiently meet: the need for human salvation.

---

80. See *SCG*, I, 4.

Salvation as the raison d'être of Sacred Doctrine

"Salvation" (*salus*) is a human need and is the guiding force of sacred doctrine. From the first sentence of the article's response, it is clear that Thomas thinks the human person is intended for salvation: "it was necessary for human salvation (*salutem*) that there be a kind of doctrine according to divine revelation beyond the philosophical disciplines."[81] The translation of "salvation" for *salus*, however, does not really capture the full meaning of the term in this article. In its normal contemporary usage, "salvation" conveys primarily (and sometimes exclusively) a sense of "redemption" that hinges on humanity's need to be delivered from sin. Thomas certainly includes the sense of *salus* as "deliverance from sin." *Salus*, nevertheless, can have an additional sense that goes beyond meaning "redemption" due to the havoc wrought by human sin. For Thomas *salus* also means the human person's "ultimate well-being."[82] The redemptive sense cannot be the exclusive sense of *salus*; in some way it is not even the primary sense here in this article. Human "well-being" regards a prior consideration of humanity's ordination to God that existed even before sin. This prior sense of ultimate human well-being is what really shapes sacred doctrine and determines its purpose.

By keeping open a sense of salvation that might have occurred had Adam and Eve never sinned, Thomas shows a reluctance to circumscribe salvation too narrowly. Admittedly, his reluctance here in the first article is somewhat under-articulated, but it appears more prominently elsewhere in the *Summa theologiae* and in greatest relief during the Christological questions of the Third Part.[83] Tellingly, his central preoccupation with the human need for salvation and Christ's role in it penetrates most deeply Thomas's articles on "the fittingness" (*convenientia*) of the Incarnation.[84]

Arguments from fittingness, in general, make rational appeals in the light of divine liberty and divine revelation.[85] When posing the question whether

---

81. ST, I, q. 1, a. 1, co.

82. White, *Holy Teaching*, 10, who helpfully translates *salus* with "weal."

83. The prologue to the Third Part indicates that *salus* is still the central preoccupation, referring immediately to Christ "our *Saviour*," who "in order to *save* 'His people from their sins' (Mt 1:21), as the angel announced, points out in himself the way of truth for us" (emphasis mine).

84. ST, III, q. 1.

85. On the place of "fittingness" in Thomas's theological method, see Gilbert Narcisse,

Christ would have become incarnate had Adam and Eve never sinned, Thomas draws attention to the fact that events like the Incarnation "arise from God's will alone . . . so that we cannot know them except insofar as they are treated in sacred scripture," that is, only insofar as they have been revealed.[86] On this specific question, it is only through divine revelation that God's will is made known. This pivotal position on the divine will and scripture explains why Thomas cites 1 Timothy 1:15 in the article's *sed contra*: "Christ came into this world to save sinners."[87] The testimony of scripture associates almost unanimously the Incarnation with God's desire to redeem fallen humanity. However, in the article's response Thomas qualifies this position somewhat. He observes that "some people" (*quidam*) say that had man never sinned, Christ still would have become incarnate. Without contradicting this view outright, he affirms that "it seems that the assertion" of Augustine and others like him "is preferable" (*quorum assertioni magis assentiendum videtur*)—that the Incarnation is for the redemption of sinners. Thomas subtly leaves the question open, while still affirming that a weighty authority like Augustine's opinion is preferable because it takes its starting point from scripture.

Thomas is not trying to constrain excessively the notions of Incarnation and salvation, knowing that our ultimate understanding of them relies on God's free will to reveal. He leaves others to have different opinions:

> Now, in sacred scripture the reason for the incarnation is in every place assigned to the sin of the first man. So, the work of the incarnation is more fittingly said to be ordered by God as a remedy for sin; so that, had no sin existed, there would have been no incarnation. *However, God's power is not thus limited; for even had sin not existed, God could have become incarnate.*[88]

Les raisons de Dieu: Argument de convenance et esthétique théologique selon saint Thomas d'Aquin et Hans Urs von Balthasar, *Studia Friburgensia 83 (Fribourg: Éditions universitaires, 1997).

86. ST, III, q. 1, a. 3, co.

87. The authority of Augustine also weighs heavy here; see ST, III, q. 1, a. 3, sc.: "Augustine says, in *Liber de verbis Domini* [*Sermones ad populum*, § 174, c. 2], commenting on Lk 19:10 'The Son of Man came to seek and to save that which had been ruined; if man had not sinned, the Son of Man would not have come.'" See Augustine, *Sermones de Novo Testamento* (157–183): In epistulas apostolicas II, Corpus Christianorum Series Latina, vol. 41Bb, ed. Shari Boodts (Turnhout: Brespolis, 2016), sermon 174, c. 2.

88. ST, III, q. 1, a. 3, co. (emphasis mine). See Jean-Pierre Torrell, *Saint Thomas d'Aquin: Maître spirituel (Initiation 2)*, new ed. (Paris: Cerf, 2017), 97–100; an English translation of the 1996 edition of *Maître spirituel* is *Thomas Aquinas*, vol. 2, *Spiritual Master*, trans. Robert

Because the question regarding the fittingness of Christ's incarnation comes up against divine necessity and divine liberty, Thomas indicates that one cannot adopt too rigid a conceptual approach to the solution. Divine liberty in sending the Redeemer points more profoundly to the prior divine liberality of creation. Torrell comments:

> In this way, the coming of the Word into the flesh is no longer caused solely by the *felix culpa*—which is sometimes hard to separate from a certain anthropocentrism—but Christ also appears as the summit and crowning of a universe entirely ruled by the communication of the Divine Being and the Good.[89]

Torrell's analysis indicates that we have hit upon a profound insight into how God is present and acts in the world. The Incarnation is indeed for our redemption, but the mission of the second person of the Trinity also regards the more prior creation of the universe through the same Word. Set in this light, one begins to appreciate how thoroughly Trinitarian Thomas's accounts of creation and redemption are.

His Trinitarian accounts of redemption and creation and of the unity of God's will for human salvation are also integrated into the theme of divine governance as a whole in Thomas's thought, and thus also into sacred doctrine. Christ's work for redemption is not understood in isolation, but already is the mutual work of the Father and Holy Spirit. Even in creation, the Trinitarian "image" is bestowed on intellectual creatures who can also cooperate with God for salvation. The work of the angels, in particular, plays a sizable part in Thomas's account of divine governance in the First Part.[90] Beyond the angels, we can point out that prophets also should be understood as individuals who have special roles in divine governance by directing people toward salvation and the theological virtue of faith.

Having considered Thomas's thoughts on the fittingness of the Incarnation, we can now return to the question of the human need for salvation with a better

---

Royal (Washington, DC: The Catholic University of America Press, 2003), 71–74. Torrell points out a parallel passage where Thomas seems even more favourable to this last qualification from his earlier *In III Sent.*, d. 1, q. 1, a. 3: "Others say that, granted what is produced by the incarnation of the Son of God is not only liberation from sin, but also the glorification (*exaltatio*) of human nature and the coronation (*consummatio*) of the whole universe, the incarnation could have occurred for these reasons, even without sin. *And this may be held as probable*" (emphasis and translation from Torrell, *Spiritual Master*, 72n49).

89. Torrell, *Spiritual Master*, 73 (*Maître spirituel*, 99).

90. See ST, I, q. 106–14.

appreciation for just where this need is located. The need is intended in the creature by the Creator, which is another way of saying that the need is designed by God. In the case of rational creatures that which is needed—the object needed—is identical with their cause in being; this singular reality is God. While human creatures are in some way orderable to their salvation, salvation is not something intrinsic to them, but it is caused from the outside by another. "The whole of human salvation" lies in God and "depends" on knowledge of the truth about Him, Thomas succinctly summarizes.[91]

This leaves a problem for humanity. If the human end is to know God, we cannot know this end by reason alone. Humans need to know their end so that their actions and intentions can be ordered to that end. For this reason, Thomas says that it was necessary for there to be a doctrine through divine revelation by which human beings could come to know God as their final end.[92] Such divine revelation comes to human beings initially through prophets, very particular people who lived at specific times in history.

Can "Singulars" Be the Object of Sacred Doctrine?

An important objection raised within the first two articles of Question One stems from sacred doctrine's treatment of these specific people and events of history. Thomas refers to all of them with the term "singulars", as opposed to generic or universal things. Singulars in this context include specific things and people like the prophet Isaiah or even individual events like those of the patriarch Abraham's life. On their own, singulars appear to create a tension within the scientific structure of sacred doctrine; singulars are unique instances of things—*this* chair, *that* tree, Abraham. The certitude of a science, however, cannot come from singulars because singulars are mutable. Science is something fixed, and this means that it can only come from necessary things, which are always the same and universal. According to Aristotle, universals, not singulars, are the only things that are intelligible.[93] One of the implications of this objection is that the

---

91. ST, I, q. 1, a. 1, co.: "a cuius tamen veritatis [de Deo] cognitione dependet tota hominis salus, quae in Deo est."

92. ST, I, q. 1, a. 1, co.: "Unde necessarium fuit homini ad salutem, quod ei nota fierent quaedam per revelationem divinam, quae rationem humanam excedunt."

93. Aristotle, for instance, thought that history could not properly be an *epistēmē* since it deals with singular facts and contingent events, not with things that must be. See Aristotle, *Metaphysics*, 1003a15, 1026a33–b11, 1027a20–21, 1065a2–7. All citations to Aristotle are

contingent events of history cannot be the basis for fixed knowledge because they are not grounded in something necessary and unchanging. This would seem to jeopardize Thomas's claim that sacred doctrine is a science; sacred doctrine is based on divine revelation which is given at discrete moments in history and relies on the testimony of particular individuals like Abraham, Moses, and Peter and their deeds. It, therefore, cannot rise to the level of universal knowledge.

How does Aquinas deal with this objection, which seems quite devastating at first glance? In his reply, Thomas acknowledges the objection's observation that the object of any science must be something immutable. Singulars by themselves cannot be known because they are not always the same and do not usually act in the same way. Thomas, however, makes a careful qualification, and in doing so, he re-rigs Aristotle's teaching on singulars and universals in such a way that allows him to admit singulars into sacred doctrine. He admits that singulars are not treated principally in sacred doctrine, but they are still brought in either to give moral examples or to announce the authority of those individuals through whom divine revelation comes.[94]

In this second way, sacred doctrine does not attempt to prove, but to "to announce" (*declarare*) the authority of prophets and apostles. By introducing singulars into sacred doctrine, Aquinas admits that in the case of revelation all one can do is start from the individual things divinely revealed. The sections on prophecy that we will examine later follow this method; Thomas starts from examples of prophecy in the Bible and moves cautiously to some general taxonomy for prophetic phenomena, all the while trying not to limit divine power and freedom.[95] His analysis does not try to demonstrate a rigid conceptual structure for prophecy but rather to reduce the individual instances back to something more general and basic. All individual instances of prophecy are reducible to some kind of knowledge (*cognitio*),[96] and this

---

to *The Complete Works of Aristotle*, ed. Jonathan Barnes, 2 vols. (Princeton, NJ: Princeton University Press, 1984).

94. ST, I, q. 1, a. 2, ad 2: "singularia traduntur in sacra doctrina, non quia de eis principaliter tractetur, sed introducuntur tum in exemplum vitae, sicut in scientiis moralibus; tum etiam ad declarandum auctoritatem virorum per quos ad nos revelatio divina processit, super quam fundatur sacra scriptura seu doctrina."

95. See Victor White, "St. Thomas's Conception of Revelation," *Dominican Studies* 1 (1948): 1–34, at 11–12. This approach acknowledges that God revealed Himself in such-and-such a way, but has or had the power to do so differently. There is also an attempt in these sections to show the fittingness of prophecy as recorded in scripture.

96. ST, II-II, q. 171, a. 1, co.

prophetic knowledge comes in degrees and has specific purposes. The medium of prophetic knowing—what Thomas calls "prophetic light"—is what makes a prophet's knowledge supernatural; this light unifies all prophetic knowledge and is, as we shall see, *the* essential element in his account of prophecy.

As in other philosophical disciplines like geometry, Thomas thinks instruction in singular things is appropriate for the beginning stages of sacred doctrine, provided one does not forget that the singulars are not the primary subject of the science: "God is truly the subject of this science."[97] This is clear, Thomas thinks, even when one looks at the individual principles of sacred doctrine—the articles of faith. Faith is ultimately not about creedal statements, but "about God." In sacred doctrine, the subject of the principles and the subject of the entire science are identical. The first principles of sacred doctrine, the articles of faith, emerge from the life of Christian religion whose own foundation rests on the divine revelation made to prophets and apostles.

Toward Human Happiness and the Moral Part of the *Summa*

This brings us back to the *raison d'être* of sacred doctrine, which is salvation, something first announced by the prophets and apostles. A deeper examination of what Thomas means by salvation requires an examination of what salvation consists in. He has already touched on this topic in Question One, but he does not fully address it until he treats happiness and the human final end at beginning of the Second Part of the *Summa*, its moral part. There Thomas will map out the return of the human person to God and what this destination consists in; he also will introduce an important theme in the Second Part's prologue: the human as created in the *imago Dei*. Created with and for this spark of divine life, the human person comes to share in the life of God through a rebirth in the life of the theological virtues. These virtues orient the person to the happiness that can only be found fully in God. Yet before turning to the critical role of faith, hope, and love in this roadmap, Thomas first explores human happiness and the final end. He does this to orient the reader to the structuring of this section—its aim is to assist in forming Christian morals, where the final end is the first principle when considering moral matters. We turn now to examine the final end, which is the essential starting point for appreciating the central role prophecy and sacred doctrine play in Thomas's Christian moral teaching.

---

97. ST, I, q. 1, a. 7, co.

2

Happiness and
the Human Final End

Based on our structural reading of the *Summa theologiae* so far, the certitude and unity of sacred doctrine must also be understood in relation to human happiness (or the final end) and the theological virtue of faith. Our discussion turns now to the relationship to happiness; this will serve as groundwork for our later discussion of how prophecy possesses an analogous certitude and unity that God gives prophets in order to promote human happiness through the gift of faith. As was seen in the preceding chapter, sacred doctrine's unique character as "an impression" of divine knowledge makes it, Thomas says, "supremely the wisdom among all human wisdoms." Standing behind this account of sacred doctrine is, of course, the reality of Christian faith. In order for sacred doctrine to exist, the light of faith must be given and accepted. Faith is that divine gift which moves a person to freely assent to the object of faith and its proposed first principles, which are received as things divinely revealed to prophets and apostles. These divinely revealed principles orient humans to their salvation that lies entirely in God, who is simultaneously their happiness and final end.

By focusing on this specific orientation to salvation innate to the human being, we hope to see how prophecy augments this natural orientation to God. At the outset of the Second Part of the *Summa*, Thomas begins to map out this orientation by examining happiness or the human final end. Later, in the *Secunda secundae*, he goes on to extend his discussion to the virtues. There both the theological virtue of faith and prophecy play an important role in orienting the person to happiness. The next two chapters look at his treatments of the human final end (I-II, qq. 1–5) and faith (II-II, qq. 1–16) in order to get a fuller picture of what Thomas only sketches for his reader in Question One when he refers to "salvation." In reading these sections side by side, two important aspects of Thomas's thought will come into view: (1) the interdependence of his account of the human final end and his accounts of faith, prophecy, and sacred doctrine; and (2) the necessity that theological faith has for human salvation. Discussion of these two aspects along with our preceding one on sacred doctrine will provide the needed background for our analysis in chapters four and five of Thomas's questions on prophecy. Special attention will also be devoted here to how the final end "functions" in human voluntary action, which is central to all moral action; this will enable us especially to appreciate how prophecy and sacred doctrine fit into Thomas's moral reflection as a whole.

Keeping Faith and Prophecy Distinct

Before turning directly to Thomas's questions on happiness and the human final end, it will be helpful to identify a potential pitfall lurking in the background. One might be tempted to confuse or conflate the things believed in faith with the things known by prophets and apostles. While there is overlap between these two categories, Thomas carefully distinguishes both. Flagging up this distinction now puts into sharper relief certain subtleties that will be encountered later in Thomas's accounts of prophecy and faith.

Failure to distinguish carefully the things believed in faith from the things known prophetically may lead one to assume mistakenly that Thomas considers prophecy to be superior to faith. The thinking behind this pitfall goes as follows. Prophecy, Thomas states, "pertains principally to knowledge,"[1] and knowledge is more certain than belief. Theological faith consists in belief and thus appears to be less certain than prophecy. Only things that are more certain lead to greater intellectual perfection in a person. Since prophecy is more certain than belief, one concludes that prophecy leads to greater intellectual perfection in a person and is, therefore, superior to the gift of faith.

Thomas responds to a similar (but ultimately defective) line of thought when addressing faith's certitude in relation to the intellectual virtues.[2] There he distinguishes between two ways of understanding "certitude." One way of speaking about certitude is relative to the perspective of the knower; according

---

1. ST, II-II, q. 171, a. 1, co.
2. See ST, II-II, q. 4, a. 8, obj. 1 and 3.

to this *subjective certitude*, faith is judged to be less certain than both prophecy and the intellectual virtues because belief does not attain the superior understanding that comes with the gift of prophecy and the intellectual virtues. In another way, one can speak about certitude absolutely (*simpliciter*) by referring to certitude's cause.[3] Since faith is caused directly by God and founded on divine truth, Thomas maintains that its cause is more certain than any intellectual virtue. This is because the intellectual virtues are caused by the light of human reason, which is fallible. Divine truth, however, is seen under the aspect of a divine light and is infallible. This divine light is not itself caused, but is the cause of the light of human reason. Since the light of faith has a greater likeness to the divine light than the natural light of reason, faith is absolutely more certain than the intellectual virtues and even more certain than the gifts of the Holy Spirit—knowledge, wisdom, and understanding.[4]

While certitude remains one of the main ways Thomas distinguishes faith and the intellectual virtues, it is not his preferred way of distinguishing faith and prophecy. The reason for this becomes apparent when one considers the respective certitude of both faith and prophecy absolutely. Both faith and prophecy share the same formal cause, God as First Truth, and considered absolutely, they are equally certain. Relative to the knower (and vis-à-vis subjective certitude), however, prophecy is more certain than faith; prophets know things that other non-prophets only believe in faith. Despite this superior subjective certitude relative to faith, prophecy is not absolutely superior to faith according to Thomas. He does not consider certitude to be their chief distinguishing factor; rather, he prefers to differentiate prophecy and faith by looking at the different ways they inhere in a person. This helps to explain partially why he tries to clarify early on in his questions on prophecy that prophets do not possess the gift of prophecy as a steady disposition or virtue (*habitus*).[5] While Thomas does think prophetic knowledge involves a perfection of a prophet's personal intellectual capacity (or power), he resists concluding that this makes prophecy superior to the virtue of faith in any way. In fact, he maintains that faith is far superior to prophecy because faith inheres in a person more permanently and stably as a virtue (*habitus*).

---

3. ST, II-II, q. 4, a. 8, co.

4. Thomas says that faith is the principal root of the gifts of the Holy Spirit in a believer. Faith causes them, and the cognitive gifts of the Holy Spirit (knowledge, understanding, wisdom, and counsel) derive their certitude from it; see ST, II-II, q. 4, a. 8, ad 3.

5. ST, II-II, q. 171, a. 2.

Faith's stability and superiority depend also on it being animated by the gift of charity, which joins the person directly to God and perfects this union. Faith's direct orientation to charity radically sets it apart from prophecy for Thomas. He thinks charity is not strictly necessary for the gift of prophecy, observing that even so-called prophets in the Bible can lack charity altogether or even be in league with demons.[6] While certainly not incompatible with charity, prophecy is not directly ordered to the prophet's personal sanctification or growth in charity; instead, it is ordered to the good of a community. Thomas in his earlier disputed question on prophecy states that "prophecy leads to faith as to an end,"[7] but as we have already seen, this statement does not mean he thinks prophecy is superior to faith.

Faith's superiority lies chiefly in the fact that it is more like God's own knowledge than prophecy. God's knowledge is not transient, but necessary to the divine nature; prophecy is transient, but faith less so. Divine knowledge is necessarily ordered to charity; prophecy is directly ordered to faith, and faith is ordered directly to charity. (In God, of course, this is because knowledge and love are essential.) The fundamental basis of faith's superiority to prophecy is that its inherence in the person is a greater likeness to God's knowledge.

It is helpful to recall here that Thomas thinks faith ranks higher absolutely than even any of the acquired intellectual virtues, because its formal cause—God as First Truth—is more certain. In order to explain why a superior cause leads absolutely to superior certitude in faith, Thomas appeals at times to faith as a mode of knowing that is a greater likeness to God's own knowledge:

> [faith] becomes for us in this life a kind of assimilation to divine knowledge and participation in this knowledge inasmuch as, through the faith infused in us, we adhere to the First Truth on account of its very self.[8]

To elaborate on what it means for faith to be "a kind of assimilation to divine knowledge" communicated to the rational creature, it may be helpful to look briefly at the natural mode of human knowing in the intellectual virtues.

---

6. ST, II-II, q. 172, a. 4; a. 6, ad 1: where Thomas cites Balaam (Nm 22).

7. *De ver.*, q. 14, a. 8, ad 13: "prophetia inducit ad fidem sicut ad finem."

8. *Super Boetium de Trinitate*, I, q. 2, a. 2, co.: "fit nobis in statu viae quaedam illius cognitionis participatio et assimilatio ad cognitionem divinam, in quantum per fidem nobis infusam inhaeremus ipsi primae veritati propter se ipsam."

Human knowledge and the intellectual virtues rely on the ability of the human person to reason. Thomas observes that, while reason is usually a reliable guide, it can still err. This is in contrast to God's mode of knowing, which is infallible. In faith, there is a kind of elevated sharing in God's mode of knowing that is caused directly by God. Thomas usually characterizes this "assimilation" to God's knowledge using the image of a "light." All humans possess the capacity to access a natural light that functions in reasoning, but certain things cannot be seen by this natural light. The things that exceed the natural light are, of course, not unimportant; they are ordered to helping the human creature realize its end, which is supernatural. Thomas thinks one's natural light can be strengthened supernaturally by the "light of faith," which itself is ordained to a higher light—the light of glory, in which the ultimate human good will be fully realized.

Thomas marks out these three lights—the light of nature (*lumen naturae*), the light of faith or grace (*lumen fidei vel gratiae*), and the light of glory (*lumen gloriae*)—as the key ways or modes in which the rational creature shares in God's knowledge. When given by God to the human person, the light of faith functions as a new principle of knowledge that inheres in the human soul and strengthens the natural light of reason. It serves as the medium by which one is disposed to knowing God supernaturally in a manner that is more like the divine mode of knowing, where God knows everything through Himself. It elevates and orients the mind to God as one supernaturally known.

As already noted, faith also resembles God's own knowledge more than prophecy by the fact that faith is more like charity, which is God's gift of Himself. Charity involves an act of the will, and when coupled with faith and hope, the three theological virtues form a new, supernatural nature in the person who receives them. They function as new principles of human operation that embrace both the intellect and will. In contrast, Thomas thinks the light of prophecy is given transiently and just enough so that prophets can know what God wants them to know at a given time. The human will is not operative when a prophet receives the prophetic gift. The only will that is operative is God's: "God gives the gift of prophecy to those to whom He judges it best to give."[9] God's will, and God's will alone, determines both those who receive the gift of prophecy and why they receive it.

---

9. ST, II-II, q. 172, a. 4, ad 4: "Deus donum prophetiae illis dat quibus optimum iudicat dare."

Thomas also thinks faith and prophecy are distinct with regards to their content. While prophets know or are said "to see" things divinely revealed, faith concerns things that are at present neither known nor seen by the believer. A veil continues to cover things believed in faith, and this, Thomas points out, implies that faith is inherently imperfect.[10] Faith's imperfection suggests that it is ordered directly to a more perfect vision: the vision or light of glory (*visio vel lumen gloriae*). This higher light consists in the complete sanctification of the person and the consummation of eternal life shared with God. In contrast, a prophet's knowledge is ordered to the good of others and not directly to the prophet's own personal sanctification. Nevertheless, prophecy can dispose both prophets and those who hear them to believe things in faith. In this way, the things divinely revealed to prophets and apostles become a starting point for the virtue of faith.

From this last observation, one begins to see a parallel between the prophet's knowledge of what has been divinely revealed and the believer's knowledge of the articles of faith, which serve as the first principles of sacred doctrine. Of course, the believer "knows" the articles of faith not as objects seen, but believed; their inner mystery remains hidden to believers, even though they adhere to these mysteries more firmly and with greater certitude than the most certain human knowledge. The prophet's knowledge in a way prepares and shapes the way things come to be believed in faith and how the individual articles of faith come to be expressed. Prophetic knowledge contributes to the material content of faith, and this material content allows faith's formal aspect to become concretized and expressed as "articles." This concretization is required for the human articulation and understanding of the faith; human understanding always starts naturally from sensible things and so depends on both sensible and mental words, which the articles of faith mediate. This material contribution of prophecy to faith accounts in part for the stability of the articles of faith as statements. In a paradoxical way, by providing the articles of faith with some stability in things that are concrete and particular—one can even say *historical*—prophecy points directly toward the immediate ordination of all creation to God: the universal and eternal common good. For human beings, the prophet's knowledge reorients their attention toward God's intention for particular creatures—for a person like Abraham, for a people like Israel, or for

---

10. ST, I-II, q. 62, a. 3, ad 2: "fides … imperfectionem quandam important, quia fides est de his quae non videntur."

the whole human race. In this way, the gift of prophecy offers "glimpses" of God's intention for certain creatures. By highlighting these particular creatures and their ordering toward God, the prophet's knowledge becomes a sort of token of God's own knowledge, which intends to draw all humans back to God by means of the particular, the concrete, and the historical.

Because what prophets see are these glimpses of divine intention in creatures, prophecy must also be understood under the rubric of divine government, as was already suggested in our preceding discussion of sacred doctrine and divine government. For Thomas divine government is a way of considering God under the aspect of His practical knowledge—a practical knowledge that is intentional and the cause of all that exists outside of God. In the light of prophecy, the prophet's mind is assimilated to the inner intentional ordering given to particular creatures by God, and in seeing this created intention it becomes a closer likeness of God's own intention *in se*, that is, how God in His practical knowledge knows and intends. The notions of providence divine government allow us to represent God's own practical knowledge as the simultaneous final and formal cause of everything. In knowing Himself and willing His own goodness, God creates everything, and since in God there is nothing composite, His acts of knowing and willing are identical. By extension, the creation of the world and its government are in God one act, and his practical knowledge, which causes everything to exist, is also one. Since creating and governing constitute one act in God, the concept of divine governance is also linked integrally to creation and its purpose intended by God. Divine government extends to all creatures and permits one to consider all of creation as intended for God, which is coterminous with God's intention to offer salvation to all rational creatures.

This discussion of divine governance could be extended further; His government encompasses His willing first and foremost the good of the whole universe. Simultaneously and secondarily, it extends down to His willing the good of every individual creature. If the good of the whole is the primary end of divine government, there is a kind of convergence of prophecy and this aspect of divine government. The convergence becomes more apparent in the light of Thomas's classification of prophecy as one of the "gratuitous graces," which are given by God primarily for the good of a community. In this respect, prophecy imitates and partakes of God's own divine governance, sharing its intentional orientation toward the good of a whole. Moreover, if divine governance reflects an aspect of God's practical knowledge, prophecy can also be understood to be an assimilation to and participation in that divine practical knowledge.

Prophecy, the Common Good, and Sacred Doctrine's "Prophetic Character"

Because prophecy is given to some individuals and not to others, it seems that some people participate more in divine knowledge and governance than others. These higher degrees of participation in divine governance, however, do not necessarily affect or perfect these prophets outside the context of fostering (or failing to foster) the common good. Differences among humans in the degree to which they share in divine knowledge and government are principally intended by God to serve the common good. Since these special differences are ordered more to the perfecting of a common good than to their recipients, the higher intellectual perfections that set prophets apart do not necessarily elevate them above others when it comes to their personal tending toward God. This last observation represents another way of expressing Thomas's concise statement that "prophecy can exist without charity"—a position he thinks is firmly rooted in New Testament teaching (Mt 7:22–23).[11] While the gift of prophecy exists as a discrete perfection in certain individuals, this perfection functions more like a common perfection or common treasury.

With its divinely-intended orientation toward a common good, prophetic knowledge has a social dimension that is meant to help orient others toward God as their final end. It is now opportune to consider whether this social dimension in prophecy enters into the virtue of faith at all. If it does, how does this happen? Also, if faith has a social dimension shaped by prophecy, how might this affect sacred doctrine and our understanding of it? Must sacred doctrine also reflect a social dimension that orients it to the good of a whole? Prophecy clearly does have a social dimension, and this social dimension does indeed enter into the structure of theological faith. As a consequence of this, sacred doctrine also possesses an inherent social structuring and orientation.

This last claim may sound especially counterintuitive. After all, one could interpret Thomas's decision to call sacred doctrine a "science" as a clear indication that he understands sacred doctrine to be an intellectual perfection or virtue (*habitus*) that only individuals are able to possess and cultivate through study;[12] indeed, Thomas reiterates this description along such lines in other contexts.[13] Sacred doctrine is in one respect an individual intellectual perfection, but this is

---

11. ST, II-II, q. 172, a. 4, sc. and co.: "prophetia autem potest esse sine charitate."
12. ST, I, q. 1, a. 3.
13. ST, I, q. 1, a. 6, ad 3.

not the entire picture. If the interpretation just outlined is pressed too hard and the sense of sacred doctrine confined too narrowly by the notion of "science," sacred doctrine's broader character as a wisdom would be lost. An important insight into how Thomas sees individual intellectual perfections as potentially serving a common good in cooperation with divine wisdom would likewise be lost. As an intellectual perfection held through the light of faith, sacred doctrine perfects not only the individuals who acquire it by study, but it also aims to perfect and benefit a common good. In fact, Thomas sees sacred doctrine as primarily ordained toward a common good; only secondarily is it ordained toward the good of an individual. Because of its principal ordination toward a common good, sacred doctrine can be said to be distinctly *prophetic*.

When seen in this perspective, what we are calling sacred doctrine's *prophetic character*—its primary orientation to a common good—also has much in common with its character as wisdom. The wise person has the task of ordering all things in light of the highest Principle, which is both the Highest Truth and Common Good of everything. The prophet has a more limited task which includes orienting a certain community of persons toward God—the same Highest Truth and Universal Common Good in whose light the wise person judges everything. From this, one can see that prophecy and wisdom have similar orderings; in fact, prophecy is ordered principally to "wisdom," but the "wisdom" spoken of here refers especially to all that is knowable through supernatural revelation. Because of its orientation to wisdom prophecy is also ordered to sacred doctrine through the charism's ordination to faith.

By instructing and correcting, prophets remind others of the need to order all things in light of the Highest Wisdom. Those who listen to a prophet's message cultivate this awareness and remembrance principally by the light of faith, not that of prophecy. Nevertheless, the light of prophecy working in a prophet helps others indirectly to receive the light of faith or, if they already possess faith, to renew and deepen their response to this light. Thus, prophets principally remind others of the need to be faithful to God. In a similar vein, teachers of sacred doctrine are also called principally to assist others by drawing attention back to the primacy of faith in Christian life. One of the ways they can do this is by helping to remove any impediments—intellectual or moral—that might hinder others from believing and loving God.

By identifying a social character common to both sacred doctrine and prophecy, we do not claim that sacred doctrine is a type of directly infused knowledge like prophetic knowledge nor that it is wisdom, the gift of the Holy

Spirit.[14] (Thomas thinks the gifts of the Holy Spirit are akin to virtues that orient all their recipients directly toward God; such gifts are even said to be "necessary" for the salvation of every believer.) Our principal observation in this context is only that sacred doctrine has more in common with the wisdom that is a gratuitous grace than the wisdom that is a gift of the Holy Spirit.[15]

Sacred Doctrine's "Social" Relation to Philosophy and Other Sciences

As a brief aside, it may be helpful to consider whether the prophetic character of sacred doctrine as just explained—its contribution toward the good of a community—has some effect on the "structures" of the human sciences and philosophy. Tentatively, one can assert that sacred doctrine's social dimension does indeed extend to the "society" of human sciences. By the "society" of the sciences, I mean here the interdependence among the sciences, which is arguably a normal feature of human knowing. We could point to Thomas's example from Question One of alternate and subalternate sciences like arithmetic and music as one such manifestation of a "social" relationship between sciences. In these "social" relations, sciences share common principles or conclusions such that one is dependent on another.

Is it really proper, however, to call these inter-scientific relationships "social"? In one sense, clearly not, if "social" means specifically the relations between individual substances or entities capable of perceiving or understanding intentions. Since sciences are not substances and lack any intrinsic capacity to perceive or know, it would be just as improper to call them "social" as it would be to call qualities like whiteness "social" or even inanimate substances like stones "social."

In another sense, however, given that sciences always depend on intellects for their existence, it could be said that sciences appropriate intentions from the persons possessing them. If this appropriated sense of intentionality can be

---

14. See ST, I-II, q. 68, a. 2.

15. By "wisdom as a gratuitous grace," we mean something different from Thomas's *sermo vel gratia sapientiae*, which is his expression for one of the gratuitous graces of speech mentioned by St. Paul as *sermo sapientiae per Spiritum / logos sophias dia tou pneumatos* (1 Cor 12:8); see ST, II-II, q. 177, a. 1–2. The gift of speech pertains to teaching but still depends in part on the knowledge of the speaker. Since knowledge is prior to speech, Thomas holds prophecy to be the higher gift and the one to which all the other gratuitous graces of speech and miracle working are ordered.

applied to sciences, then it appears there may be a meaningful way of speaking about "social" relations between sciences, provided one remembers that these "social" relations derive ultimately from concrete persons and not from the sciences as such. The relating of one science to another—in other words, their "socializing"—occurs because a particular mind desires to consider one thing in relation to another or to develop one science from principles discovered in another science known prior. If the human sciences cultivated by reason alone can be said to interrelate or be "social," it seems reasonable to extend this way of speaking to sacred doctrine.

Sacred Doctrine's "Social" Relation to God and the Saints: A Trinitarian Aside

Looking at the "social" relations that can exist between sacred doctrine and the other human sciences also brings to mind its "sociality" as a subalternate science whose principles derive from the knowledge of God and the blessed. Thomas chooses memorably to highlight sacred doctrine's own scientific character in this way: "sacred doctrine is a science, since it proceeds from principles known by the light of a superior science, which is namely the *scientia Dei et beatorum*."[16] Sacred doctrine is not just the individual's sharing of God's knowledge as if it were only a binary relationship, but divine knowledge itself appears to be inherently "social." We can analyze divine knowledge's sociality under two chief aspects, each of which reflects a different way one can choose to consider the divine nature in general: God *in se* and God *ad extra*. Under the first aspect, God's knowledge *in se* is "social" because God is a Trinity; under the second, God's knowledge *ad extra* is said to be "social" because intellectual creatures can participate in it. Regarding the first, since God's knowledge is identical with His nature and His nature as Triune is essentially a communion of persons, divine knowledge can also be said to be inherently "social" on account of the intra-Trinitarian communion. An analysis of knowledge in the Trinity and its "social" aspect deserves a much fuller treatment than we can hope to give here, and needless to say such an analysis would lead us deeper into Thomas's Trinitarian theology.

Without intending to be comprehensive on the issue, we can observe how this first "social" aspect of God's knowledge *in se* is reflected in the way a prophet

---

16. ST, I, q. 1, a. 2, co.

knows by the light of prophecy. The prophet's participation in divine knowledge highlights a parallel between two sets of relationships. The first relationship is between God's knowledge and the prophet's knowledge. Running parallel to this is the Trinitarian relationship between the Father and the Word, the latter being understood as the intention of the Father or "the eidetic pattern of the divine intellect" and model for every inspired word.[17] By participating in divine knowledge, the prophet's mind is made into a more perfect image of God's own knowledge. Just as the person of the Son is a perfect likeness and image of the Father, prophets through their likeness to the divine mind are said especially to be participating in the person of the Son. Thomas writes in his *Commentary on John*:

> at one time, the only Son of God revealed knowledge of God through the prophets, whose proclamation was measured to the extent to which they had been made participants in the eternal Word.[18]

The prophet's knowledge is understood here to be derived from and modelled especially on the Son.

In addition to this Christological identification of prophetic knowledge, Thomas also highlights in the *Summa*'s Third Part the Word as the Wisdom of the Father. Strikingly, he does this in the course of his article on the fittingness of the Incarnation:

> The Word of God has a special affinity with human nature, because he is a concept of the eternal wisdom, from which all human wisdom comes. And this is why a human being is perfected in wisdom— which is the perfection belonging to him as a rational being—in the measure that he participates in the Word of God; just like the disciple is instructed by receiving the word of his master. Hence it is said in Ecclesiasticus, *The Word of God on high is the fountain of wisdom* (1:5). And so to lead humanity to its perfection, it was fitting that the Word of God personally united himself to humanity.[19]

---

17. *SCG*, IV, 13, 11 (cited by Gilles Emery, *The Trinitarian Theology of St. Thomas Aquinas*, trans. Francesca A. Murphy [Oxford: Oxford University Press, 2007], 201); the full passage runs: "oportet igitur quod per verbum Dei, quod est *ratio intellectus divini*, causetur omnis intellectualis cognitio" (emphasis mine).

18. *Super Evangelium S. Ioannis lectura* (hereafter *In Ioan.*), ed. R. Cai, 6th ed. (Turin: Marietti, 1972), 1.18, no. 221 (cited by Emery, *Trinitarian Theology of St. Thomas*, 202).

19. ST, III, q. 3, a. 8, co. (cited by Emery, *Trinitarian Theology of St. Thomas*, 202).

From these roots, one can trace his identification of sacred doctrine as wisdom and see how it too comes from and is a participation in the eternal Word. Emery aptly notes how Thomas "puts his presentation of the whole work of revelation, right up to the beatific vision, under the light of the Word."[20] When commenting on the text of Jn 14, Thomas also shows how the Word's action is shared with the Holy Spirit:

> Just as the mission of the Son was to lead to the Father, so the effect of the mission of the Holy Spirit is to lead the faithful to the Son. Now the Son, since he is begotten Wisdom, is Truth itself: *I am the way, the truth, and the life* (Jn 14:6). And so the effect of this mission is to render men participants in the divine Wisdom and knowers of the truth. Since he is the Word, the Son gives us teaching; and the Holy Spirit makes us able to grasp it.[21]

This passage helps to pin-point prophecy's unique role as leading others to faith under the mission of the Holy Spirit, who illuminates the prophet's mind and whose work always accompanies the work of the Son.

When it comes to the second aspect (i.e., the capacity of intellectual creatures to participate in God's knowledge *ad extra*), the "sociality" of God's knowledge is reflected imperfectly. Even under this second aspect, God's knowledge can still be understood to be "social." This is what Thomas is alluding to when he describes sacred doctrine as depending on the knowledge of God and of the blessed. The blessed at present have a share in the beatific vision, which is a perfect communion with the Trinity. From this communion, they see and share now in God's intentions for the governance of the universe. Their presence to the communion of divine persons reminds us that sacred doctrine and faith are both socially mediated—principally by God, who is Triune, but also instrumentally through others, especially prophets and apostles—and socially oriented, that is, they aim primarily at a common good. In order to elaborate this second social orientation to a common good, it is now necessary to turn to the issue of the final end in Thomas's thought and his *Summa* questions on the subject.

---

20. Emery, *Trinitarian Theology of St. Thomas*, 203.

21. *In Ioan.*, 14.26, no. 1958 (cited by Emery, *Trinitarian Theology of St. Thomas*, 203).

Happiness and Human Salvation: Entry Points

We have already introduced the idea that both prophecy and faith share a common orientation to happiness (or the final end) and salvation. Question One set down that because the human end is supernatural, a knowledge that is beyond what can be reached by human reason alone is required. In order to have access to this supernatural knowledge there must be a kind of supernatural teaching. Divine revelation offers access to such a teaching allowing the human person to perceive the final end as supernatural and ultimately to move toward it. While Thomas's notion of the human final end is woven into his notion of salvation, it is now necessary to try to identify and discuss the thread of the final end on its own.

He considers the human final end in various ways, but perhaps the most penetrating is through final causality. As a final cause, God is that which all human beings are ordered to. Final cause and final end coincide for all creatures, and for intelligent creatures their final end must be foreknown in some respect; otherwise, they would not be able to orient their intentions and actions to it.[22] If God is the final cause and end, can human beings actually know God who *in se* exceeds the comprehension of human reason? Thomas insists that humans cannot know and attain their final end through the use of their reason alone, and because of this, there must be another way of knowing God that is supernatural and divinely revealed. While Thomas's insistence on this last point appears initially to rest on an epistemological claim since it speaks to the limits of human knowledge, it is rather at its root a metaphysical claim about the rational creature and its relationship to God as its cause.

The metaphysical core of this claim is perhaps brought out more succinctly in the *Summa contra Gentiles* than in the *Summa theologiae*. While the purpose, structure, and occasion of the former is markedly different from the latter,[23] there are certain structural affinities between the two works when it comes to Thomas's arguments that human beings need divine revelation to be happy.[24] Scholarship

---

22. ST, I, q. 1, a. 1, co.: "Finem autem oportet esse praecognitum hominibus, qui *suas intentiones et actiones debent ordinare in finem.* Unde necessarium fuit homini ad salutem, quod ei nota fierent quaedam per revelationem divinam, quae rationem humanam excedunt" (emphasis mine).

23. For an overview of the major scholarship on the *SCG*, see Jordan, *Rewritten Theology*, 89–115; Torrell, *Initiation*, 140–57 (*The Person and His Work*, 115–37).

24. For parallels, see ST, I-II, q. 3, aa. 6–8 and *SCG*, I, 3.

on the *Summa contra Gentiles* is just as vast and complex as the literature on the larger *Summa*. Many different and sometimes conflicting opinions have been put forward to account for some of the unique features of the *Contra Gentiles*. Our intention here is not to resolve these oft-conflicting accounts, but merely to appeal to parallel structures that may help us in understanding some of the background behind the much more condensed questions in the *Summa theologiae*. The latter's broader pedagogical aims account partially for why Thomas's questions on the final end (I-II, qq. 1–5) must be more constrained than his treatment of the same issue in the *Contra Gentiles*. By keeping the larger *Summa*'s pedagogical structure in mind, some of these parallels become easier to see.

Metaphysical Account of the Final End and the "Need" for Divine Revelation

At the beginning of the *Contra Gentiles*, Thomas states that he intends to set forth the truth "professed by the Catholic faith" and resolve errors raised against it by those who do not accept the entirety of divine revelation. In this task, he says he will make recourse "to natural reason, which everyone is bound to assent to."[25] This preference in the *Contra Gentiles* for natural reason explains to some extent why it is easier to appreciate in that text the metaphysical structure of Thomas's arguments for the necessity of divine revelation to attain one's final end. In the *Contra Gentiles*, Thomas observes that truth in itself can be made manifest in various ways.[26] Concerning the truth about God, there is a twofold path. Some truths can be grasped through the exercise of reason; others, however, are beyond reason's reach, and these must be divinely revealed. Thomas maintains that according to natural reason itself "the evidence clearly indicates" (*evidentissme apparet*) that certain truths lie beyond human ken, and he offers three arguments to show this. The first argument is based on the mode of human knowing. The second considers different grades of intellectual creatures and has some structural similarities to Thomas's Fourth Way in the *Summa theologiae*. The third argues from the defects of the human intellect from the perspective of everyday experience.

In the first argument, Thomas offers an analysis of how humans know. He starts off by distinguishing the principles of knowledge from the mode by which

---

25. *SCG*, I, 2, 2–3.
26. *SCG*, I, 3.

something is grasped as understood. How we come to know something affects what we know about it.[27] Human knowledge in the present life depends on our senses. Things that are beyond our senses like angels, who are immaterial, are strictly speaking beyond our knowing. We can have knowledge of the existence of immaterial beings from the evidence of their effects on and in material creation, but this does not translate into knowledge of the essences of immaterial beings. The things we can know about them like certain angelic powers come through a sort of negative knowledge wherein we apply to them a dissimilarity that has reference to something that we already know of through our senses. In this way, Thomas thinks that the human senses can sometimes lead us back to reflect on the existence of immaterial beings and to consider them negatively, but this still only happens because the material effects of these immaterial beings are perceived by our senses. This, of course, does not preclude another possible way of knowing immaterial beings by a mode that is supernatural and beyond natural reason. Back in the *Summa theologiae*, Thomas makes a parallel observation and goes on to show how the human limitation in knowledge is rooted metaphysically in a discrepancy between the human mode of existence (*modus essendi*) and the mode of existence of the objects that are known, which exceed this human mode:

> The knowledge of any knower is according to the mode of its nature. Therefore, if the mode of existence (*modus essendi*) of any known thing exceeds the knower's mode of nature (*modum naturae*), then knowledge of that thing must be above the nature of the knower.[28]

This passage illustrates that Thomas's point about the limitation of human knowledge is not at its root epistemological, but rather it reflects his understanding of the prior dependence of knowledge on being—a point he highlights here by appealing to the different modes of existence (or nature) between knower and object known. The essences of things that exist above human nature are only knowable through a *super*natural mode. This point will be critical to hold onto for our later discussion of Thomas's understanding of the prophet's and believer's knowledge as a kind of participation in God's knowledge.

The second argument from the different grades of intellectual creatures requires a good deal of analysis to unpack, but the majority of its presentation

---

27. *SCG*, I, 3. Compare ST, I-II, q. 3, a. 6.
28. ST, I, q. 12, a. 4, co.

can be passed over for the purposes of our discussion here, since one of its main points is reiterated in the third argument: the relative weakness of the human intellect. This third argument starts from the observable weakness of the human intellect, which, Thomas notes, is so feeble that we remain ignorant even of many sensible things knowable through reason.[29] In the *Summa theologiae*, Thomas also highlights the weakness of the human intellect insofar as things such as "whether God exists," which he thinks is knowable by reason, must be taught also by means of divine revelation. He points out that only a very limited number of human beings ever discover these divine truths by reason alone, and even if they do, they often only reach them after a long period time and "mixed with many errors."[30] If the human intellect is fallible in very basic points about material things, how much more will it be open to error when it comes to knowledge of immaterial and divine things. Because the human intellect is so weak in its present state, Thomas concludes that even certain naturally knowable truths about God also need to be divinely revealed.

Through the instruction of divine revelation, Thomas says, humans will arrive "both more fittingly and more certainly" at the knowledge of God, wherein lies their salvation.[31] He makes this claim to "fittingness" and "certitude" both in light of the existence of divine revelation and about divine revelation. To say that salvation comes "more fittingly" (*convenientius*) through revelation is to appeal to the divine will—God's motive for creation and salvation. Since God's will is one with His nature, it is unknowable in itself given our human limitiations. We only have incomplete and imperfect knowledge of it from creation and through divine revelation. Thus, Thomas's judgment that humans will arrive "more fittingly" at salvation through divine revelation is based not on an apodictic demonstration, but on an inference from creation and revelation that God wills to reward those who seek Him. It is out of God's willing and loving of Himself as the highest good that His love overflows into creation. Creation, in turn, reflects His will for the good, which is perceptible to creatures, even if imperfectly.

Thomas's point about humanity being saved "more fittingly" through divine revelation thus reflects a broader insight about all created goodness being derived ultimately from God's goodness. Human beings find and perceive that

---

29. *SCG*, I, 3.

30. ST, I, q. 1, a. 1, co; see also ST, II-II, q. 2, a. 4, co.

31. ST, I, q. 1, a. 1, co.: "et convenientius et certius."

every created good they encounter is in some way imperfect. These goods are imperfect because their goodness ultimately depends on God as their cause. God makes these goods good, and they simply participate finitely in God's infinite goodness. As imperfect likenesses of divine goodness, created goods serve to orient the intellectual creature back to God. By "more fittingly" orienting humanity back to God, divine revelation through prophecy *intensifies* what created goods are already meant to do: lead one to God. Thus, divine revelation accomplishes "more fittingly" God's will to save and share His goodness. One also gets the sense that what Thomas means here by this expression is a "better" accomplishment of God's will for human salvation, because it makes manifest more fully divine goodness. In manifesting His goodness more fully, God allows Himself to be more readily perceived as desirable. Through divine revelation, He elicits more intensely the human desire for God and draws the rational creature more closely to Him, all the while respecting the human person's freedom to turn away from God through sin.

By also saying humanity is saved "more certainly" (*certius*) through divine revelation, Thomas indicates an inherent link between God's manifestation of His goodness and His manifestation of truth, to which certitude principally points. Divine revelation allows humanity to know more fully the picture of the human final end—an end which even reason tells us cannot be known in its essence by reason alone, except by a kind of negative knowledge. Prophetic revelation represents a partial assimilation of this end in the order of knowledge. More specifically, prophecy is a more intense participation in God's knowledge, which the truth dwells in. In talking about the need for a firmer knowledge of God for salvation, Thomas does not see divine revelation supplanting natural reason, but rather assisting and perfecting it.[32] He does not say that revelation alone is "more certain"—although perhaps if pushed he might admit that based on its source, divine revelation must be more certain absolutely—but rather that reason left by itself is less certain than when assisted by divine revelation. It is the mutual kinship between reason and divine revelation—received as a principle of knowledge in faith—that makes up sacred doctrine. In order to see more clearly how sacred doctrine functions as a real principle of knowledge under the light of faith, we must now look at how Thomas thinks faith makes known the final end and helps to orient the human person to happiness.

---

32. See ST, I, q. 1, a. 8, ad 2.

Faith as Revealing Happiness and the Human Final End

Faith is the principle of knowledge that builds on and perfects reason's grasp of the final end. For this reason, in the *Summa theologiae*, Thomas treats the object of the human final end first not as an object knowable in faith, but as an object accessible—albeit imperfectly—to natural reason. He treats both sets of questions on the human final end and on faith within the Second Part, making up its backbone. The prologue to the Second Part gives a sense of Thomas's overall intention and purpose. The location of the questions on the human final end immediately after the Second Part's prologue is also of critical importance. Due to their location, these questions exert an enormous influence and controlling force on how subsequent questions are read. For instance, later in the *Secunda secundae* appear the questions on faith and prophecy; both sets of questions are set in parallel positions in relation to the questions on the human final end so that all three sets of questions immediately follow a critical prologue that reiterates the Second Part's central consideration of "the human being made in the image of God."[33] Thomas, therefore, signals a parallel relationship between the questions on the final end and on faith. Examining and discussing these parallel relationships among the three sets of questions will enable us to see more clearly how Thomas accentuates the fundamental orientation of faith and prophecy toward the final end.

The Prologues in the Second Part

While all the prologues in the *Summa theologiae* are important signposts for how to understand Thomas's intention and purpose in a given section with respect to his overall intention of the work, the prologue to the Second Part is particularly important. It contains several interpretive keys for discerning how the notions of prophecy, faith, and the human final end relate to the structure of the *Summa* as a whole. In other words, it is integral for our understanding of how prophecy, faith, and the final end fit into sacred doctrine. The three prologues of the Second Part that we will examine all have the human person's knowledge of the final end as a central theme.

---

33. ST, I-II, prologue: "quia, sicut Damascenus dicit, homo factus ad imaginem Dei dicitur, secundum quod per imaginem significatur intellectuale et arbitrio liberum et per se potestativum." On the *imago Dei*, see also ST, I, q. 93.

The opening prologue to the Second Part marks the transition between Thomas's treatment of God as first and exemplary cause of all creation and his turning toward the human being as a rational creature made in God's image. Thomas is signaling that in this new part of his work he is considering God principally as He is the formal and final cause of the human person. He cites an important passage from St. John Damascene to disambiguate the "image" to which he refers: The image in question is "an intellectual being both free in will and self-directed."[34] The Damascene passage flags up succinctly the fact that it is the human creature's intellectual nature that allows it to be free and a principle of its own actions.

Early on in the Second Part, Thomas homes in on the will (*voluntas*) or rational appetite as that which specifically makes the actions of a human being "human." The will is the principle of action that allows human acts to be self-determined. But before launching into questions on the will and on voluntary and involuntary action, Thomas addresses the human final end, as both the ultimate object of desire and intellection and that which orients the human will as a first principle of action. It is because the human appetite can have reference to this final end in an act of deliberation that Thomas says humans can act voluntarily. If deliberation in reference to this final end is absent, a human appetite remains subhuman strictly speaking; it is only rational and voluntary through an act of deliberation wherein a person weighs the goodness of a course of action in ultimate reference to this final end.

To understand Thomas's ordering of these questions immediately following the prologue to the Second Part, we need to look briefly at what he says earlier about the human will in the First Part (qq. 82–83). He explains there that the will's object always involves some good perceived and then desired. Prior to any deliberate motion toward some good—a motion, which in rational creatures is caused by the will—there must be some perception of a good. Taken alone, this perception is an intellectual act. Human voluntary acts depend on this prior perception of an object before they are partially moved by that object as an object of desire that attracts the rational creature to move toward it through deliberation and choice.

The good, Thomas says, is the will's proper object, and goodness is an aspect of anything that exists. All goods, Thomas thinks, have causal dependence on the one Good; they must be caused by one Highest Good from

---

34. ST, I-II, prologue: "secundum quod per imaginem significatur intellectuale et arbitrio liberum et per se potestativum." The foundation for Thomas's assertion that man is made in God's image comes from Gn 1:26–27; see ST, I, q. 93, a. 1, sc.

which they derive their particular goodness.[35] He understands goodness metaphysically as a kind of participation in God's highest goodness. Such an understanding implies the corollary that all goods other than the Highest Good are themselves deficient in their goodness. Because they cannot cause or account for their own goodness, they must necessarily lack some goodness. Beyond the Highest Good, there is no other good to be desired, and in the Highest Good, all desires are satisfied. It is only here, then, that the human will can rest. From this, Thomas can draw the threads together between the human will and final end: since the only actions of a human being that are worthy of being called "human" stem from the will, the proto-principle of human action must always be this Ultimate Good, which is God.[36]

The starting point of actions that are properly human is the divine goodness that sets the the will in motion in creation. From the human perspective, the will is a principle of human action.[37] An important feature of all human action is that it already has an orientation built in, so to speak. This orientation, which comes from its principle, is toward the final end, which is goodness, as seen above. Thomas also calls the final end the "final cause," and it is final causality that is reflected in the will's orientation to the final end. The human final cause is the final cause of everything: God.

God as final cause controls the scope of the *Summa theologiae* in a more explicit way in the Second Part than in the First, even though we have seen this theme already present latently in Question One's introduction of salvation as the *raison d'être* of sacred doctrine. Thomas's attention for the remainder of the Second Part focuses on the different principles in the human being that lead to or away from the final end, which he identifies toward the end of the questions on the final end as the beatific vision.[38]

Accompanying its introduction of the central theme of the human creature made in God's image is the prologue to the Second Part's elaboration that this image is located exclusively in the soul. Thomas says he will consider the human

---

35. See ST, I, q. 2, a. 3, co.: the Fourth Way; compare ST, I, q. 6, a. 4.

36. ST, I-II, q. 1, a. 1, co.: "Illae ergo actiones proprie humanae dicuntur, quae ex voluntate deliberata procedunt. Si quae autem aliae actiones homini conveniant, possunt dici quidem hominis actiones; sed non proprie humanae, cum non sint hominis inquantum est homo."

37. A principle denotes simply the first thing from which other things proceed; see ST, I, q. 33, a. 1, co.: "hoc nomen principium nihil aliud significat, quam id, a quo aliquid procedit; omne enim, a quo aliquid procedit quocumque modo, dicimus esse principium, et e converse."

38. ST, I-II, q. 3, a. 8.

body in sacred doctrine only insofar as it has a relationship to the soul.[39] A soul, he observes, possesses its own principle of activity. Yet, because the human end is supernatural and humans suffer from the wounds of sin, the soul's own interior principles are not sufficient; people need exterior principles to assist them: law and grace.[40] Thomas devotes the last cluster of questions in the *Prima secundae* to these exterior principles of law and grace.

The *Secunda secundae* follows immediately from the questions on grace, and the analysis begun in the *Prima secundae* restarts now with the questions on faith and reiterates the central themes of beatitude and the final end. Only now Thomas incorporates and integrates into the account grace as an exterior principle interiorly at work in human persons in the infused virtues and gifts of the Holy Spirit. Just as the *Prima secundae* begins by looking at the final end in general, the *Secunda secundae* starts by examining faith, which by grace orients the human person's understanding to grasp and move toward the final end as it is supernaturally revealed. While centered primarily on an intellectual act, faith also involves the will, and indeed Thomas will insist that an act of the will is essential to the act of faith. Without denying the role of the will in the act of faith, Thomas still conceives of faith as having a distinctly intellectual focus. By this, I mean that Thomas sees faith as the theological virtue that deals more with orienting the human intellect—the grasping of first principles—than with orienting the will; the latter task is taken up in his *Summa* schema by the theological virtues of hope and charity. He thinks faith serves as the starting point for Christian life and action precisely because it reveals to the human mind its supernatural end. Without this primarily intellectual orientation, humans cannot direct their voluntary actions and intentions toward God as their final end.

The Necessity of the End:
The Moral Part as the Nexus for Faith and Prophecy

In the *Prima secundae*, Thomas outlines how "moral consideration, since it is about human acts, must first be treated in general [*in universali*], and then second in particular [*in particulari*]."[41] As a whole, the Second Part follows this gener-

---

39. ST, I, q. 75, prologue: "naturam autem hominis considerare pertinet ad theologum ex parte animae, non autem ex parte corporis, nisi secundum habitudinem quam habet corpus ad animam."

40. ST, I-II, q. 90, prologue.

41. ST, I-II, q. 6, prologue.

al-to-specific model; there is first a general treatment of virtues, vices, and "other things pertaining to moral material" followed by a specific treatment of the same moral material.[42] Human happiness requires that people know in what way their acts help them arrive at beatitude and which acts impede them. In themselves, actions and works are never general things but are particular events involving particular people and objects. For this reason, "the science that deals with action" (*operativa scientia*) is perfected only in the consideration of particulars.[43]

Throughout all the subsequent questions in the *Prima secundae* starting from voluntary acts and their principles and ending with law and grace, the human final end remains Thomas's controlling idea, and the pull of the final end moves the entire structure of the part along. In one sense, the final end is what makes Thomas's treatment of morals "scientific" as opposed to exhortative or merely exemplary.[44] At the same time, there is some validity in Mark Jordan's observation that Thomas's notion of a "moral science" (*scientia moralis*)—a term he does occasionally employ—is much more self-limiting than some readers of Thomas have maintained.[45] While the final end as the first principle

---

42. Thomas does not cite any authority at ST, I-II, q. 6, prologue for this method of moral consideration, but an inspiration for this general-to-specific model was likely Aristotle, *Nicomachean Ethics*, I, 6, 1096b30.

43. ST, I-II, q. 6, prologue. Thomas does not explain fully here how and why *scientia operativa* is perfected in the consideration of particulars. It is also not entirely clear whether by "particulars" Thomas means "contingents." Presuming that he does, is Thomas in this statement modeling moral consideration too strictly on the process of speculative reason (or analysis), which starts from the general and ends in the particular, without considering the difficulties in knowing the particular and contingent? His statement here seems to be in some tension with what he says later in the questions on law (ST, I-II, q. 94, a. 4). There he makes a distinction between speculative and practical reason according to their differing matter. Speculative reason handles necessary things, and in its conclusions, truth is held without fail and is equally accessible to everyone. In contrast, practical reason handles contingent things, and while there are necessary and general principles in practical reason, the more one gets down into the contingent realm of human action the more one finds defects and contrary conclusions. Hence, Thomas writes: "in matters of action (*in operativis*) the same truth or practical rectitude are not held by everyone with regard to particulars (*ad propria*), but only with regard to general things." Even when there is the same rectitude in everyone with regards to particulars, Thomas observes that sometimes not everyone knows it. For more on the issue of the particular in Thomas's moral thought, see the somewhat unbalanced, albeit thought-provoking, treatment in Jordan, *Rewritten Theology*, 142–43. It could be that Thomas's remark reflects a commonplace that he does not adequately question or consider here.

44. An exemplary account would be one where the treatment of morals is based on a narrative or analysis of the lives of particular individuals.

45. Jordan, *Rewritten Theology*, 149–53.

in practical reasoning does have bearing on universal necessity, this universality rarely extends down to the particulars of human action. Jordan observes aptly that for Thomas moral science is "more taxonomy than exhortation, more causal classification than spiritual direction."[46] The way one speaks about necessity in moral considerations is thus slightly different from the way one speaks about it in speculative and theoretical subjects like mathematics and physics, where apodictic demonstrations are the expectation. This difference in necessity reflects on one level the difference between God as final cause and God as formal cause. We will focus primarily here on this notion of final necessity and the constitutive part it plays in voluntary action and desire.

While God has given humans the ability to be the master of their own acts, the final end according to Thomas is not really something that a person chooses to desire: our desire to be happy (*felices*) does not pertain to free will, but rather to a natural instinct.[47] The human desire to be happy is something constitutive of human nature, Thomas thinks.[48] He attempts to describe its functioning in the human person as a kind of natural instinct. This instinct is the first motion of the will that makes possible other subsequent acts of the will. "Subsequent" means here not temporally subsequent, but causally subsequent. When defining the natural instinct for happiness, Thomas initially takes the term "happiness" in a general way to be the object of a desire for a "perfect good" that satisfies the will completely.[49] Because a perfect good is that which satisfies the will completely, it can also be called the "final good," he thinks.[50] Thus, the will's natural instinct for happiness is the same as its natural instinct for the final good or end, which everyone desires necessarily. This natural instinct for the final good contributes causally to every other act of the will in a person, and in this way, the will in its functioning is said "to adhere" to the final end, just as the intellect adheres to first principles in its functioning.[51] The final end comes to be functional in the human person through the natural instinct of the will, which is not only determined necessarily to the final good taken generally, but

---

46. Jordan, *Rewritten Theology*, 152.

47. ST, I, q. 19, a. 10, co.: "non enim ad liberum arbitrium pertinet quod volumus esse felices, sed ad naturalem instinctum."

48. ST, I, q. 83, a. 1.

49. See ST, I-II, q. 5, a. 8, co.

50. See ST, I-II, q. 5, a. 8, ad 2.

51. ST, I, q. 82, a. 2, co.: "sicut intellectus naturaliter et ex necessitate inhaeret primis principiis, ita voluntas ultimo fini."

is also elicited or drawn out by God through specific, concrete created goods that one encounters.[52]

Under its general aspect, the final end or good functions within human deliberation like a first principle in speculative thought. Thomas gives a very condensed reason for this in the First Part. He explains: "that which is by nature always suitable (*convenit*) for something"—suitable for something's final good or end—"must be the foundation and principle of everything else in that thing."[53] This means that the final good acts as the foundation for the nature of something through its formal cause. The formal cause is the inherent principle that causes something to move toward what is suitable to that thing's nature: something's natural end. Thomas in this compressed passage is trying to highlight a parallel between formal and final causes. He sets up two parallel relationships: (1) that which is always fitting for a nature—a final cause; and (2) a thing's natural acts—its formal cause. From these, he shows that the final cause has a controlling relationship over all the acts of a nature, but it has this because it causes the formal cause from which all the acts of a nature derive. In other words, the final cause is that which causes and directs something's formal cause. The formal cause remains the root of a thing's nature as it moves itself to its natural perfection, but because the formal cause is itself caused by the final, every motion or act that comes (immanently) from some nature is also said to be caused by the final cause, just as "every act must come from something immovable."[54] The final cause of the human will is the final good; thus, all voluntary action is simultaneously both caused by and oriented to this final good, which serves as the will's immovable and necessary first principle.

Clarification about "Necessity"

Because the will is necessarily joined to the final good, Thomas thinks it follows that everyone desires happiness—the attainment of that final good—necessarily. But what does Thomas mean by "necessarily"? How is it necessary? A

---

52. On the distinction between the specific notion of the good and the general notion of the good, see ST, I, q. 5, a. 8, co. and ad 2–3.

53. ST, I, q. 82, a. 1, co.: "Oportet enim quod illud quod naturaliter alicui convenit et immobiliter, sit fundamentum et principium omnium aliorum, quia natura rei est primum in unoquoque, et omnis motus procedit ab aliquo immobili."

54. ST, I, q. 82, a. 1, co.

brief clarification about "necessity" is required. Necessity, he explains, can be spoken of in various ways.[55] A frequently employed general definition is that the necessary "cannot be otherwise." Necessity can apply to either internal or external principles. If applied to intrinsic principles, two types of necessity are possible one material, the other formal. For instance, the necessary corruption of any composite by its opposite is a materially intrinsic necessity; this type does not concern us as much as the second type. As an example of formal necessity, Thomas gives the example of a triangle whose three angles must necessarily add up to two right angles; such necessity he calls "natural and absolute."[56] For external principles, there is "the necessity of coercion." This is when someone is forced by another agent to do something and, thus, cannot act otherwise. External necessity is incompatible with the human will because it goes against its natural inclination for self-determination and self-preservation. Lastly, things can be necessary by their end; this is the type of necessity we need to pay most attention to.

Thomas's example of a necessary end is when someone cannot achieve (or cannot achieve well) an end without another thing. This other thing can be said to be necessary by virtue of the end. He notes, for example, that we commonly say food is "necessary" for life. Without food, we cannot live, or at the very least we cannot live well or for very long. The necessity of end, he says, is also "sometimes called utility."[57] Despite what one may initially think, the necessity of end is not repugnant to a person's free will according to Thomas. To illustrate this he draws an analogy between the will and the understanding: "just as out of necessity the understanding adheres to first principles, so the will out of necessity adheres to the final end, which is beatitude."[58] He cites Aristotle's *Physics* (II, 9, 200a21) here: The end pertains to morals as first principles relate to speculative matters. In the order of knowledge, first principles are foundational insights grasped initially by the intellect which underpin all subsequent conclusions based on those principles. One has knowledge (*scientia*) only when the conclusions follow necessarily from some principle known prior. When he compares the final end to a kind of principle in the mode of practical reason,

---

55. ST, I, q. 82, a. 1.

56. ST, I, q. 82, a. 1, co.

57. ST, I, q. 82, a. 1, co.

58. ST, I, q. 82, a. 1, co.

Thomas is considering this principle to be "necessary" by virtue of an end.[59] Even though human practical reason is determined necessarily by the final end, this does not mean that the human person lacks freedom. Thomas thinks the human capacity for free choice (*electio*) is compatible with the will's being necessitated, in another respect, with regard to the end:

> We are masters of our actions according to the fact that we can choose this or that thing. Choice, however, is not about the end, but "about those things which are to the end" (*ad finem*), as said in the *Nicomachean Ethics* [1111b26]. Hence, the appetite for the final end (*appetitus ultimi finis*) is not about those things of which we are masters.[60]

Thomas thinks that all voluntary action has this inherent orientation to the final end, and this orientation is at least perceivable by reason, even if it is not perfectly understood or properly applied to further reasoning. It is the necessity of the end as grasped as the first principle in practical reason that also allows the human appetite to be rational.

Taking the time to appreciate this background into Thomas's account of voluntary action will help us to appreciate later why he sees such a clear distinction between prophecy and faith. Prophecy in itself will not involve any act of the will for Thomas; the prophet is a passive recipient of the light of prophecy, which is unmerited and perhaps not even necessarily desired. While the light of prophecy allows the prophet to see clearly certain things in a godlike manner, this resulting knowledge does not necessarily determine the prophet to a particular course of action. Hence, someone like Jonah (1:1–3) runs away after receiving God's message to go to Nineveh and preach. Prophets remain free to use the gift for good or for evil or not at all, provided they are aware they have received it. The gift does not function directly as external assistance to the human will to move toward God; this is more the function of sanctifying grace in Thomas's doctrine of grace. Prophecy acts more like an invitation to both prophets and those who hear them to seek their final end in God with their whole heart (or will) and mind and to be open to the gift of faith.

---

59. See ST, I, q. 82, a. 1, ad 2: the will, when it wants something naturally, corresponds more to "the understanding of natural principles" (*intellectui naturalium principiorum*) than to "reason" (*rationi*).

60. ST, I, q. 82, a. 1, ad 3.

How "Human" Is an Act?
The Human Act's Proximity to Beatitude

One final insight we can take from this first cluster of questions in the *Prima secundae* is how happiness and the final end are not afterthoughts in Thomas's anthropology, but are rather central components of it. Conceived entirely at the heart of sacred doctrine, his anthropology is first and foremost that of a theologian's, concerning itself with appropriating a deeper understanding of how all human actions and intentions can be oriented toward God and the enjoyment of God—an enjoyment that will culminate in a face-to-face vision.[61] The extent to which an act derives from a person's heart and mind and is oriented to this beatific vision determines the degree to which an act is properly human. In distinguishing between acts that are proper to humans and acts that are common to both humans and animals, Thomas draws on the insight that the human final end and ultimate good consists in beatitude.[62] Acts that are more closely related to beatitude are ones that are more properly human. The inverse of this also holds true; acts that are common with animals are less human and, by extension, further from beatitude.[63] Yet, this beatitude, because it is above human nature, can only become an object of the will if it is grasped by the mind.

This grasping by the mind of the object of beatitude only comes about through the theological virtue of faith according to Thomas. In order to grasp how the final end becomes operative in human life and activity, we must now turn directly to his questions on faith. This will provide the last piece of background needed to situate prophecy within sacred doctrine and his thought as a whole.

---

61. ST, I-II, q. 5, a. 7–8.

62. ST, I-II, q. 6, prologue.

63. This position seems to reflect a commonplace in Thomas's thought that he has inherited from earlier traditions of moral consideration but fails to question deeply. On its own, it appears to be in tension with certain aspects of his hylomorphic doctrine with regard to the human person and his insistence on the presence of the human body in the beatific vision along with heaven's existence as a place; see ST, I, q. 102.

3

Faith, Happiness, and the Final End

The preceding chapter detoured from the larger discussion of Thomas's account of happiness and the final end to consider his analysis of voluntary action. This was necessary in part to be able to appreciate adequately the voluntary dimension which sets the act of faith apart from prophecy. Thomas does not think prophecy is a human voluntary act in and of itself,[1] and he explicitly denies that it is a virtue or *habitus*.[2] Faith's voluntary character allows him to call it both an act (*actus fidei*)[3] and *habitus* or virtue (*habitus vel virtus*).[4] As a voluntary act, faith already refers to the final end. In addition to its voluntary dimension, faith is comprised also of an intellectual act wherein the human mind perceives the human final end as supernaturally revealed. Faith thus ordains the human person immediately to beatitude and functions as eternal life in an inchoate form.[5] It will now be profitable to take a closer look at Thomas's treatment of the act of

---

1. ST, II-II, q. 172, a. 4; compare *De ver.*, q. 12, a. 5, ad 3. Thomas uses the phrase *actus prophetiae* a number of times (7) in the *De veritate*, and most often in reference to issues regarding the moral status of an act of prophecy—its being good or evil. This line of questioning allows Thomas to distinguish between the "act of prophecy," which being caused by the Holy Spirit is good in and of itself, and its "use," wherein a person may use prophetic gifts immorally to seek ends that are contrary to the Holy Spirit's. The phrase *actus prophetiae*, however, is entirely absent from his questions on prophecy in the *Summa theologiae* and the article on whether prophets need good morals (ST, II-II, q. 172, a. 4).

2. ST, II-II, q. 171, a.2.

3. ST, II-II, q. 2.

4. ST, II-II, q. 4, a. 5.

5. See ST, II-II, q. 4, a. 1: "fides est habitus mentis, qua inchoatur vita aeterna in nobis."

faith and the virtue of faith in general from his questions on the subject (II-II, qq. 1–16); this will help us further to distinguish faith from prophecy, which lacks this voluntary dimension.

An understanding of the human final end as something necessary for knowing and attaining beatitude can also be seen in the way sacred doctrine needs to relate to salvation and to its divinely revealed first principles—the articles of faith. It is the light of faith that structures this parallel ordering in sacred doctrine. Faith perfects reason and the will without supplanting them, and it should be recalled that Thomas thinks the ordination of human reason and the will to the final end through faith is something already reflected naturally because of the human person's formal dependence on God as cause.

Devoting attention now to Thomas's questions on the theological virtue of faith (II-II, qq. 1–16) in this chapter will enable us also to identify a kind of mirroring between sacred doctrine and prophecy that will be seen most clearly when prophecy is distinguished from the act of faith. In his analysis of the latter, Thomas maintains that every believer's act of faith relies on an implicit appeal to prophetic testimony; this gives the act both a social dimension and a rootedness in history. Given that the light of faith is also required for sacred doctrine, an analogous, implicit appeal to prophetic testimony is also found there, the beginnings of which were already seen during our discussion of Question One in the First Part. When these parallel ordinations to theological faith are discovered in sacred doctrine and prophecy, a common and shared function of both becomes apparent; they both are structured so as to communicate supernatural knowledge received through divine revelation. This in turn orients the human person to God as Highest Good and source of happiness.

The incompleteness of both prophecy and faith will also figure prominently. In the act of faith, the mind comes to a stable resting, but this stabilization is not the final rest of beatitude, because the intellect can still enquire into things it does not know about God. It grasps onto the things to be believed in faith, the *credenda*, as the new limits of faith's horizon. It is prophetic testimony that lends shape to these limits by grounding them discretely in history.

The Prologue to the *Secunda secundae*

As was already seen with the prologue to the *Prima secundae*, the prologue to the *Secunda secundae* is equally pivotal for getting one's bearings. Thomas says there that he will analyze human actions with respect to both particular things and universals. The human final end can be analyzed particularly and universally as well. The reason for ending his analysis with particular things is that humans attain their final end through particulars. This accounts for why he thinks it "less useful" (*utile minus*) to have "universal moral discussions."[6] Such discussions relate less directly to the manner by which humans attain beatitude, which is through a concrete act assisted by grace. Particularized moral discussions about this or that act are ultimately more useful because they have more similarity to actual human circumstances. As was seen earlier, Thomas observes that another name for the "necessity of end" is *utilitas*, and the "utility" he is speaking of here in the prologue to the *Secunda secundae* refers again to the necessity of the human final end.[7] Singulars contribute more to our knowledge of actions than universal discussion on their own; and knowledge that is more complete is more "useful," because surer knowledge about acts helps to direct us with more certainty and precision toward our final end.

Having established why he will consider moral matters in the particular, Thomas goes on to subdivide his analysis into two further parts; these divisions make up the two major sections of the *Secunda secundae*. The first section of questions (qq. 1–170) considers particular virtues and vices that can be held by all people. The second section (qq. 171–89) looks at a number of special cases involving certain particular types of individuals, such as recipients of certain charisms (in the first place, prophets), ecclesiastical rulers or subjects, and active individuals or contemplatives. Thomas places his questions on prophecy in this second section as it is a gift given only to certain individuals and is not held by everyone. This last section of the *Secunda secundae* offers a number of different taxonomies as he examines the differences between humans and classifies specific actions that appear to fall outside the common course of human life shared by everyone.

The Questions on Faith

Given that faith is necessary for everyone's salvation, Thomas treats it in the first major section of the *Secunda secundae*; indeed, it makes up this section's first cluster of questions. Thomas outlines there that faith is a supernatural virtue given by God that orients the human intellect to the final end as knowable

---

6. ST, II-II, prologue: "sermones morales universales."
7. ST, I, q. 82, a. 1, co.

through divine revelation. Through faith humans come to know that their beatitude consists in something supernatural, in a God who has revealed Himself. Humans are also given the gifts of theological hope and charity, which allow them to trust in God as their Highest Good and to confidently believe that through the truths divinely revealed they will be united to God face-to-face. Thomas will follow up his questions on faith with clusters on hope and charity. The remainder of the first section is completed by additional clusters organized around the four cardinal virtues: prudence, justice, fortitude, and temperance.

The structure of the cluster of questions on faith adheres closely to the structure proposed by Thomas in the prologue, which he repeats for every major virtue-cluster. He first treats the virtue of faith: its object (q. 1), its internal and external acts (qq. 2–3), and its status as a steady disposition or virtue (*habitus*) in the human person (q. 4).[8] He then considers those who have faith (q. 5), which is followed by questions on faith's cause (q. 6) and effect (q. 7), and on understanding (q. 8) and knowledge (q. 9) as gifts of the Holy Spirit that correspond to faith and related beatitudes from the Sermon on the Mount. He concludes this cluster with articles on the corresponding vice of unbelief and other vices that oppose faith (qq. 10–15) and on the precepts of the Decalogue that correspond to faith (q. 16).

Question One:
The Object of Faith Is God as First Truth

The first question identifies the object of faith to be God as First Truth. We must first address what Thomas means by "object" here. He says that in the other cognitive habits (*habitus*), there are two things that can be identified as objects: (1) "that which is known materially," which he calls the "material object"; and (2) "that through which something is known," which is called the "formal object." An example from geometry illustrates these two objects at work. Geometric conclusions are the material objects of geometry. The means of demonstration through which these conclusions are known are its formal objects. Faith's formal object, says Thomas, is God as "First Truth" (*veritas prima*).[9] The means by which the human intellect adheres to the material objects of faith is God Himself revealing them. Hence, due to faith's formal object a

---

8. ST, II-II, q. 1, prologue.
9. ST, II-II, q. 1, a. 1, co.

believer does not assent to something "unless it is revealed by God."[10] Because faith "rests (*innititur*) on divine truth itself as a medium,"[11] it can already be said to share in God's own perfect self-knowledge. Faith's material object is also God, but it includes many other things as well: for example, the articles of faith or the covenant with Abraham. There is potential for a wide variety of secondary material objects of faith after the primary object, God.

In this distinction between the formal and material objects of faith, one finds a parallel also with sacred doctrine. Sacred doctrine's primary subject is God. Its secondary subject extends to other things as they relate to God. Similarly, the secondary material objects of faith do not fall under faith "unless they have some order to God," says Thomas.[12] Things other than God—what Thomas broadly calls "his effects"—ought to assist human beings "to tend toward divine enjoyment," that is, toward their final end.[13] If such effects do not help believers by ordering them to God, the light of faith will not move a person to assent to them as material objects of faith. Likewise, the formal object in sacred doctrine is based on God's revelation. It is, however, not the same formal object as faith: God as First Truth. Because of this, we cannot say that what is known in sacred doctrine is directly known by a sharing in God's self-knowledge; instead, the "demonstrations" from divinely revealed first principles are sacred doctrine's formal object. "Demonstrations" are within quotation marks here to highlight the fact that they are not exclusively logical or apodictic demonstrations. Unlike other sciences, sacred doctrine's principles are divinely revealed and rest on the knowledge of God and the blessed. They come to be expressed or "articulated" as the articles of faith, and in sacred doctrine these articles of faith are analogous to the self-evident first principles of natural knowledge.[14] The human intellect adheres to the articles through faith's formal object, the light of faith. Likewise, the intellect adheres to naturally knowable things through reason's formal object, the light of reason.

The formal object in both faith and sacred doctrine also serves as a first principle. Just as much as optics cannot properly be called a "science" without principles from arithmetic, so too sacred doctrine needs the articles of faith as its principles. Likewise, faith has God as First Truth as its necessary first principle.

---

10. ST, II-II, q. 1, a. 1, co.: "nisi quia est a Deo revelatum."

11. ST, II-II, q. 1, a. 1, co.

12. ST, II-II, q. 1, a. 1, co.: "nisi secundum quod habent aliquem ordinem ad Deum."

13. ST, II-II, q. 1, a. 1, co.: "ad tendendum in divinam fructionem."

14. ST, II-II, q. 1, a. 7, co.: "ita se habent in doctrina fidei articuli fidei sicut principia per se nota in doctrina quae per rationem naturalem habetur."

In sacred doctrine, the mode under which the articles of faith are received and held in a person is the formal light of faith. Thus, faith's formal light is necessary for sacred doctrine to achieve its status as a science. Since sciences are stable dispositions that deal with necessary relationships between the knower and the thing known, the human intellect's adherence to the articles of faith must also be equally firm. Faith gives the human mind this stability necessary to acquire a science and wisdom because faith is also habitual (*habitus*). Having recourse to both the light of reason and the light of faith, sacred doctrine can employ reason to unfold further truths from the objects of faith.

A link between faith and sacred doctrine can also be seen in their final causes. Just as in sacred doctrine, everything falling under faith that is not God must be "ordered to God."[15] This is because the formal object of faith—as a principle of understanding—is ordered to hope, which orients a person's will toward God as unseen. Faith's formal object is caused and oriented by God as final cause, and the final cause brings about the motion of the will toward God as the supernatural final good through the theological virtues of hope and charity. Thomas states that faith's formal object simultaneously corresponds to the final good and first truth:

> The act of faith is to believe, which as shown earlier is an act of the intellect determined to one [object] by the command of the will. Thus, the act of faith is ordered both to the object of the will, which is the good and the end, and to the object of the intellect, which is the true. Since faith as a theological virtue … has the same object and end, the object of faith and the end must proportionately correspond to each other. Moreover, earlier we saw that the object of faith is the First Truth insofar as it is not seen and is the object of and reason for (*propter ipsam*) [a believer's] adherence. Because of this, the First Truth itself must be related to the act of faith by means of the end under the aspect of something not seen, which pertains to the definition of a thing hoped for.[16]

Faith's formal object and final end correspond to each other: both relate to God but under the different aspects of First Truth and ultimate good. Thomas need not refer to faith as either an intellectual or moral virtue; he calls it a "theological virtue" because it is entirely ordained to God as its end. In a similar way, the

---

15. ST, II-II, q. 1, a. 1, co.: "in ordine ad Deum."
16. ST, II-II, q. 4, a. 1, co.

distinction between sacred doctrine's final end (human salvation in the beatific vision) and its formal object (the "demonstrations" from divinely revealed first principles) is modelled on faith's final and formal cause.

With this understanding of God as the final cause of faith, Aquinas can answer the objections of those who claim that things like Christ's humanity and the sacraments do not fall under faith. Such things, he says, are material objects of faith, and it is through these material objects that "we are ordered to God."[17] The believer assents to them because they have been revealed by God, who cannot err. In this way, everything in scripture also comes under faith because scripture comes from divine revelation. What Thomas says here about the material objects of faith finds a parallel in his identification of sacred doctrine's secondary subject matter—the things that are not of God. Back in Question One of the First Part, he observes that some people, when determining the subject of sacred doctrine, look "to that which is treated" in sacred doctrine and "not to the formal aspect under which it is considered."[18] When they do this, they assign other subjects to sacred doctrine, such as the distinction between "things and signs," the "works of reparation," or "the whole Christ." Thomas insists that sacred doctrine treats all these things, but only "with regard to their ordination to God."[19] We can see now in the light of the questions on faith that sacred doctrine's structuring of its subject matter is caused by the virtue of faith. Faith will also cause a similar structure in Thomas's notion of prophecy.

Material Objects of Faith Are Known through Propositions

From the believer's perspective faith's object can be considered as "something complex through a proposition" (*aliquid complexum per modum enuntiabilis*).[20] In general, as humans we come to know truths through the use of our reason and intellect. Reason functions "by composing and dividing."[21] One consequence of this mode of knowing is that God, who is absolutely simple,[22] comes to be known to us "through a certain complexity."[23] God's own mode

---

17. ST, II-II, q. 1, a. 1, obj. 1 and ad 1.

18. ST, I, q. 1, a. 7, co.

19. ST, I, q. 1, a. 7, co.

20. ST, II-II, q. 1, a. 7, co.; see also ad 2.

21. ST, II-II, q. 1, a. 2, co.

22. See ST, I, q. 3, a. 7.

23. ST, II-II, q. 1, a. 2, co.

of knowing, however, is not complex because it is identical with the absolutely simple mode of divine being.[24] From God's perspective, the objects of faith are known simply, although for us complexly. Now, propositions as logical entities or verbal statements are by definition complex. In order to understand how propositions function in faith, Thomas looks to how they are used in other sciences. In other sciences, propositions are formed only "to have knowledge (*cognitionem*) about realities."[25] The same is true in faith, he thinks. The act of belief uses propositions to get beyond the positions themselves. Faith's act does not terminate in propositions, but in a reality (*ad rem*). Propositions remain the vehicles by which we know things; they are not what the act of knowing ends in. This will remain important for Thomas's understanding of prophetic testimony, which must rely on human speech and propositions to convey the contents of prophetic knowledge. Just as in the articles of faith, prophetic testimonies bear witness to truths that go beyond propositional statements and extend to realities themselves—and especially to God.

Nothing False Can Come under Faith

Due to its formal object, Thomas also thinks that nothing in faith can be false.[26] Everything believed in faith can only be believed as something caused by faith's formal object. As the formal object of faith, the First Truth is the medium by which something is believed in faith. Because the First Truth cannot be false, anything that is believed in faith cannot be incompatible with the First Truth and thus cannot be false.

Faith's infallibility, which rests on divine infallibility, explains in part why Thomas says earlier that sacred doctrine is more certain than all other human sciences.[27] Several of the objections from the article on faith's infallibility suggest this link to sacred doctrine.[28] The third objection begins by looking at those "ancients" who believed that Christ would be born. These people's faith endured up until the time of the preaching of the Gospel. Yet, there was a period of time in between Christ's birth and the preaching of the Gospel when he was publicly

---

24. See ST, I, q. 14, a. 4.
25. ST, II-II, q. 1, a. 2, ad 2.
26. ST, II-II, q. 1, a. 3, co.
27. See ST, I, q. 1, a. 5.
28. ST, II-II, q. 1, a. 3, obj. 3 and obj. 2.

unknown. Those who believed that Christ would be born during this interim period would seem to have believed something false, namely, that Christ would be born, when in fact he already was born. The objection turns on the problem of human judgments (or conjectures) and their relationship to faith. Thomas resolves this objection by clarifying what faith in Christ's birth actually implies. After his birth but before his public preaching, faith means belief that he would be born at some time. Some ancient believers, Thomas explains, tried to predict that Christ would be born at a determined time, but their predictions, unless divinely revealed, came not from faith but from human conjecture. Human conjectures, of course, can be false, and some of these ancient believers were wrong not because their faith was false, but because their estimation about the time of the nativity was based on conjecture. However, Thomas thinks "it is impossible to judge (*aestimet*) anything false from faith." This is due again to faith's formal object, God as First Truth, which informs judgments through the light of faith—a kind of sharing in God's own judgment. The certitude of sacred doctrine is similarly derived "from the light of divine knowledge" which also "cannot be deceived."[29] This "light of divine knowledge" in sacred doctrine is mediated for the believer by faith. Critically, this does not translate into infallibility for sacred doctrine. It can try to judge whether something—a proposition, for example—follows necessarily from faith.[30] If this judgment is found to be true, the proposition shares in the certitude of faith and becomes a part of sacred doctrine; if a proposition is judged to be contrary to faith, it must be false, although one might not be able right away to show why the given proposition is false.

Prophecy, however, shares in the same infallibility as faith, and this is because the formal object of prophecy is the same as faith's formal object: God as First Truth.[31] Just as in faith, prophets do not see God *in se* as the First Truth, but they do share in God's knowledge through the medium of the light of prophecy. In receiving the light of prophecy, prophets receive a principle that makes their knowledge temporarily more like God's. Thomas compares this to the knowledge of students, which becomes "a likeness (*similitudo*) of

---

29. ST, I, q. 1, a. 5, co.

30. See ST, I, q. 1, a. 8, co.: Thomas's example is St. Paul basing the truth of the general resurrection on Christ's resurrection.

31. ST, II-II, q. 171, a. 4, co.: "principium autem eorum quae divino lumine prophetice manifestantur, est ipsa veritas prima, quam prophetae in seipsa non vident."

[their] teacher's knowledge."[32] While their knowledge is not identical with the teacher's, "the truth of this knowledge" (*veritas cognitionis*) is the same.[33] Just as the truth of the teacher is the same as that of the student, Thomas thinks "the truth of prophetic knowledge and announcement" is the same as God's truth. This truth comes "from the divine knowledge," which is infallible, and hence, prophecy too cannot be false. Thomas for this reason calls prophecy "an impressed likeness or sign of divine prescience."[34]

Given this account of prophecy's infallibility, Thomas devotes a fair amount of attention to several cases of biblical prophecy that are difficult to explain.[35] These problematic cases add nuances to his general position outlined above. Many of these involve difficulties that arise when future contingents are prophesied. They help to accentuate just how radically different God's knowledge of future contingents is from ours. God, for example, knows future contingents both presently in themselves and through their causes. While both of these aspects of God's knowledge of future contingents are present simultaneously in the divine mind, in prophetic revelation, it happens sometimes that prophets know future contingents only in themselves or only through a series of causes. Thomas explains that these two aspects of future contingents—which God knows perfectly—lead to two different ways for understanding how prophetic revelation bestows knowledge of future contingents. He explains:

> Although future contingents, as they are in themselves, are determined to one [outcome], nevertheless, insofar as they are [known] in their causes, they are not determined [to one], since they could come about otherwise. And although this double knowledge is always united in the divine intellect, it is not always united in prophetic revelation, since the impression of an agent does not always yield its same power. Hence, on the one hand, sometimes prophetic revelation is a kind of impressed likeness of divine foreknowledge insofar as it regards those future contingents in themselves; and these [contingents] come about just as they are prophesied, as when in Isaiah (7:14) [it says], *Behold, a virgin shall conceive.* On the other hand, sometimes prophetic revelation is an impressed likeness of divine foreknowledge insofar as [God] knows

---

32. ST, II-II, q. 171, a. 6, co.

33. ST, II-II, q. 171, a. 6, ad 1.

34. ST, II-II, q. 171, a. 6, co.

35. ST, II-II, q. 171, a. 6, ad 2.

the order of causes to effects; in these latter cases, sometimes something comes about differently than it was prophesied. Still, such a prophecy is not false, because the meaning of the prophecy (*sensus prophetiae*) here is that there is a disposition of inferior or natural causes or of human acts so that such-and-such an effect would come about. In this way, the saying of Isaiah (38:1) is understood: *You will die and not live*, that is, there is a disposition in your body that is ordained to death. Also, it is said in Jonah (3:4), *Yet forty days, and Nineveh will be overthrown*, that is, Nineveh's merits will be weighed and may result in her being overthrown. Moreover, God is said "to repent" metaphorically inasmuch as He acts like one who repents insofar as He changes his sentence (*sententiam*) but does not change his counsel.[36]

Knowing future contingents in this double aspect is natural to God, but for humans and even for prophets, the two are not normally joined together. Prophets sometimes know future contingents in themselves without knowing the order of causes that lead up to them; at other times, they may only know the order of causes to effects, while remaining ignorant of the contingent outcome itself. Despite this radical distinction between divine knowledge and the prophet's, Thomas insists that prophecy, even of this latter type, is still infallible. Our understanding of a prophecy may shift and alter inasmuch as it is possible for prophecies to have more than one sense (*sensus prophetiae*), but Thomas denies this results in prophecy's fallibility. Given that most of Thomas's examples are biblical prophecies, it is not surprising to find in his analysis of prophesied future contingents and his appeal to the "sense of prophecy" a structural parallel to what he says earlier about the multiple senses of scripture in sacred doctrine: "something false can never come under the literal sense of sacred scripture."[37]

The Object of Faith Is Unseen: Faith's Psychology

One of the common features of prophecy and faith is that their formal object— God as First Truth—is never seen. In faith, the human person assents to God, which involves both an act of the intellect and will. Thomas pays close attention to the psychology of this assent. Spending some time looking at it will allow us

---

36. ST, II-II, q. 171, a. 6, ad 2.
37. ST, I, q. 1, a. 10.

to appreciate another link between sacred doctrine and prophecy and how the first principles of the former are received by believers.

Faith, Thomas says, is not based "on sight," but rather implies "an assent of the intellect to what is believed."[38] He explains that there are two general ways a person may assent to something. In the first way, the intellect is moved to assent by the very object as understood. In this case, the object can be known either *per se*, as first principles, or it can be known through something else (*per aliud*), as conclusions. It is paramount to note the passivity of the intellect in this type of assent. The intellect "is moved" (*movetur*) by the object and does not move itself. In other places, Aquinas even says the intellect "is compelled" to assent to things seen through demonstrations.[39] A person can assent in a second way when the intellect is moved not by an object seen but through some "choice" (*electionem*). In an act of choosing, the will turns the intellect toward affirming or denying a proposition. If this turning happens "with doubt and fear" of the opposite being affirmed, "opinion" results. If, however, the intellect is turned to one object "with certitude without such fear," the assent is faith. The absence of "fear" (*formido*) specifically differentiates the assent of opinion from that of faith.[40] In an assent made by choice, the object perceived cannot compel the intellect to assent because the intellect does not fully grasp it. Faith and opinion, for this reason, demand that objects remain unseen.

Yet this seems to create a problem: What exactly is the believer assenting to? If the object of belief is not fully grasped, how can one know whether the object is worthy of assent? This problem is initially raised in one of Thomas's objections where he presents a particular interpretation of 1 Cor 13:12, "we see now dimly through a mirror."[41] St. Paul, the objection notes, says that we see "now" (*nunc*). Does he mean that the believer has "knowledge of faith" (*cognitio fidei*) in this life? Thomas thinks that this passage makes it clear that there is something seen in faith, but what is seen cannot be the formal object of faith;

---

38. ST, II-II, q. 1, a. 4, co.

39. See ST, II-II, q. 2, a. 9, ad 2.

40. Scripture also repeatedly speaks of the incompatibility between faith and fear and between charity and fear. See 1 Jn 4:18: "he who fears is not perfected in charity." See also Lk 12:4, 32; Mt 28:10; Jn 14:27. The "fear" Thomas is speaking of here is *formido*, not *timor*. *Timor* is a gift of the Holy Spirit. See ST, II-II, q. 19. See also Marie-Dominique Chenu, *La parole de Dieu, 1: La foi dans l'intelligence* (Paris: Cerf, 1964), 92–93, who notes the absence of any equivalent notion of *formido* in Aristotle.

41. ST, II-II, q. 1, a. 4, obj. 2 and ad 2.

this would imply the beatific vision. Instead of seeing faith's formal object, in this life we see "things that ought to be believed," *credenda.*

To tease out the difference between knowing faith's object and knowing *credenda,* Thomas identifies two ways something can fall under faith. Under the first way, something falls under faith "in particular." Thomas emphatically denies that some particular thing can be both seen and believed at the same time and in the same way.[42] Other things can fall under faith "in general, that is, under the common aspect of the believable (*credibilis*)."[43] In this general way, certain things are "seen" by a person who believes:

> One would not believe unless he were to see (*videret*) the things that
> he ought to believe [the *credenda*], either on account of the evidence
> of signs or on account of something similar.[44]

This concise passage holds quite a bit in it. Thomas seems to be asserting here that a certain type of knowledge, knowledge specifically of the *credenda,* underpins the act of faith. But how does the believer see these *credenda*? The believer sees them "on account of the evidence of signs" or something similar.[45] In other contexts, "signs" often denote miracles, but Thomas is deliberately being more inclusive here. While miracles certainly are signs of God's power at work in an individual, not all signs are miracles. The "signs" of this passage could also refer to prophecy, which Thomas sometimes calls "a sign of divine foreknowledge."[46] Thomas's subsequent phrase "or on account of something similar" also suggests that he is speaking broadly here, not exclusively about miracles. If prophecies fall under the category of signs as articulated in this passage, then it would seem that prophecies act as a kind of medium for communicating knowledge of the *credenda* to believers. These signs and prophecies allow the *credenda* to be seen under the aspect of "believability" (*credibilis*), and in this way, they function analogously to apodictic demonstrations; however, unlike demonstrations, these signs do not compel assent necessarily, but rather

---

42. ST, II-II, q. 1, a. 5, co.: "non autem est possibile quod idem ab eodem sit creditum et visum."

43. ST, II-II, q. 1, a. 4, ad 2.

44. ST, II-II, q. 1, a. 4, ad 2: "non enim crederet nisi videret ea esse credenda, vel propter evidentiam signorum vel propter aliquid huiusmodi."

45. ST, II-II, q. 1, a. 4, ad 2: "propter evidentiam signorum."

46. ST, II-II, q. 171, a. 6, ad 1: "prophetia, quae est divinae praescientiae similitudo impressa vel signum."

induce the assent of faith. Thus, the demonstration-like character of signs like prophecy functions as a structural parallel to apodictic demonstrations but with an additional affective appeal. Nevertheless, the structure of both demonstrations and signs or prophecies as inducements to faith aim ultimately at the same end: truth and certitude. For signs or prophecies, however, certitude is properly mediated by something other than the object itself. The testimony of others enters the realm of intellectual certitude. A similar structural "demonstration" is also apparent in sacred doctrine and especially when it employs arguments from convenience (i.e., fittingness), which appeal directly to this notion of God as final cause but without apodictic certitude. Arguments from convenience thus seem to have a close structural parallel to the way signs like prophecy function as inducements to faith, since both faith and sacred doctrine aim at the same end—salvation.

The word "sign" in the New Testament as well in Thomas's writings is often associated with the working of miracles.[47] Without doing an entire word study, it may be helpful to look briefly at what Thomas says about the gift of working miracles. He treats the question in the section on the gratuitous graces, the same section where we find the questions on prophecy.[48] There he explains that miracles function primarily as "confirmations" of prophecy. When miracles are understood in this way, Thomas helps us see why St. Paul also teaches that prophecy is superior to the gift of miracle working. This also sheds light on Paul's teaching about the superiority of prophecy to the gift of tongues: "tongues are a sign not for believers but for unbelievers, while prophecy is not for unbelievers but for believers" (1 Cor 14:22). The gifts of charismatic speech (including tongues) and miracles are meant to orient an unbeliever to the message of a prophet who presents things to be believed, certain *credenda*. Hence, when St. Paul says "we see now through a mirror," he is not referring to the object of faith, but to these *credenda* which someone has been led to believe by being induced to accept the gift of faith through signs like miracles and tongues. This knowledge of the *credenda* is compared to seeing dimly an object in a mirror. The credibility of the *credenda* is ordered to seeing the object imperfectly as through a mirror; the *credenda* shed an imperfect light on the object of faith not indeed because of an error in the *credenda*, but because of the weakness of the

---

47. The phrase "signs and wonders" (*sēmeia kai terata*) occurs 16 times in the New Testament and seems almost always to refer to miraculous events.

48. ST, II-II, q. 178.

light of faith. This mode of seeing the object of faith dimly and imperfectly in this life is due to the relative imperfection of the light of faith when compared to the light of glory. Hence, faith's grasp is only "a beginning" that is oriented to full knowledge in the beatific vision.[49] Being the ultimate object of what He reveals (that is, God's self-revelation), God is also the basis for the credibility of what He reveals through signs and prophecies. In faith, people assent to this divine testimony identifying God precisely as the reason for and guarantee of the truth to which they assent.

The Light of Faith as the Formal Cause of the Assent of Faith

Another striking feature of Thomas's account of the assent of faith is his reliance on the image of light. No doubt, as with the image of the mirror, his usage of light is partially inspired by scripture and especially John's Gospel (1:4–9, 8:12). The "light of faith" (*lumen fidei*), he explains, causes us to see what we ought to believe.[50] In receiving this light, one's mind is inclined to assent to things that correspond with correct faith and to withhold assent from things that do not. The light of faith acts as a kind of internal compass or standard, which Thomas compares to a moral *habitus*. A temperate person, he says, simply "sees" what is in accord with temperance and acts accordingly without having to think much about it. Similarly, a person who has the light of faith "sees" the things that accord with faith.[51] The metaphor of visible light helps Aquinas speak to this formal aspect of faith whereby things are simply grasped or "seen" by the intellect. Just as visible light enables the eye to see an object's color, so too does the light of faith enable the human mind to see what God has revealed. Once one has faith, there is no need to seek out further justification or to demonstrate how one sees this. Even if one desires to know how one has come to believe, this can be undertaken under the light of faith as part of sacred doctrine.

The mode of this desire to know, however, must accord with charity, Thomas thinks, if such an undertaking is to be meritorious and not detrimental to faith's complete lack of "fear" (*formido*). More critically, if the desire to know why one believes is motivated by "fear" and not charity, Thomas

---

49. See *In III Sent.*, d. 24, a. 2, q. 1a; *De ver.*, q. 14, a. 9.

50. ST, II-II, q. 1, a. 4, ad 3: "lumen fidei facit videre ea quae creduntur."

51. This is a type of judging "by inclination"; see ST, I, q. 1, a. 6, ad 3.

thinks a degree of personal human freedom is lost. To seek to understand faith out of fear and without charity paradoxically lessens a person's freedom with regard to the assent of faith. While for humans the act of faith must always be chosen freely, Thomas does seem to think there are degrees of freedom in one's assent to faith's object. Faith is the foundation for one's participation in the divine nature, and God's nature is absolutely free. Any participation in God's nature is going to be greater the more a person is said to imitate this nature. If one were to put conditions on the assent of faith, this would be analogous to placing conditions on God's freedom. By extension, one would participate less perfectly in God's nature and would also participate less perfectly in God's own freedom. Implied in this understanding of freedom is the premise that human freedom is only understood as a kind of participated likeness of God's absolute freedom. Hence, Thomas thinks faith's merit can decrease if people seek to know why they believe out of fear or lack of charity. Fear is a sign that their act of faith could be freer and more informed by charity. In being freer, we mean that the person's act of faith could be more informed and animated by abundant self-giving, which is an imitation of God's own freedom to give being and goodness out of His superabundance. The more a person's assent of faith becomes conditioned out of a necessity compelled by the intellect or will, the less perfectly this assent reflects divine freedom—the less the assent is a free response to God. Moreover, to question why one believes is to seek out the motives of credibility. But to seek these out of fear and lack of charity would be to ignore precisely the fact that God is also the ultimate source of the credibility of what He has revealed.

An assent of faith conditioned more by necessity than by freedom and love would be, in the final analysis, a less godlike act. God is absolutely necessary and Truth Himself. At the same time, He is also perfectly free and absolutely good—willing His own good and, out of this willing, creating everything else. In the divine nature, necessity and freedom find perfect unity, and in our way of speaking about the two, we cannot stress divine necessity over divine freedom because we only know necessity from things that have already been freely created and conditioned by God's loving will. Everything that exists that is other than God did not have to exist; we cannot impose our notion of necessity, which ultimately depends on creatures, onto the divine will. In its most radical sense then, the assent of faith is "an obedience" (Rom 1:15) to God's absolutely superior knowledge and will. To place conditions shaped by fear or lack of charity onto the assent of faith through intellectual inquiries into why one believes would go against this obedience; it would in turn decrease the act's likeness to God and, by extension, its merit. From this, Thomas's well-known observation that "love of God is something greater than knowledge of Him especially in this life" comes into sharper relief.[52] This statement acknowledges the radical distinction between divine knowledge and freedom and human knowledge and freedom, between God's necessity and our human conception of necessity.

That the light of faith causes the assent of faith formally also reveals another critical feature of faith: its *dialogical character*. Admittedly this dialogical feature is not expressed directly in the light of faith as the formal cause of the assent; however, if we recall our earlier discussion about the causal role played by the final cause in voluntary acts with regards to their formal cause, we see that within the very structure of faith's formal cause—the light of faith—there is a prior orientation toward God as final good due to Him being the final cause. This final cause actualizes faith's formal cause, and since it is causally prior compared to the formal cause, the final cause can be said to be more essential to the act of faith. It is this priority of the final cause in the act of faith that we call faith's dialogical character, since it brings the human creature into an immediate union and dialogue with God as final cause and highest good. Hence, charity, which stabilizes the will by uniting it immediately to God by grace, informs (*informat*) and perfects the act of faith, just as the final cause informs and perfects a formal cause.[53] That through which something works is called its form, and because faith works through charity, charity is faith's form. While Thomas does not himself explicitly call this interaction of charity informing faith a "dialogue," the phrase is nevertheless helpful on three counts. First, it is a convenient place-holder term for indicating the complex and dynamic structuring of formal cause to final cause. Second and more critically, the term serves as a reminder that faith is fundamentally a relationship between two persons with respect to their *logoi* or intellects. Third, the term highlights the fact that faith's assent can never be compelled but must be an entirely free response to God's equally free gift. Freedom is uniquely appropriate to the relations between persons and especially to dialogue. In God freely offering the gift of faith, the human person has the radical freedom either to accept or reject God.

Prophecy too can lay claim to a certain dialogical character, but not in this third respect, since a prophet never chooses to receive the gift of prophecy.

---

52. ST, II-II, q. 27, a. 4, ad 2.
53. ST, II-II, q. 4, a. 3, co.

Nevertheless, precisely because prophecy lacks this third dimension of what we are calling "dialogue," it becomes all the more useful for putting into sharper relief the second sense of dialogue: the relationship between two persons on the level of the intellect. In this second sense, prophecy is the dialogue *par excellence* between man and God in this life. On another level, because both prophecy and faith possess this dialogical character, sacred doctrine can also be said to be dialogically structured both in its matter (in its inspired writings and in the creeds) and in its formal ordering to the manifestation of truths necessary for the salvation of others (a call to dialogue with others).

Clarification on How Sacred Doctrine Functions as a Science

Sacred doctrine as a science assumes the gift of faith because faith provides it with its principles. Thomas outlines faith's capacity to "scientifically" structure in these terms:

> From the principles of faith, namely, the authority of sacred scripture, something is proved (*probatur*) among the faithful, just as from principles known naturally something is proved among all. Thus, we see that theology (*theologia*) too is a science (*scientia*), as shown at the beginning of the work.[54]

Theology assumes that these principles of faith reside "among the faithful" (*apud fideles*) as things known as *credenda*. Earlier in the same article, Thomas claims that the saints do not really offer demonstrations of what belongs to faith to someone who does not recognize (or at least grant within an argument) some of the principles of faith. Saints who do offer reasons concerning the faith do this not because they think they can demonstrate what ought to be believed, but rather to persuade someone that what faith proposes is not false or impossible. Showing that the articles of faith are not impossible becomes a part of sacred doctrine by relation to the principles of faith, which cannot be false.

---

54. ST, II-II, q. 1, a. 5, ad 2. "Principles of faith" (*principia fidei*) is not a phrase used frequently by Thomas in the ST (12 occurrences). He employs it a few times in his *Sentences* commentary and once rather notably at *In Ioan.*, IV, l. 5: "fides habet certitudinem ex lumine infuso divinitus, scientia vero ex lumine naturali. Nam sicut certitudo scientiae habetur per prima principia naturaliter cognita, ita et *principia fidei* cognoscuntur ex lumine infuso divinitus" (emphasis mine).

Without the light of faith, sacred doctrine loses its status as a science. For instance, in apodictic demonstrations, if one only grants a principle for the sake of argument rather than understanding it *qua* principle, any demonstration that follows from that principle would lack the force needed to elicit the intellect's assent. At best, such a demonstration could only show that a necessary logical relation exists between the granted principle and the conclusion being demonstrated. In sacred doctrine, where the principles are divinely given, the light of faith is precisely that which enables a believer to assent both to the principles (seen as divinely revealed) and to the conclusions shown to follow from these principles. All demonstrative force in sacred doctrine depends on the light of faith. While faith does not remove the usefulness of apodictic demonstrations to establish necessary logical connections in the natural light of reason, in sacred doctrine these demonstrations get taken up by the light of faith and become oriented toward the final end of manifesting truth for salvation. All the while, the believer does not know the principles of sacred doctrine in their full, but believes them. Their inner core remains a mystery whose very purpose is not to confound or confuse, but to bring believers into deeper dialogue with God. Within this new relationship brought about by faith, the principles of faith point back to the object of faith as their cause, which remains an unseen mystery. They function like signs of God's own knowledge, and since their ultimate reference point remains hidden, believers can seek their inner truth in various ways through the other things divinely revealed. The things God has revealed are known by the believer under the light of faith as firm truths. Thus, things shown to follow necessarily from the articles of faith—conclusions of a sort—make up for the believer a real knowledge or science.[55]

All the while, the content of faith's starting principles is given to particular individuals who do not believe them, but know them. Thomas again thinks it impossible for the same person to simultaneously know and believe the same thing. However, it can happen that what is seen and known by one is believed by another. The blessed angels, for example, have a vision of the Trinity, but we do not; what we believe about the Trinity they simply see. Aquinas stretches this example further to human beings:

---

55. See *De ver.*, q. 14, a. 9, ad 3: "fidelis potest dici habere scientiam de his quae concluduntur ex articulis fidei."

And similarly it can happen that what is seen and known by one human being, *even in this life,* is believed by another who does not know it demonstratively.[56]

While Thomas does not explicitly state that he is speaking about prophets here, it appears to be a safe assumption that prophets make up some of those who, "even in this life," know certain things which others only believe. Even though certain individuals may know things where others only believe in faith, Thomas is quick to clarify:

> That which is commonly (*communiter*) proposed to all people to believe is not commonly known. And it is these things that come under faith absolutely (*simpliciter*).[57]

This distinction prevents all the things that might be known by prophets from coming under faith as it is "commonly" proposed to everyone. As Thomas makes clearer in a later article on the necessity of explicit faith for salvation, this consideration of the faith as "commonly proposed" is structured by the more prior consideration of salvation.[58] Not everything that prophets come to know supernaturally and announce is necessary for salvation even if it may help lead others to faith. The distinction, then, between the things commonly proposed to all to believe and the things divinely revealed to prophets is itself structured by the final end considered as the ultimate common good.

Types of Credibilia

Thomas thinks that the "things believed in faith"—its *credibilia*—ought to be distinguished by fixed articles. At the outset, it is important to note that this article (a. 6) and the following three (aa. 7–9) all share aspects of arguments from fittingness. In the eighth and ninth articles, the fittingness arguments are explicit, but they need to be carefully teased out of the sixth and seventh. Living in the thirteenth century, Aquinas had already received Christian faith as "articulated." Thus, in posing the question of whether faith's *credibilia* ought to be distinguished into articles, he is not trying to cast radical doubt on the contemporary form of the articles of faith. The spirit behind these articles is

---

56. ST, II-II, q. 1, a. 5, co. (emphasis mine).
57. ST, II-II, q. 1, a. 5, co.
58. See ST, II-II, q. 2, a. 5.

more to show how the articles of faith make perceptible to us what God has already freely chosen to reveal.

Thomas begins by citing a definition of an article of faith which he mistakenly attributes to St. Isidore of Seville: "an article is a perception of divine truth that aims at that very truth."[59] This definition characterizes the articles of faith as dynamic realties that both capture some truth as revealed by God and at the same time confess ignorance of the ground of that truth by highlighting the process of "tending toward." "To tend toward" implies that there has yet to be an arrival. It may help to see this characterization by splitting the definition into two parts. The "perception of divine truth" speaks to some prior receiving of divine truth. This reception is constitutive of there being any articles at all. It also points to a reality external to the perceiver, since one cannot have a perception of something unless there exists something else perceivable. In this case, what is being perceived is divine truth. But how is this possible? Elsewhere, Thomas has insisted that God is "supremely knowable."[60] Our failure to perceive God can only be due to a limitation of our intellect. Because of our intellectual limitations, divine truth cannot be perceived in itself; we can only perceive it "by some kind of distinction" or division. We only perceive the divine truth as fragmented, and God has helped us to do this by revealing Himself. Although we perceive this revelation in a fragmented way, in God's mind truth is absolutely simple.

The second half of the definition—"that aims at that very truth"—speaks to the orientation of the divine truth received (as revealed) to the final end. The divine truth that an article of faith captures is not in itself self-explanatory but points beyond itself to a Truth which we do not yet see or know. This ultimate Truth is both the object of belief and the very cause of our believing.[61] Believers do not see the First Truth, yet it is precisely out of this absence of sight that the articles of faith emerge. Aquinas observes that one

---

59. ST, II-II, q. 1, a. 6, sed: "Isidorus dicit, articulus est perceptio divinae veritatis tendens in ipsam." On the mistaken attribution, see Mark D. Jordan, *On Faith:* Summa theologiae, *2-2, qq. 1–16 of St. Thomas Aquinas* (Notre Dame: University of Notre Dame Press, 1990), 45n43: "this definition is also attributed to Isidore in Albert the Great and Bonaventure, but it appears in an earlier work by Philip the Chancellor without attribution."

60. ST, I, q. 12, a. 1, co.

61. See *In III Sent.*, d. 25, q. 1, a. 1, qc. 1, ad 4 "perceptio divinae veritatis quae fit per rationem naturalem, tendit, sicut in id cui innititur, in intellectum principiorum; sed perceptio divinae veritatis quae est articulus, tendit in primam veritatem non solum sicut in finem, vel obiectum, *sed sicut in id in quod resolvitur sicut in causam suae credulitatis*" (emphasis mine).

finds a specific article wherever there is something which "for some specific reason is not seen." The articles of faith, then, are the human response to the unknown, but not just any unknown. They are a response to God as a mystery—an unknown who is freely chosen and loved out of a response to an invitation. We would not be entirely wrong in saying that the articles of faith are the human response to encountering God as He has revealed Himself. From this perspective, we see too that they are intrinsically dialogical. God speaks "in many and various ways" (Heb 1:1), initially to humans "by the prophets" and then "by a Son," and the human person answers God in the articles of faith which make up the creeds.

In this way, the articles of faith actually resemble scripture because, as St. Gregory says, "in one and the same sentence, while telling a fact," they reveal a mystery.[62] That Thomas understands the articles of faith as being very near to scripture helps make sense of the objection that argues that faith ought to regard everything contained in scripture equally.[63] If faith regarded everything in the Bible equally, then it would only make sense to list everything contained in the Bible as articles, but the sheer number of articles that would result makes this an absurd prospect. In his reply to the objection, Thomas explains that faith does not regard everything in scripture equally; instead there is a hierarchy of belief which is ordered by nothing other than faith and the final end:

> Since faith is principally about those things we hope to see in heaven, as Heb 11:1 says, *faith is the substance of things hoped for*, those things which order us directly to eternal life pertain to faith *per se*, such as the three Persons, God's omnipotence, the mystery of Christ's incarnation, and other such things. And these make up the distinct articles of faith.[64]

Many of the things related in scripture are not things that directly order us to eternal life, although they may indirectly order us to it. Thus, such things do not become articles of faith.

After establishing the fittingness of having articles of faith, Aquinas goes on to distinguish two types of *credibilia*. The *credibilia* are the things "known" by the believer as worthy of belief, "known" taken here not apodictically, but

---

62. ST, I, q. 1, a. 10, sed.

63. ST, II-II, q. 1, a. 6, obj. 1.

64. ST, II-II, q. 1, a. 6, ad 1.

under the analogy of faith. Believers must know that they ought to believe these things, yet the question remains: how do they precisely come to know them? They come to know the *credibilia* first because they have been proposed. If prophets and apostles announce them verbally, they may be able to communicate the words, but because the prophetic mode of knowing is beyond human nature, they cannot directly cause other people to know them. All prophets can do is propose what they themselves already know as something that ought to be believed because it has been revealed by God. Believers do not assent to the prophet's knowledge as such, but rather they assent to what the prophet knows only as something rooted in God's testimony.[65] Once the *credibilia* have been announced, the light of faith is required for them to be "known" under the analogy of faith as being rooted in God's infallible testimony entrusted to prophets.

Among the *credibilia*, there are some that are about faith "absolutely" (*secundum se*), while others do not pertain directly to faith but rather are ordered "to other things."[66] To clarify this distinction, Thomas draws an analogy between science and faith's *credibilia*. In a science there are certain things that are proposed as *per se* intended, which is to say they are proposed as having a direct bearing on the science. Other things are proposed so that even more things can become clear. The things that order us directly to the beatific vision pertain to faith *per se*. The articles of the creed thus deal only with *credibilia* that pertain to faith *per se*. This is not to say that non-*per se* *credibilia* need not be believed. The purpose of Thomas's distinction is both to explain the provenance of the articles of faith and to emphasize that their determination as articles relies on our final end. The other secondary things do not order us directly to our final end, such as certain facts contained in scripture like Jacob having twelve sons. These secondary things help to shed light on the *per se credibilia* but do not merit or require a specific article.

---

65. See *De ver.*, q. 14, a. 8, co.: "faith cannot thus stand as a virtue, deriving from the evidence of things, since it deals with things which do not appear. Consequently, it must derive this infallibility from its adherence to some testimony in which the truth is infallibly found. But, just as every created being of itself is empty and liable to fail, unless it is supported by uncreated being, so all created truth is liable to fail except in so far as it is regulated by uncreated truth. Hence, to assent to the testimony of a man or an angel would lead infallibly to the truth only in so far as we considered the testimony of God speaking in them" (McGlynn trans., *Truth* [Indianapolis: Hackett, 1994]).

66. ST, II-II, q. 1, a. 6, ad 1.

Progress in the Knowledge of Faith

After affirming that the *credibilia* ought to be divided into articles, Thomas goes on to ask whether the number of articles has increased over time. He approaches this question by introducing a distinction between the substance of the articles and their explication. As far as the substance of the articles goes, there is no increase over time. Anything which later generations believed "was contained in the faith of the preceding Fathers, although implicitly."[67] As far as their explication, however, there is an increase in the number of articles, and he cites Ephesians 3:5 to support this: "to other generations the mystery of Christ was not acknowledged as it is now revealed to his holy apostles and prophets."[68]

Aquinas proceeds to analyze the distinction between stability and development causally. He begins by drawing an analogy with natural generation.[69] In natural generation, parents precede their offspring and have perfections that their offspring do not yet have. From this case of natural generation, Thomas makes the following metaphysical observation: That which is more perfect is prior. Another way of applying this is to say that "nature takes its beginning from perfect things."[70] This leads him to distinguish between two different types of causes involved in generation: pre-existing active causes and material causes. In generation, the parents are the active cause, while the offspring are the material. If one observes generation from the perspective of the active cause, one can see that the more perfect being precedes a less perfect one. On the other hand, from the perspective of the material, the less perfect is prior to the perfect. Offspring require something more perfect to cause and sustain them, namely, parents as active causes.

Having outlined this distinction, Aquinas returns to the articles of faith. In faith God is the active cause who makes the *credenda* visible to mankind. The material cause is mankind, receiving "an influx" (*influxum*) of divine action under the modality of intellect. Now, God's own knowledge is absolutely perfect.[71] Divine knowledge perfects the intellect of a believer, just

---

67. ST, II-II, q. 1, a. 7, co.

68. See *Super Epistolas S. Pauli lectura*, vol. 2, *In ad Ephesios*, ed. R. Cai, 8th ed. (Turin: Marietti, 1972), III, l. 1.

69. ST, II-II, q. 1, a. 7, ad 3.

70. ST, II-II, q. 1, a. 7, ad 3.

71. On divine perfection, see ST, I, q. 4, a. 1.

as the perfect causes the less perfect. From the human perspective, however, "knowledge of faith" (*cognitio fidei*) goes from what is less perfect to what is more perfect.

Thomas makes an important refinement to this exposition of the knowledge of faith. There are some people, he explains, who are also active causes of the knowledge of faith. These are "the doctors of faith," who have received a special spirit or "gratuitous grace."[72] All the gratuitous graces are ordered to the sanctification of the whole community rather than to the individual who receives them. The doctors of faith, Thomas thinks following St. Paul, play a special function in the Church. The special grace they receive enables them to be active causes for the knowledge of faith in others. They can help "give birth" to new Christian disciples. However, in calling the doctors of faith "active causes" of the knowledge of faith Thomas is only speaking analogically to the case of natural generation. The doctors are not sufficient active causes for knowledge of the faith, because they cannot bestow the light of faith on their students and hearers; only God can do this. Nevertheless, doctors still have a role to play in the building up of the community of believers. In receiving the gift of prophecy as a gratuitous grace, the prophet has a role similar to that of the doctor in building up the community.

Thomas also thinks that the Old Testament patriarchs were given "knowledge of the faith," and while they lived, they acted as doctors of the faith. The patriarchs handed over to the people what was necessary "at that time."[73] The fullness of truth was not revealed all at once. A sudden complete revelation of all truth would seemingly go against the natural way humans come to know things, which is gradually. Instead, certain truths were revealed only as they became necessary and when God deemed them ready to receive them. The Old Testament patriarchs who acted as the doctors of the faith handed over this knowledge either "plainly or figuratively," depending on the circumstances. Many of them could also be considered prophets according to Thomas's broad definition; pre-eminent among them, he thinks, was Moses.[74]

---

72. ST, II-II, q. 1, a. 7, ad 3: Thomas cites 1 Cor 12:7, "the manifestation of the Spirit is given to such men for common use." In addition to tying this passage to the doctors of faith as active causes of the knowledge of faith, Thomas often associates this Pauline passage with the gratuitous graces; see ST, II-II, q. 171, prologue.

73. ST, II-II, q. 1, a. 7, ad 3.

74. ST, II-II, q. 174, a. 4.

Question Two: Faith's Interior Act and the Kind of Thinking Involved in Faith

The second question on faith treats the interior act of faith which is to believe (*credere*). Thomas's definition of belief as a kind of "thinking with assent" (*cogitare cum assensione*) sets the tone for the type of thinking that happens in sacred doctrine.[75] In its assent, faith does not move a person to hold "an inquiry of natural reason" that attempts to demonstrate the *credenda*, as if they were demonstrable apodictically.[76] As seen already, to try to do this would violate the very nature of faith as a free act and would thus decrease its merit; it would also fail to recognize that the credibility of the *credenda* is ultimately dependent on God's absolute necessity and infallibility, in which human notions of necessity only participate imperfectly. Instead, faith moves a person to acknowledge and accept God and the things believed in faith as mysteries in this life. Hence, Thomas thinks there can be no apodictic demonstration that God is Trinity. Nevertheless, under faith one can hold "a kind of inquiry" about things that lead a person to believe. If undertaken out of charity and not out of fear or doubt, such an inquiry would seek to ask about what sort of things lead to faith—things *ad fidem*. For example, we could ask whether certain things are examples of divine testimony or, if not directly divine testimony, would they be at least confirmed by God. Taken under the light of faith, such inquiries would fall under sacred doctrine.

It remains unclear whether Thomas thinks that someone before receiving the gift of faith and assenting to it ought to inquire into things *ad fidem*. It seems unlikely that this is his position based on what we have already observed about the ideally free nature of the assent of faith. Believers are at liberty to hold an inquiry into how they came to believe what they believe under the light of faith, provided it be motivated by charity and not by fear. Unbelievers, however, should not be encouraged to inquire into the things *ad fidem* since it may diminish the merit of faith by causing their assent to be "more necessary" and less radically free. At the same time, if unbelievers seek to understand the things *ad fidem* out of charity and goodwill and not out fear, then it would seem that faith is already being offered to them. Such individuals should be encouraged to continue to seek with an open heart the things *ad fidem* and be helped to see

---

75. ST, II-II, q. 2, a. 1.
76. ST, II-II, q. 2, a. 1, ad 1.

how their desire to seek further may already be a sign that God is freely offering them the gift of faith. Thomas does not address explicitly these considerations, and since they touch more on the realm of pastoral theology, one would not expect Thomas to treat every single case that might arise involving a pastor's care of individual souls.[77]

Some of Thomas's own pastoral judgments regarding the virtue of faith have been realized in hindsight to contain serious errors. There is, for instance, his now infamous position that relapsed and obstinate heretics ought "to be compelled," that is, physically punished at the hands of the civil authorities, to believe—a position, it should be added, that was widely shared and largely unquestioned among Thomas's contemporaries and predecessors.[78] Errors like these should be readily acknowledged and studied more widely precisely because of their instructive value. They help one to appreciate his own distinction between what is essential in faith and what is less essential. The things that are less essential may reflect to a greater degree the particular historical contingencies of believers or certain groups of believers and thus be subject to change. In this way, his errors are illustrative of both his own theological method and his further position that sacred doctrine develops and in practice remains fallible due to its dependence on human reasoning.

Taking the limitations of his pastoral judgments into account, Thomas's hesitancy to acknowledge the value of having unbelievers inquire into things *ad fidem* is a reflection of his awareness of the limitations of pastoral knowledge when it comes to judging who exactly is and is not seeking God with an open and sincere heart motivated by a good will. His quietness on the point shows his real concern that such inquiries have potential dangers for both unbelievers and believers who undertake them motivated by fear or doubt and not by charity. Illustrated here in miniature is the Pauline model cited explicitly by Thomas in the general prologue of the *Summa theologiae* of giving milk to those who are "young" in the faith and not solid food before they are able to digest it. This pedagogical concern, which is ultimately concern for the salvation of a person, is the reason why Thomas states that believers ought not to inquire

---

77. Thomas addresses, although not frequently, very specific cases of pastoral theology in the *Summa theologiae*. Consider, for example, his article on whether the children of unbelievers ought to be baptised compulsorily (II-II, q. 10, a. 12). His answer is "no" based on the fact that it would violate the natural right of the children's parents to raise their children freely, and faith, while elevating nature, can never violate this right.

78. ST, II-II, q. 11, a. 3, co.

into the things *ad fidem* in order to prove the mysteries of faith; not only is such an inquiry doomed to failure, but it also potentially decreases the merit of one's personal act of faith; in other words, it may be a sign that one's inquiry is not motivated by charity and may be leading one away from God—and this is exactly the opposite of what sacred doctrine is meant to do. In place of an inquiry that seeks apodictic certitude about the things believed in faith, Thomas suggests that believers consider generally the contingent circumstances that lead people to belief. This initial restriction to the general circumstances is important because it allows the inquiry to be framed in such a way so as to be potentially useful not only to the person studying, but also to others by helping them toward faith. Unsurprisingly, we see how Thomas's very decision to begin the Second Part with a parallel consideration of the general circumstances of moral action reflects a similarly motivated pastoral concern to help others come closer to God in their moral life.

A general consideration of contingent circumstances *ad fidem* aims primarily at confirming for believers that their faith rests not on their own opinions or on something naturally knowable, but on God's own testimony alone. Now, God's testimony has been entrusted to certain individuals who function as prophets and apostles. Inquiries *ad fidem*, if they are to be a part of sacred doctrine, must point to the divine origin of this testimony and cannot call it into question; any attempt to do the latter or to prove the necessity of divine testimony would be "unscientific" with respect to sacred doctrine.

Since inquiries *ad fidem* aim at confirming for believers that faith rests ultimately on divine testimony, it may not be surprising that prophecy plays an important part in such inquires. The opening lines of the Letter to the Hebrews contain the basic outline of an inquiry or argument *ad fidem* in miniature when its author explains how in the past God spoke to the chosen people "through the prophets," but now has spoken through His incarnate Son (Heb 1:1–3). In the past, the prophets were entrusted with and communicated God's testimony to Israel, but in the incarnate Son, we encounter the unique instance where divine testimony and testifier are the same person. Seen in this perspective, prophets function as a kind of indicator or sign specifically of Christ's role as divine testimony becoming incarnate. One observes here an additional parallel between prophets—and especially prophets of the Old Testament—and Christ's apostles. Both testify to the incarnate Son's testimony. Old Testament prophets testify to the coming mission of the Christ. The apostles testify to the birth, life, passion, and resurrection of Christ. From the apostolic perspective, Christ is no longer foretold, but they still testify to another divine testimony that Christ will come again in glory. Because those who have received and accepted the apostolic testimony—believers in faith—still await the coming testimony of Christ in glory, there is still a place for prophecy in postapostolic times to remind people of Christ and his testimony. Thomas in his questions on prophecy leaves open the possibility that God can continue to give prophecy, if He wants, to certain individuals so that they might help others order their lives to Christ. Hence, Thomas thinks prophets in the postapostolic age function largely as guides to human actions and morals and, intriguingly, especially as guides to acts of divine worship (*cultus divinus*).[79]

The testimony of the Son, of course, is at its heart Trinitarian. While Thomas does not explicitly make this link between the prophet's testimony and the Son's testimony of his coming from and identity with the Father in the questions on faith and prophecy in *Summa theologiae*, the theme is present in his *Commentary on John*. I suspect there is much fruitful material here as Thomas reflects on the Johannine theme of the Son's testimony together with some of the New Testament's richest theological and Trinitarian language. I equally suspect such material has only just begun to receive the contemporary scholarly attention it deserves.[80] While we cannot adequately examine his *Commentary on John* at present, we can still appreciate how a discussion of prophecy reveals a path for further work to gain access into the Trinitarian notion of divine testimony in Thomas's thought through the dialogical character of both faith and prophecy.

Just like the apostles who are chosen by Christ (Jn 15:16), God freely chooses the prophets; they do not choose Him. There is, however, a sense in which prophets could still choose to cooperate with God or not in a specific prophetic mission, just as much as an apostle like Judas could choose to betray Jesus. Certain individuals may receive the gift of prophecy, but they may choose to use it for evil deeds or not to share it at all.

---

79. ST, II-II, q. 172, a. 1, ad 4.

80. See Serge-Thomas Bonino, "'*Propheta et dominus prophetarum*': Prophétologie et christologie dans la *Lectura super Ioannem*," in *Études thomasiennes* (Paris: Parole et Silence, 2018), 157–86; Serge-Thomas Bonino, "The Role of the Apostles in the Communication of Revelation according to the *Lectura super Ioannem* of St. Thomas Aquinas," in Dauphinais and Levering, *Reading John with St. Thomas Aquinas*, 318–46, where Bonino focuses largely on the role of the apostles as transmitters of revelation and less directly on the gift of prophecy. The reason for this should be obvious; apostolicity is superior to prophecy due to the apostles' proximity to the life of Christ. Their testimony is more fundamental to the faith and to the constitution of the Church than any prophet's.

Somewhat analogously, faith can be held without charity. Thomas refers to such faith as "lifeless" (*informis*) or "dead" (*mortua*), and faith loses this "life" or form as a result of mortal sin.[81] Lifeless faith and living faith are not separate habits, but they are the same habit under different orientations of the will. The will can either be oriented to God or not, and the human person remains free with regards to this orientation even under the light of faith. This is because ultimately in the assent of faith a person's intellect is determined to one thing "not through reason but through the will."[82]

Moreover, the human will, while a necessary contributor to faith's assent, is not sufficient for its accomplishment. In his *Sentences* commentary, Thomas makes this more explicit. Human reason is insufficient to move the will to adhere to its supernatural object; rather the will is moved directly by God's "speech":

> The reason why the will is inclined to assent to those things it does not see is *because God has spoken them* (*quia Deus ea dicta*), just as a man in those things which he does not see believes the testimony of another good man, who sees the things which he himself does not see.[83]

This passage offers a nice summary of how Thomas conceives of faith as a kind of dialogue between the human person and the person of the divine Word, through whom the Father speaks.

Faith's Necessity

Thomas's article concerning the need to believe something beyond the human rational capacity is a linchpin for the entire *Summa theologiae*.[84] Commentators have often noted the parallels between this article in the questions on faith and Question One of Part One.[85] The latter's treatment of the need for a supernatural teaching almost seems to presume at times the *Secunda secundae*'s subsequent treatment of faith. Just as in Question One, in this article on the need for faith is present the idea that any created, rational nature must have an

---

81. ST, II-II, q. 4, a. 4.

82. ST, II-II, q. 2, a. 1, ad 3.

83. *In III Sent.*, d. 23, q. 2, a. 2, q. 1a, 2c (emphasis mine).

84. ST, II-II, q. 2, a. 3.

85. For a summary of the commentary tradition on this parallel, see Van Ackeren, *Sacra doctrina*, 20–24.

immediate ordering to God as final end. This idea represents one of the main conclusions taken from the questions on the final end.[86] Why are only rational natures ordered to God? In one sense, all creatures, rational or non-rational, are ordered to God as the cause of their existing. Thomas observes that non-rational creatures like animals are perfected in the mode of knowing in ways different from rational creatures, and this is because they have different capacities for perfections. Animals, for example, are only perfected by the perception and attainment of sensible things; they are not capable of abstracting universals from sensible substances and thus cannot consider (and be perfected by) being (*ens*) as a universal. Rational creatures, in contrast, are capable of being perfected by universals through abstraction, and it is the human capacity to know universals via abstraction that indicates rational creatures are perfected by being itself. This means their highest perfection is to be perfected by the highest being, who is God as subsisting being (*esse ipsum subsistens*).[87]

Another helpful way to understand this distinction between rational and non-rational ordering to God is to analyze how creatures participate in divine goodness. A cow participates "in existing" (*in essendo*) just as an inanimate chair does, but cows participate in God's goodness more than a chair does because cows know singulars in addition to existing. There is, however, an aspect of God's goodness which cows do not participate in. Cows have no share in God's knowledge of universals. To perceive universals cows would need a rational faculty, but it seems that they do not have one. The rational faculty in humans has a specific purpose, Thomas explains: "inasmuch as it knows the universal notion (*ratio*) of the good and being," the rational faculty "possesses an immediate ordering to the universal principle of being."[88] The end of a rational creature, then, is to know goodness and being absolutely and not just to know beings that participate in God's goodness and being. In other words, humans are meant to know God as the universal principle of being and goodness.

However, human reason by itself cannot know the divine essence *in se*. This is due to the identity in God of essence and existence. In creatures, essence and existence are always distinct principles—that which is and that by which something is. By nature human beings come to know any unknown thing by abstracting it first from its matter (if it is material) and then by abstracting the

---

86. ST, I-II, qq. 1–5.

87. See ST, I, q. 4, a. 2, co.

88. ST, II-II, q. 2, a. 3, co.: "immediatum ordinem ad universale essendi principium."

resulting intelligible species from its particular mode of existing in our mind. Because God's essence is identical to His existence, we are unable to abstract His essence from His existence, who He is from how He is; they are the same reality.[89] Because we cannot know God *in se* through abstraction and the use of our reason, we can only come to know God through some mode of knowing that exceeds our natural capacity.

In order then for humans to know God *in se*, they need to be lifted up beyond their natural mode of knowing:

> Through a mode of learning from God as teacher (*per modum addiscentis a Deo doctore*), just as according to John (6:45), *all who hear from the Father and learn, come to me*. The human being becomes a participator in this instruction not immediately, but gradually (*successive*) according to the mode of human nature. Moreover, it is necessary that every learner believe so as to arrive at perfect knowledge.[90]

Faith is what enables the human person to participate in this superior mode of knowing. Thus, faith is necessary for knowing God in such a way as to participate in His knowledge. At the same time, the other aspect of faith's necessity—necessary for attaining one's final good—is also in play:

> The perfection of the rational creature consists not only in that which is suitable according to its nature [its formal perfection], but also in that which is attributed to it from a kind of *supernatural participation in divine goodness*.[91]

Faith enables the human as a rational creature to have a share not only in God's knowledge, but also in divine being and goodness as a final end.

Admittedly, at this stage of our study this last phrase still requires additional explanation concerning what Thomas means by "participation." He gives us an initial clue when he evokes the image of the student and teacher. The teacher possesses a perfection that the student does not yet have—some perfection in knowledge. Through instruction, the student becomes increasingly like the teacher, who assists the learner by first proposing things to be taken or *believed* on the basis

---

89. See ST, I, q. 3, a. 4, co.

90. ST, II-II, q. 2, a. 3, co.

91. ST, II-II, q. 2, a. 3, co.: "perfectio ergo rationalis creaturae non solum consistit in eo quod ei competit secundum suam naturam, sed etiam in eo quod ei attribuitur ex quadam *supernaturali participatione divinae bonitatis*" (emphasis mine).

of the teacher's authority. Gradually, students become increasingly like their teacher because they come to possess the same knowledge. In this sense, the students are said "to participate" in their teacher's knowledge. Analogously, humans come to participate in divine knowledge and goodness "according to the mode of human nature." Hence, the light of faith elevates but does not replace the natural light of reason. When humans start to learn new things by the light of reason, novices normally begin by believing what their teacher says. This is especially true when it comes to learning the first principles of a human science. Thomas attributes this insight to Aristotle who says that a student "must believe in order to arrive at perfect knowledge [*perfectam scientiam*]."[92] Faith closely resembles the natural way human beings come to have knowledge (*scientia*), and structurally both faith and reason are oriented toward knowledge of the universal principle of being; except in the case of faith, humans are taught by divine revelation. Because they cannot naturally know the universal principle being, humans must believe God "as a student believes his teacher" so as to arrive at the perfect vision of beatitude.

As a final addendum to this discussion of faith's necessity, the belief in God spoken of here cannot exclusively or even directly be interpreted as a statement about the necessity of believing in God's existence (*esse*). The type of believing that Thomas is talking about here assumes that one already believes God exists or at the very least is open to acknowledging God's existence; if it were otherwise, there would be no strict "need" to speak about a teacher to be believed and from whom to learn. This explains why Thomas calls things like belief in God's existence "preambles" of faith, rather than something directly belonging to faith.[93] In lieu of the preambles of faith, Thomas is more concerned to address the virtue and act of faith through which comes a person's radical openness to God's plan to teach and guide rational creatures to their ultimate happiness.

Explicit Faith:
Its Necessity and the Order of Divine Revelation

Thomas's question on whether all are equally bound to have explicit faith also requires attention. This question hinges on his understanding of the word "explication" (*explicatio*), from which "explicit" derives. The term is closely associated

---

92. ST, II-II, q. 2, a. 3, co.; see Aristotle, *On Sophistical Refutations*, II, 2, 161b3.
93. ST, II-II, q. 2, a. 10, ad 2.

with the unfolding of divine revelation: "An explication of things that ought to be believed happens through divine revelation."[94] The sense of this statement is that revelation itself provides an explanation of the *credenda*. The *credenda* again are neither self-evident nor self-explanatory. While they can be understood in their literal sense, their deepest meaning ultimately lies beyond the scope of human reason. The only way to know these deeper and hidden meanings is "through divine revelation." The *credenda* as propositions are meant to help humans come to know these deeper truths, just as the literal meaning in a text is meant to help a reader come to know the text's spiritual sense.[95] The *credenda* thus are concrete expressions of something divinely revealed which themselves point to the need for a higher revelation to be fully grasped.

Thomas thinks that all divine revelation comes to mankind "by a kind of order." This order goes from higher to lower as a metaphysical necessity. He even extends this order to angelic creation. Citing Pseudo-Dionysius's *Celestial Hierarchies*, Aquinas gives examples of how humans receive messages ("explications") from angels. In this unfolding of revelation through the angels, prophets will often be the ones receiving angelic messages. He thinks that angels being the "intermediaries [*medii*] between God and humans" always serve as the mediators of prophetic revelation to human beings.[96] This is part of their angelic "ministry" which reflects "God's order" (*ordo divinitatis*) where lowers things are disposed by mediators to higher things.[97]

Having outlined the order of this "unfolding of the *credenda*," Thomas next turns to "the unfolding of faith" (*fidei*), which is the true subject of the article. Just as the angels communicate knowledge from higher to lower hierarchies, so also "the unfolding of faith must come from higher humans to lower ones."[98] He draws on another example from Pseudo-Dionysius: Just as higher angels

---

94. ST, II-II, q. 2, a. 6. *Explicatio* often is used by Thomas to describe the "unfolding" of divine providence; see *Compendium theologiae seu Brevis compilatio theologiae ad fratrem Raynaldum*, Leonine Edition, vol. 42 (Rome: Editori di San Tommaso, 1979), I, 138. On the "unfolding of truth" from *rationes seminales* as a model for implicit-to-explicit things in faith, see also *Super Boetium de Trinitate*, I, prologue 6.

95. On this latter relationship between the literal and spiritual senses in scripture, see ST, I, q. 1, a. 10.

96. ST, II-II, q. 172, a. 2, co.

97. Thomas also cites Pseudo-Dionysius for this *ordo* of higher to lower in the article on angelic mediation in prophecy; see ST, II-II, q. 172, a. 2.

98. ST, II-II, q. 2, a. 6, co.: "ad inferiors homines per maiores."

enlighten the lower ones and have a fuller knowledge about divine things, "so too higher humans, to whom it pertains to instruct [*erudire*] others, are bound to have a fuller knowledge about the *credenda* and are bound to believe more explicitly." Thomas seems to suggest these higher individuals will know numerically more *credenda*; the so-called "higher" are bound to believe "more things" (*plura*) than the lower. Teachers of the faith too will require a more explicit knowledge of the faith, and this observation would seem to suggest that sacred doctrine plays a critical role in deepening and expanding the teacher's knowledge of faith through study.

Yet not everyone is bound to have equal knowledge of the *credenda* to be saved.[99] Only those who teach others are required to have a deeper knowledge of the faith and to believe more things. We can note in passing that operative in this question is again the notion of the necessity of the end. Only that which is "necessary for salvation" determines what must be believed explicitly by all.

Does this mean that the lower beings taught about the *credenda* by the higher are instructed only according to what their teachers know about the faith? If so, would not this put faith on insecure grounds due to the personal fallibility of human teachers? Aquinas carefully addresses this concern in his third reply: "Simple people do not have implicit faith in the faith of the higher, except to the extent that the higher adhere to God's teaching [*doctrinae divinae*]."[100] The higher (as teachers) are only instruments in a causal chain of teaching and explaining the faith. The first cause and primary teacher is God whose "divine truth" remains the real "rule of faith (*regula fidei*)."[101] If some of the simple are led unwittingly into error by their teachers, this does not prejudice their faith, because they think what they believe is true on the authority of their teachers. The case changes, Thomas says, when the simple obstinately persevere in error against "the faith of the universal Church" after being corrected.[102] In such a case, their faith would be prejudiced.

---

99. ST, II-II, q. 2, a. 6, ad 1: "explicatio credendorum non aequaliter quantum ad omnes est de necessitate salutis."

100. ST, II-II, q. 2, a. 6, ad 3.

101. ST, II-II, q. 2, a. 6, ad 3: "unde humana cognitio non fit regula fidei, sed veritas divina." See *De ver.*, q. 11, a. 1.

102. ST, II-II, q. 2, a. 6, ad 3. Thomas maintains that the universal Church's faith cannot be defective, citing Lk 22:32.

The Merit of Faith

It will help us later on to make sense of why prophecy lacks a principle of merit if we address now why Thomas thinks believing is meritorious. The heart of faith's merit lies in the will and its acceptance of the motion of grace, which orients the human person to God as final end. In the questions on faith, Thomas reiterates the basic understanding of merit which he treated earlier in the *Prima secundae*:

> Our acts are meritorious inasmuch as they proceed from a free will moved by God through grace. Hence, every human act that is subject to free will, if it is related to God, can be meritorious.[103]

He simultaneously summarizes belief as "an act of the intellect assenting to Divine Truth from a command of the will moved by God through grace." Because an act of belief depends on "a command of the will moved by God," faith is meritorious. In corresponding to grace, which orients its recipient to God as one's final good loved and desired, the act of belief also receives the form of charity, which is the measure of merit.[104]

When we turn to prophecy in the chapters subsequent, this definition will be important to keep in mind. Prophecy, as Thomas will explain, is a gift that can be had without charity. Therefore, to be a prophet is not a sign of merit. While the gift of prophecy does not necessarily exclude charity, it does not guarantee that a prophet will use the gift out of love of God and neighbor. That prophecy lacks an intrinsic principle of merit comes from the fact that it deals principally with knowledge and does not directly engage the will. The act of knowing something is not meritorious in itself because it does not directly involve the will. Any intellectual assent that involves knowledge "is not subject to free will because one who knows *is compelled* [*cogitur*] to assent through the efficacy of a demonstration; and thus, the assent of knowledge is not meritorious."[105]

Thomas, however, makes a subtle distinction between "the assent of knowledge" and the "actual consideration" of things known that has important ramifications for sacred doctrine. Unlike the assent of knowledge, an actual

---

103. ST, II-II, q. 2, a. 9, co.; see ST, I-II, q. 114, aa. 3–4.
104. On charity as the measure of merit, see ST, I-II, q. 114, a. 4.
105. ST, II-II, q. 2, a. 9, ad 2 (emphasis mine).

consideration is subject to free will. For example, I can choose to consider my knowledge of triangles, or I can choose not to.[106] Considering things already known or "believed" in faith can be meritorious "if it is referred to the end of charity, that is, to God's honor or the utility of neighbor."[107] This allows sacred doctrine, which results "through study" (a kind of actual consideration), to be potentially meritorious.[108]

Conclusion

Placing faith and prophecy in juxtaposition brings into relief something which remains quite muted in Thomas's own treatment of faith: its dialogical character. Faith constitutes a living relationship between God and the believer which participates in an intimacy that is similar to the intimacy God has with prophets. In the remaining two chapters, we will explore how this dialogical character is also a structural feature of Thomas's notion of prophecy. By providing theological background to the questions on prophecy, it is now easier to appreciate how the doctrinal content and expression of the articles of faith and Christian creeds are particularized at given moments in Church history. The articles and symbols share in the dialogical character of faith as they expound the things to be believed and point toward the mystery of God. Whence, it will be seen that sacred doctrine itself, by taking its principles from the articles of faith, also possesses a dialogical structure.

This dialogical character is already reflected partially in sacred doctrine's structure as a subalternated science, but this now needs to be expanded. Because sacred doctrine through faith has access to this shared relationship between God and the human creature, "doctrine" itself comes to be more properly understood not as some static proposition or formulation of truth, but as a dynamic expression of a living relationship given by God. At its core this living relationship is what it means to be taught by God. This calls to mind the striking words of John 6:45, where Jesus (himself citing Isaiah) proclaims, "It is written in the prophets, 'And they shall all be taught by God.' Everyone who has heard and learned from the Father comes to me." In teaching his disciples, Jesus shows

---

106. To actualize my knowledge of geometry means to be actively thinking about some geometric demonstration or axiom.

107. ST, II-II, q. 2, a. 9, ad 2.

108. ST, I, q. 1, a. 6, ad 3.

himself to be fulfilling the Old Testament prophetic tradition. For Thomas, it is clear that Christ's living teaching extends to all, not only those who lived during Christ's earthly mission. The Holy Spirit having been poured out continues to teach and give the lights of faith and of prophecy to the Church during her pilgrim journey.

4

Prophecy as a Gratuitous Grace and Entry into Ecclesial Faith and Wisdom

With the structural background of the last three chapters in place, Thomas's questions on prophecy in the *Summa theologiae* can now be properly situated (II-II, qq. 171–74). Again, an important prologue opens this last major section of the *Secunda secundae* that analyzes how special individuals contribute to human morality and the journey to salvation brought about by the theological virtues of faith, hope, and love.[1] As has been seen already with Thomas's earlier prologues, this noteworthy prologue similarly signals a recapitulation of the major structural themes of the *Summa*, which we have already identified: faith, the final end, and divine revelation as a sharing in God's knowledge. In this chapter, focus will be on Thomas's account of the essence and cause of prophecy, and the next on his analysis of prophetic knowledge and judgment.

Following the Latin scholastic rendering of St. Paul's *charisma* (1 Cor 12) as *gratia gratis datae*, Thomas classifies prophecy and other spiritual gifts like inspired speech and miracle working as "gratuitous graces." Within this special class of graces, prophecy functions as a sort of keystone, Thomas thinks, since all the other gifts are in some way ordered to it. Among the gratuitous graces listed by St. Paul in 1 Cor 12, prophecy is the one that "consists first and principally in knowledge," according to Thomas.[2] This cognitive starting point coupled with

---

1. See Serge-Thomas Bonino, "Charisms, Forms, and States of Life (*IIa IIae*, qq. 171–189)," in *The Ethics of Aquinas*, 340–52.

2. ST, II-II, q. 171, a. 1, co.: "prophetia primo et principaliter consistit in cognitione."

121

the general setting of the prologue indicates that his treatment of prophecy is in direct relationship with his wider framework of the human being's knowledge of the final end as a kind of assimilation to divine knowledge. The identification of this framework comes as one of the fruits of our earlier discussions of the *Summa*'s background in the first three chapters.

The formal cause of prophecy according to Thomas is a supernatural light, the light of prophecy, that is given transiently to certain individuals for the good of the ecclesial community. Upon the recipient of this light, it bestows sure knowledge about what God wants to be revealed. Prophetic knowledge is a kind of sharing in God's own knowledge that he thinks is always mediated by angels. The involvement of angels in mediating the light of prophecy is a helpful reminder of an important theme that has already been introduced: that prophetic knowledge is for Thomas ordered for sharing with others; it is ordered to the building up of a community whose individuals are seeking to live lives shaped by happiness and for happiness through the virtue of faith. Because its social ordering is primary, prophecy does not require the prophet to possess good morals; rather, the prophet's knowledge is meant to guide and order others collectively to faith and charity's full integration into their moral lives. This social aspect reveals a strong functional dimension to Thomas's notion of prophecy, which is governed by God's free choice to reveal Himself to humanity via supernatural knowledge that is meant to be conducive for eternal salvation.

Situating the Questions on Prophecy in the *Secunda secundae*

The prologue to the questions on prophecy situate the cluster of four questions within the work's larger scheme and links prophecy to the *Secunda secundae*'s earlier sections on the virtues and vices. The first part of the *Secunda secundae* had set out to examine morals from the perspective of moral material that is common to all human beings. Shared by all humans is the fact that they are made in the image of God; they have the potential to be the principle of their own actions and operations through their intellect and will. Even still, the exercise of human freedom in voluntary acts always remains determined and metaphysically grounded by one object: the end which is also the ultimate good that shapes all human moral decisions and action. This final end is for humans also the object of beatitude, which Thomas describes as a single "operation" (*operatio*) accomplished through acts of both the intellect and will that aim at God as ultimate truth and goodness.[3] Human acts, for this reason, are considered and classified by Thomas with respect to their orientation to the final end, that is, by whether they lead one closer to or away from beatitude. The theological and cardinal virtues (*habitus*), which Thomas uses to structure the first part of the *Secunda secundae*, are human qualities that actively dispose one to act more readily and effectively in accordance with the will's natural orientation to the final end. Vices do the opposite, by hindering people from attaining happiness.

In the second major section of the *Secunda secundae*, Thomas now turns to "special states" within his analysis of Christian morals, and here prophecy is treated first. This is because prophecy functions in a way analogous to faith in the first part of the *Secunda secundae*. Thomas indicates this structurally by treating both faith and prophecy first within their respective sections. To reiterate, this positioning is not coincidental. Both faith and prophecy serve to help orient humans to their final end. In faith this is accomplished through sanctifying grace—a divine gift and promise that is communicated interiorly to the believer by a movement of the Holy Spirit and indicated externally by public confession. Faith itself is not complete knowledge (*scientia*) of the divinely revealed truths confessed in faith's *credenda*—"we walk by faith not by sight" (2 Cor 5:7); instead, it is an elevated sharing in God's way of knowing that assists in orienting believers' minds, hearts, and actions toward their supernatural final end, which is impossible for them to know without divine assistance. Received as a promise, faith illuminates the mind so that it can order a person to act for the final end; the virtue of hope strengthens the human desire to seek this end above all else, and charity is the unity of friendship between Creator and creature. In all of this, prophecy is the place where certain individuals receive knowledge about the final end in order to communicate it to others for their well-being and salvation. Prophecy, for this reason, is foundational for faith and provides faith with aspects of its material content.

Thomas indicates that his analysis of the aspects of morality shared universally by humans is not sufficient; another consideration is needed that goes further into particulars. Christian moral reflection must also consider "the special states of human beings" and what role these play in the human journey to God.[4] These special states are no afterthoughts in Thomas's scheme that are crammed in at the end of the Second Part; they are integral to his vision of

---

3. See ST, I-II, q. 3, a. 2.
4. ST, II-II, prologue: "quantum ad speciales status hominum."

the return of the human creature to God, and they address especially aspects of human sociality and the place of the Church in this. Thomas lists three major sub-groups among these "special states": among gratuitous graces, among forms of life (active or contemplative), and among the offices one could hold in the Church.[5] Within the sub-group of gratuitous graces, prophecy ranks first.

Among the gratuitous graces, Thomas makes a further division. Gratuitous graces can be divided into three groups: those that pertain to knowledge (*ad cognitionem*), to speech (*ad locutionem*), and to operation (*ad operationem*).[6] All the gratuitous graces that fall under the first group pertaining to knowledge "can be comprehended under prophecy." Thomas asserts prophecy's relationship to knowledge immediately and quickly expands on it:

> Prophetic revelation extends not only to the future events of human beings, but also to divine things, both with respect to those things proposed to all for believing (*credenda*), which pertain to faith, and with respect to higher mysteries, which belong to the perfect [and] pertain to wisdom. Prophetic revelation is also about those things which pertain to spiritual substances [that is, angels], who induce us either to the good or to the bad, and this pertains to the discernment of spirits. It even extends to the direction of human acts, which pertains to knowledge (*ad scientiam*), as will be made clear below. Therefore, first there must be a consideration about prophecy and then about rapture, which is a certain grade of prophecy.[7]

One observes initially the breadth of Thomas's outline of prophecy; it extends to very many things. He identifies first that "prophetic revelation" is not strictly limited to knowledge about future events. In denying this limitation, Thomas is immediately going against a trend common among some of his thirteenth-century contemporaries who thought the term "prophet" should only properly designate someone who knows and foretells future events.[8] While Thomas distances himself from this narrow definition, he obviously does not

---

5. ST, II-II, q. 171, prologue.

6. ST, II-II, q. 171, prologue.

7. ST, II-II, q. 171, prologue.

8. See, for example, Hugh of Saint-Cher, q. 481, *De prophetia*, a. 1, ad 9: "dicimus quod proprie prophetia est de re futura, sumitur tamen aliquando communiter pro revelatione qualibet occultorum facta a Deo sive preteritorum sive presentium sive futurorum" (text in Torrell, *Théorie de la prophétie*, 16, lines 1–4).

abandon it; he will still affirm that the revelation of future events belongs "most properly" (*propriissime*) to prophecy due to the remoteness of this knowledge from ordinary human experience.[9] The issue of prophetic knowledge of future contingents raises a number of problems surrounding how prophetic knowledge is classified, and Thomas devotes an entire article to future contingents (q. 171, a. 3) to serve as a sort of entry point for classifying the additional things to which prophetic knowledge can extend. This later listing of classifications is representative of Thomas's method in general which one sees already in the prologue to the questions on prophecy. There having introduced and acknowledged what would be considered by most of his thirteenth-century audience to be the typical object of prophetic revelation—future contingents—he goes on to expand the list. Prophecy extends also to things proposed for everyone to believe (*ea quae proponuntur omnibus credenda*), to higher mysteries (*altiora mysteria*), to things relating to angels and demons (*spirituales substantias*), and to the direction of human acts (*ad directionem humanorum actuum*).

At the same time, Thomas compiles a corresponding list that introduces a sub-classification scheme that seems to be inspired by St. Paul's catalogue of the Holy Spirit's manifestations (1 Cor 12:8–10). The "things proposed for everyone to believe" belong to faith (*ad fidem*); "higher mysteries" to wisdom (*ad sapientiam*); "angels and demons" to the discernment of spirits (*ad discretionem spirituum*); and the "direction of human acts" to knowledge (*ad scientiam*). On closer inspection, however, this corresponding list does not fit quite so neatly with the Pauline list. While "faith" and "the discernment of spirits" are clearly part of the 1 Corinthians 12 catalogue, "wisdom" and "knowledge" seem slightly out of place. In fact, in St. Paul's text Thomas would have found the phrase "the word of knowledge" (*sermo scientiae*) and "the word of wisdom" (*sermo sapientiae*). Is Thomas directly referring here to the Pauline "word of knowledge" and "word of wisdom"? The answer is likely no because he treats this word of knowledge or wisdom pair independently in a different group of articles on the gratuitous gifts that "consist in speech" (*in sermone*), not in prophecy. This later discussion about gifts of speech explicitly cites the Pauline passage (1 Cor 12:8)—*to some are given by the Spirit the word of wisdom, to others the word of knowledge.*[10] The word of knowledge and word of wisdom as speech gifts are given to certain individuals so that they can speak "efficaciously" (*efficaciter*) for

---

9. ST, II-II, q. 171, a. 3, co.

10. ST, II-II, q. 177, prologue.

the benefit of others and especially "to communicate their own faith to others."[11] They thus relate more to effective communication or speech than to a grace of knowledge, which prophecy principally is. It seems unlikely then that it was St. Paul's precise list that Thomas had in mind.

This second corresponding sub-list may actually signal a deeper structural level present in Thomas's classification of prophecy. To recall, faith and wisdom are loosely paired in the sub-list and correspond to the prophetic revelation of "divine things." These "divine things" (*res divinas*) are not just any type of supernatural knowledge; the term, as Thomas uses it here, refers especially to supernatural knowledge of God as the human final end. Faith is the virtue that first ordains believers to God as their supernatural end. Within it, prophetic revelation presents knowledge of the "things proposed for everyone to believe," of faith's *credenda*. Wisdom here means knowledge of the highest principle, and it corresponds to prophetic revelation of "higher mysteries." Thomas revealingly adds that these higher mysteries "belong to the perfect" (*quae sunt perfectorum*). By saying this, he means that they belong to the saints in heaven who behold divine Wisdom itself. Prophetic revelation thus extends to knowledge that relates to the beatific vision and extends to things that touch upon the inner life of God that would otherwise be unknowable to humans by nature, such as God being Trinity. From this first corresponding pair, the picture is already emerging that prophetic revelation for Thomas is concerned primarily with knowledge that has a bearing on the human final end.

The second pair—the discernment of spirits and knowledge—extends this picture and confirms it. Here Thomas signals how these two objects of prophetic revelation extend unambiguously into the realm of human morality and action. Discernment of spirits corresponds to prophetic revelation about angels and demons, but again Thomas does not mean here generic knowledge about the angelic creation. Prophetic revelation in this specific context provides knowledge about how angels and demons are external principles of human acts, "who induce us either to the good or to the bad" (*a quibus vel ad bonum vel ad malum inducimur*). It is helpful to recall that Thomas does not think that humans in this life can acquire natural knowledge of spiritual substances in themselves or knowledge of their natures.[12] This puts humanity at a moral disadvantage, given that angels and demons can influence human acts—something itself only known

---

11. ST, II-II, q. 177, a. 1, co. and ad 4: "quod autem aliquis fidem suam aliis communicet, fit per sermonem scientiae seu sapientiae."

12. ST, I, q. 88, a. 1.

definitively by divine revelation. Because of this, Thomas thinks humans need to know how to "discern" and distinguish the inducements of the good angels from those of the bad so that they may more effectively orient their own intentions and actions to God. The moral function of prophecy is at the forefront. Finally, Thomas's discussion of knowledge (*scientia*) in prophetic revelation confirms that he conceives prophecy as having a moral telos. Knowledge corresponds specifically to the direction of human acts. That human acts can "be directed" implies that prophetic revelation provides a kind of moral guidance that allows humans to know more concretely how they ought to direct their actions as intermediate steps on their pilgrimage to beatitude. Knowledge in this context is especially knowledge about human acts, which allows people to choose with greater freedom and efficacy courses of action that can be meritorious of eternal life.

To sum up, this corresponding sub-list from the prologue confirms how Thomas conceives of prophecy as the medium for supernatural knowledge that is meant first and foremost to orient humans to their final end. Without this hermeneutic perspective rooted in faith and the final end, it is difficult to discern any rationale behind Thomas's choice of what to list as objects of prophetic revelation. The prologue gives a preliminary overview of how prophecy relates to the whole expanse of human morals and how it will provide certain objects of knowledge. These objects fall under Thomas's classification scheme thanks to their integral orientation to human morals. The knowledge prophetic revelation provides is as follows: (1) the knowledge of faith and the things to be believed in order to attain beatitude (knowledge of *credenda*), (2) the knowledge of the saints in heaven and, by extension, the knowledge of sacred doctrine as a wisdom that shares in the knowledge of the saints, (3) knowledge relevant for discerning how angels and demons influence human acts, and (4) knowledge concerned directly with human morals.

As a special case of prophecy, Thomas adds rapture, but one can already see by its placement at the very end of the prologue that it does not quite fit into the scheme that comes before. While rapture does relate to a kind of momentary "glimpse" of the divine essence, the fact that Thomas does not fully integrate it into his prologue treatment suggests that he already does not see it as directly contributing to knowledge that helps humans orient themselves to their final end. On top of this, the question on rapture has its own set of very technical and laborious difficulties relating to how Thomas understands the essence of rapture or ecstasy to lie in the mind's temporary "standing outside" (*extasis*) of the body. Characteristic of rapture then is the violent and, in some sense, *coercive* lifting out of the human mind from the body by divine power.[13] This coercive quality makes it difficult to integrate it satisfactorily within a classification scheme of human action, especially when one considers how the rapt person remains purely passive in every respect; human acts, after all, are only properly "human" when they are voluntary. In rapture, voluntary action seems to be absent and the sole agent is God who "acts upon" the rapt in separating the mind from the body, thus temporarily disrupting the normal functioning of the principles of human action that normally presuppose the substantial unity of mind and body. Perhaps it is not surprising then that Thomas hesitates to integrate rapture fully into his scheme for prophecy and the other gratuitous graces. Because of this peculiarity and a whole set of other complexities (historical and philosophical) that touch upon the medieval scholastic treatment of this topic, a discussion of Thomas's question on rapture would lead too far afield; it will not be a major focus.

Q. 171, a. 1—Prophecy Is Ordered to Supernatural Knowledge of the Final End

Most of our attention must be guided by what Thomas himself says sets prophecy apart from other kinds of knowing, as outlined in his first question on prophecy (q. 171). There he refers to that which sets prophecy apart as "its essence."[14] In the first article, he establishes firmly that "prophecy consists primarily and principally in knowledge." As already seen in the prologue, Thomas's treatment must be read in the light of his other questions on supernatural knowledge. While in many respects speech is closely related to knowledge, Thomas separated the two in the prologue's scheme. The gratuitous graces that relate to speech he treats after the questions on prophecy, since the content of supernatural speech or communication depends on what a speaker knows. In this way, prophets for Thomas are not just God's dictation machines; to some degree, they have assimilated what God has revealed to them through the gift of prophecy into their own understanding. Of course, due to God's infinite power and knowledge, no one—not even a prophet—can ever assimilate in this life the full import of even the smallest expression of divine testimony.

---

13. ST, II-II, q. 175, a. 1, ad 3.

14. ST, II-II, q. 171, prologue: "de prophetia autem quadruplex consideratio occurrit, quarum prima est de essentia eius."

Thomas establishes that the framework to best understand prophecy is principally knowledge. Under this aspect, prophecy is understood initially as a kind of perfection of the intellect. An interesting contrast is seen in scripture, where prophecy is often discerned and defined in relation to false prophecy. This biblical dialectic between true and false prophecy, which Thomas himself is conscious of, indicates to him that prophecy ought to be examined primarily as it relates to truth and falsity, which principally exist in the intellect.[15] In the first article's third objection, he cites Hosea 9:7 that refers to the prophets of Israel as "fools"—*you will know, Israel, that the prophet is a fool and insane*. Being a fool, however, seems to imply an intellectual imperfection, and this would exclude prophecy from being about knowledge, which is an intellectual perfection. Thomas responds by pointing out that in scripture being a fool or losing control of one's senses is a sign of false prophecy, not of true prophecy.[16] The notion of the prophet as a kind of manic seer whose mental capacities are overwhelmed and overthrown by divine inspiration is ruled out almost immediately.

In the same article's fourth objection, Thomas introduces a standard definition of prophecy attributed to Cassiodorus: prophecy is an "inspiration or revelation" (*inspiratio vel revelatio*). The objection notes that the word "inspiration" seems to imply an affective movement, while "revelation" refers to an intellectual perfection. If the affective element in prophecy is just as strong as the intellectual, it seems that Thomas would have little basis for claiming that prophecy relates primarily to the intellect. In his response to the objection, Thomas reinterprets the word "inspiration" emptying it of any affective dimension. "Inspiration" refers more to the elevating of the "mind's intention" (*intentio mentis*) than to a moving of the will toward some good:

> It is necessary in prophecy that the intention of the mind be raised so as to perceive divine things: thus, it is said (Ezek 2:1–2): *Son of man, stand on your feet, and I will speak with you*. This elevation of the intention (*elevatio intentionis*) is brought about by a motion of the Holy Spirit, wherein the same [text] goes on to say: *And the Spirit entered into me and set me upon my feet*. After the mind's intention has been elevated to heavenly things, it perceives divine things; hence the text continues: *And I heard Him speaking to me*. Therefore, inspiration is

---

15. See ST, I, q. 16, a. 1, co.: "veritas principaliter est in intellectu; secundario vero in rebus, secundum quod comparantur ad intellectum ut ad principium."

16. ST, II-II, q. 171, a. 1, ad 3.

necessary for prophecy with respect to the mind's elevation, according to Jb 32:8, *The inspiration of the Almighty gives understanding.* Meanwhile, revelation is necessary with respect to the very perception of divine things, wherein prophecy is completed; and through it the veil of darkness and ignorance is removed, according to Jb 12:22, *He reveals profound things out of the shadows.*[17]

This passage illustrates again how Thomas's concept of prophecy is governed more by its end, which he identifies with the revelation of truths that are above human knowledge, that is, "divine things" not accessible to human natural reason. His redefinition of "inspiration" around this elevation of "the mind's intention" puts on display how his thinking is structured by this central consideration about the end.

In this raising of "the mind's intention" in inspiration, one also sees a structural parallel with Question One on sacred doctrine. In that question's first article, Thomas tries to show that a knowledge that is "beyond" the philosophical disciplines is necessary. What precisely is this supernatural knowledge necessary for? It is necessary for human salvation—the fulfilment and resting of every desire in the beatific vision. Humans, however, are not normally given salvation at one discrete moment in time. For humans, salvation is worked out gradually, and they are oriented to their salvation by faith, which is the orientation of the mind to God through grace—a sharing in God's own intentions. The inspiration of prophets provides some of this orientation as they try analogously to elevate the intentions of the minds of those who hear them, becoming for them occasions of faith.

The first article in q. 171 also reflects some of the background structure that is taken for granted in the same article on sacred doctrine. Given that a supernatural knowledge is necessary, there must be a way for that knowledge to reach human beings. Prophecy is the primary way human beings come to know the supernatural truths that are presented in faith, but this gift only needs to be given to a few individuals, Thomas thinks. Thus, when he says that prophecy deals primarily with knowledge, the knowledge that he has in mind is knowledge of truths that orient human beings and society toward their supernatural end.

Including the orientation of society among the aims of prophetic knowledge is not an attempt at an interpretive sleight of hand. It is true that Thomas does not yet speak in this first article (q. 171) of prophecy's function

---

17. ST, II-II, q. 171, a. 1, ad 4.

as a social orientation. Nevertheless, there are passages later in the questions on prophecy that indicate that Thomas sees prophetic revelation as being more essential for a community than for the prophet. The type of knowledge dealt with in prophecy is operative at a communal level, but like all knowledge it must be rooted at the psychological level of the individual. Thomas knows this, and it is reflected in how his analysis relates initially to the individual's gift of prophecy. But taken in its fuller view, this analysis on the individual level is embedded structurally within his more foundational framework of the common good as the primary sense of good and the role the prophet has in orienting both the individual and society toward that common good, understood supernaturally. The two dimensions—the individual and the social (or ecclesial)—function like x-and-y axes in mapping out Thomas's notion of prophecy.

Admittedly, some difficulties arise with this interpretation. A simple glance at many of the article headings from this section reveals that most of Thomas's attention is devoted to the individual axis. This is undeniable. Taken by themselves, the individual articles leave the social (or ecclesial) axis of prophecy somewhat underdeveloped. However, if these articles on prophecy are read structurally with appreciation for their particular location within the *Secunda secundae*, one begins to see how the social axis or structure is built into the account through key structural terms like "gratuitous graces" (gifts ordered primarily to a common good) and "faith" (an ordination of humans to their supernatural good through an act of the intellect but one mediated, in part, socially through others) and through the overall moral nexus of the Second Part (centered on beatitude which consists solely in the contemplation of God as a shared common good, who is as Trinity essentially "social").

The Dynamic between the Individual and Social Dimensions of Prophecy

To elaborate this "social" dimension of prophecy, it may help to consider one of Thomas's recurring analogies, that of the teacher and student. Unsurprisingly, one finds it frequently in his discussions of faith and sacred doctrine, too. He employs the analogy of a teacher instructing students to characterize this individual relationship between God and prophets. God illuminates the mind of a prophet in a way similar to that in which a teacher instructs a student about the particular areas of a subject. Thomas extends this teaching analogy beyond the external act of instructing and hits upon the more profound inner likeness between the mind of the teacher and the student's mind that is the heart of teaching. To attain to truth, the student's knowledge must become "a likeness" (*similitudo*) of the teacher's knowledge.[18] Expanding this to the social level, Thomas also draws attention to how the chief task of the prophet is to communicate the divine testimony to a community. Here again, the teacher instructing students is Thomas's preferred analogy for capturing how prophets "instruct" others by proposing certain things to be believed under the virtue of faith.

This multilayered and dynamic analogy of teacher-student, structured at both the individual and social levels, has the potential to cause confusion when we try to reconstruct how Thomas employs both elements to describe prophecy as a whole. To allay such potential confusion, the interaction between the individual and social elements can be clarified through another analogy Thomas employs—namely, to the human mind and voice. The audible voice expresses what is conceived antecedently in the mind, just as the social element of prophecy expresses and flows from the individual element possessed by prophets.[19] However, one finds that this mind-voice image also maps onto prophecy's inner element as it relates to the act of knowledge itself. The inner prophetic word—as understood by the prophet—is received by means of God's "external" voice that speaks inwardly to the prophet;[20] this external voice is a "divine locution" that the prophet receives as an inner word, and existing as an inner word in a prophet's mind, it is not the divine essence itself, but an expression of it. It is a likeness or sign of God's speech. More precisely, the divine locution is a likeness of God as He expresses Himself. Now, God's act of "expressing" Himself *ad extra* is appropriated to the person of the Word, who is the intra-Trinitarian intellectual "expression" or "word" of the Father. Because this inner word existing in the prophet's mind serves as a sign of God's speech and especially of the person of the Word, Thomas also thinks it appropriate to call it "a kind of spiritual likeness of [God's] own

---

18. ST, II-II, q. 171, a. 1, co.

19. See ST, II-II, q. 3, a. 1, co.: "exterior enim locutio ordinatur ad significandum id quod in corde concipitur." To my knowledge, Thomas never explicitly brings together these two images—the teacher-student analogy and the mind-voice analogy—within the context of his discussions of prophecy. Nevertheless, it seems that the one complements the other when trying to distinguish what we are calling the "social" element in prophecy. In the context of his discussions on faith, he does explicitly relate the image of inner speech (or mental word) and outer speech to the relationship of faith's preachers to its hearers; this latter relationship comes quite close to the teacher-student dynamic.

20. "External" means here "not belonging to the prophet as a subject."

Wisdom."[21] Thus, the relationship between the inner word and the external expression or word can be understood on multiple levels. To avoid overlapping these comparative models altogether is impossible, and it seems that one must acknowledge that "being in relation" is a structural feature of prophecy.

This essentially "relational" character of Thomas's notion of prophecy is reflected acutely in his determination that prophetic knowledge is not meant to perfect the individual prophet's mind alone, but is always ordered and in relation to something beyond the individual's mind—toward some common supernatural good. As something rooted in individual prophets, prophetic knowledge serves as the initial orientation for personal knowledge of one's supernatural end. Simultaneously, it serves as part of prophecy's social element—its relating to others their supernatural final end, in other words, its leading of others to theological faith. In prophecy's social element, one appreciates how the knowledge of individual prophets is ordered to the gift of faith. That which is revealed in the light of prophecy establishes the things to be believed commonly in faith, and the things to be believed under faith become the chief conceptual (or dogmatic) content which the teacher of sacred doctrine must articulate. The social character of prophecy thus indicates a certain degree of interdependence among Thomas's concepts of communal faith and doctrine, which consequently both become commonly structured by and oriented to the common good of salvation.

Q. 171, a. 2—Whether Prophecy Is a *Habitus*

The second article brings prophecy into dialectical tension with Thomas's notion of a virtue or stable disposition (*habitus*). Through this dialectic, Thomas is able to elaborate on prophecy's unique feature of being a "transient

---

21. *De ver.*, q. 18, a. 3, co.: "Est enim quaedam locutio exterior, qua nobis Deus per praedicatores loquitur; quaedam autem interior locutio, qua nobis loquitur per internam inspirationem. Dicitur autem ipsa interna inspiratio locutio quaedam ad similitudinem exterioris locutionis: sicut enim in exteriori locutione proferimus ad audientem non ipsam rem quam notificare cupimus, sed signum illius rei, scilicet vocem significativam; ita Deus interius inspirando non exhibet essentiam suam ad videndum, sed aliquod suae essentiae signum, quod est *aliqua spiritualis similitudo suae sapientiae*" (emphasis mine). My attention to this passage was drawn by Jean-Pierre Torrell, "Le traité de la prophétie de S. Thomas d'Aquin et la théologie de la Révélation," in *La doctrine de la révélation divine de saint Thomas d'Aquin: Actes du Symposium sur la pensée de saint Thomas d'Aquin tenu à Rolduc, les 4 et 5 novembre 1989*, ed. Leo Elders, Studi Tomistici 37 (Vatican City: Libreria Editrice Vaticana, 1990), 171–95, at 192n25.

impression." The article also serves to distinguish prophecy from the moral, intellectual, and theological virtues, which up to this point have been the central framework of the *Secunda secundae*.

The first objection introduces Aristotle's tripartite division of the soul, which possesses powers, passions, and *habitus*. This division offers a framed definition of a *habitus*, that is, a definition that can draw on oppositions to the notions of powers and passions. Thomas will subsequently employ this framed definition of *habitus* to situate prophecy. Prophecy, the objection claims, must belong to one of these three divisions, since as something that consists in knowledge—something shown in the previous article—prophecy must necessarily involve the human soul. The objection asserts that prophecy cannot be a power, because it is not found in all human beings; only a few people ever exercise it. It also cannot be a passion, because passions involve the appetite, which for humans implies an act of the will; the previous article already denied that prophecy is voluntary by locating it in the intellect. If the will is not operative, prophecy then cannot relate to the appetite; it also cannot be a passion. This leaves the category of a *habitus* as the only one left.

In the objection's reply, Thomas qualifies this use of Aristotle's tripartite division. While he does not deny that *habitus*, powers, and passions are all found in the soul, Thomas questions whether these three categories as described in the objection exhaust absolutely everything found in the soul.[22] He moves beyond the objection's definitional framing and maintains that this specific tripartite division applies only to the "principles of moral acts." He admits that moral acts can and do emerge from passions, *habitus*, and naked powers of the soul. But by not limiting the soul's activity to one of the three, Thomas signals that prophecy by itself is not a moral act; nor is it, by extension, morally blameworthy or praiseworthy in and of itself. Having limited prophecy primarily to the cognitional sphere, the moral sphere only enters into the framework at a secondary level when one begins to consider how prophecy is ordered and used. Considered by itself, then, prophecy is not a moral act because it requires no use of the will. It follows from this that, since prophecy does not directly involve a human will, it also has no direct link to charity.[23] If one is chosen by God to be a prophet, it is still possible to live charitably, Thomas thinks, but prophecy by itself does not guarantee this.

---

22. ST, II-II, q. 171, a. 2, ad 1: "illa divisio philosophi non comprehendit absolute omnia quae sunt in anima, sed ea quae possunt esse principia moralium actuum."

23. This issue is dealt with fully at ST, II-II, q. 172, a. 4.

Prophecy's lack of a voluntary dimension, however, does not exclude it completely from being a *habitus*; after all, the intellectual virtues do not depend on the will for their perfection. An intellectual virtue is still a *habitus* because it exists as "an enduring form" in a person; prophecy, in contrast, is "a kind of passion or transient impression."[24] The light of prophecy temporarily illuminates the mind of the prophet who receives it passively without it inhering permanently. Instead of a *habitus*, Thomas thinks prophecy "can be reduced to a passion" (*passio*), but he is careful here to qualify what he means by "passion."[25] A "passion" as defined in the first objection was restricted to "a force of the appetite." This sense is impossible to ascribe to prophecy. If, however, the sense of "passion" is simplified to mean "any kind of receiving" (*pro qualibet receptione*)—a sense that implies no volitional dimension—then Thomas thinks one can call prophecy a "passion." He finds this simplified sense of passion even in a passage from Aristotle's *On the Soul*: "To understand is something suffered (*pati*)."[26] Thomas gets a good deal of mileage out of this passage by considering every act of intellection as involving a kind of passivity. This passivity is such a basic feature of intellectual acts that Thomas decides to identify it as a principle (or a starting point) in human intellection. He calls this principle "the possible intellect" (*intellectus possibilis*) and explains how:

> in natural knowledge the possible intellect suffers [*patitur*] from the light of the agent intellect; similarly in prophetic knowledge the human intellect suffers from the shining of divine light.[27]

This passage gives us a clue into how closely Thomas structures his basic account of prophetic knowing on the natural mode of human intellection. The chief difference in prophecy is the additional *lumen divinum* that shines in the prophet's mind. This new light functions like the light of the agent intellect in natural intellection. The key difference, he notes, is that, unlike the light of reason, the *lumen propheticum* does not exist permanently in prophets. Prophetic knowledge is only impressed on a mind when the light of prophecy is given. Once the light ceases to be given, the passion disappears, and active prophetic knowing must also cease.

---

24. ST, II-II, q. 171, a. 2, co.: "Lumen propheticum insit animae prophetae per modum cuiusdam passionis vel impressionis transeuntis.... Habitus autem est forma permanens."

25. ST, II-II, q. 171, a. 2, ad 1.

26. See Aristotle, *On the Soul*, III, 4, 429a14.

27. ST, II-II, q. 171, a. 2, ad 1.

At the same time, the mind's potential to be illuminated by supernatural light (its passivity) does not by itself account for why prophecy cannot be a *habitus*. Faith is also given passively through a supernatural light, but it is given as a *habitus*. The case of faith, however, already has a layer of complexity beyond prophecy because faith as a *habitus* involves not only the mind, but also the will. Thomas also denies that prophecy corresponds to an intellectual *habitus*. He bases this, again, on the transient existence of the prophetic light in prophets—a transience that he roots ultimately in scriptural testimony. An intellectual virtue like a *scientia* requires a steady intellectual light wherein a person can regularly and reliably draw conclusions from given principles seen in that light.[28] Even though prophets never lose their natural light of reason, they still do not possess the prophetic light in the same way as they possess their natural light. Thomas thinks this happens because the very principle of prophetic knowledge, the prophetic light, is not given permanently to prophets. Thus, their minds cannot continually lead their conclusions back to the first principle seen in the prophetic light, nor can they do this whenever they want. If a prophet's mind could continually lead its conclusions directly back to a first principle seen in the prophetic light, Thomas thinks this would be the equivalent of the prophet seeing the divine essence, because God is the principle of the prophetic light. Thomas, however, firmly denies that prophets see the divine essence when they receive the light of prophecy;[29] instead, they only receive a likeness of the divine essence, "a likeness of the First Truth."[30] Prophets' minds are united to this likeness of the divine mind only temporarily and transiently. Since the human mind continually requires illumination for its activity—even with respect to natural reason's activity—the prophet's mind falls back into passivity (and relative "darkness" with respect to the supernatural light) when the light of prophecy is no longer given.

Thomas also highlights that those who become prophets in scripture do not necessarily choose to be prophets; God's will ultimately determines whether someone is a prophet. That such light depends entirely on God's will leads him to conclude that a prophet relies on a constant influx of prophetic light to prophesy. He confirms this when he says that people are called prophets ultimately "by divine appointment" (*ex deputatione divina*), even sometimes after light has

---

28. ST, II-II, q. 171, a. 2. On *scientia* as a *habitus*, see ST, I-II, q. 57, aa. 1–2.
29. ST, II-II, q. 173, a. 1.
30. ST, II-II, q. 173, a. 1, ad 2.

ceased to be given.[31] This total reliance on God's will enlarges prophecy to a kind of divinely bestowed gift that cannot be confused with a natural ability or *habitus*. Someone like Jeremiah, for instance, is chosen in his mother's womb to be a prophet, even before he has received the use of his reason or ability to speak. Even when referring to Jeremiah in his mother's womb, scripture refers to him properly as a prophet, says Thomas, because God has chosen him; hence, it is appropriate to call Jeremiah a prophet even when he is not actively being inspired by the prophetic light. Thus, the name "prophet" maintains in Thomas's thinking the essential aspect of "being chosen and called" by God, an aspect that is especially prominent among Old Testament prophets like Jeremiah and Moses. The fact that someone cannot choose to be a prophet but is only one by divine election reveals another aspect of how prophecy is structured "socially"; it requires an external call—something essentially relational. This simultaneously is a call to serve for the good of others—another essentially relational feature as well as again a prominent feature of Old Testament prophecy.

This aspect of a divine "appointment" in the service of others allows Thomas to highlight another essential feature of prophecy: its *super*naturalness. Prophecy is a not something acquired for oneself by the dint of work or personal effort; it is a gratuitous gift given by God that is above human nature.[32]

Passivity to Supernatural Light and Faith's "Deposit"

A brief return to the issue of the passivity of the human mind to supernatural light will highlight another parallel between prophecy and theological faith that bears on the biaxial aspect of the act of faith and on faith's deposit as hope. The parallel is rooted in the essentially supernatural and gratuitous nature of both lights. Similar to the light of prophecy, Thomas maintains that only God can bestow the light of faith on individuals, wherein they take on a more perfect likeness of God's mode of knowing by beginning to know what and how God knows. They also begin to know what they ought to believe (that is, faith's *credenda*) in response to the external invitation of prophets and apostles. This makes their resulting act of faith a response to a biaxial invitation to believe things divinely revealed and taught initially to prophets. The believer's response in turn is

---

31. ST, II-II, q. 171, a. 2, ad 2: "potest tamen dici quod aliquis dicitur propheta etiam cessante actuali prophetica illustratione, ex deputatione divina, secundum illud Ierem. [1:5], 'et prophetam in gentibus dedi te.'"

32. ST, II-II, q. 171, a. 2, ad 3.

working on two planes. On the first plane, it is directed primarily toward God as the initial inviter, who remains a mystery but now a mystery most intimately loved. On the other plane, creedal and doctrinal propositions or statements received in preaching or teaching make up the secondary external invitation; under the light of faith the believer responds to these statements by affirming them to have their terminus and ultimate meaning in the first plane. While these propositions and statements are true for all times, there always remains room for growth in our understanding of them and in their expression—in other words, there can be development in how they are understood among believers.

Considered on the second plane of the biaxial act of faith, prophecy is a transient light given to certain individuals that can over time influence what comes to be recognized by believers as pertaining to the object of faith. New things can be affirmed as following from the initial deposit of faith entrusted to the apostles by Christ, and new dimensions of the initial teaching can be renewed or reiterated under the steady light of faith and the occasional flashes of light given to certain prophets. Following the Incarnation and the death of the last apostle, the expansion of what comes to be recognized as the measure of what belongs to faith with regard to its essential content has ceased. This limitation of the content of faith to a fixed "deposit," which serves as a measure for everything else that comes after, reflects structurally the "fixed" status of the prophet's knowledge as received under the light of prophecy. This knowledge, which is absolutely certain, remains the fixed point of reference for all subsequent things known in the light of faith. The benefit of highlighting this structural parallel comes when we realize that the deposit of faith, just as the "fixed" things prophets know, is meant to be a sign of God's promise of salvation—a "deposit" which God desires to pay out in full. Just as the prophet's knowledge is meant to orient humans to the promise of faith, faith's deposit serves as a sign of hope meant to orient humans to God's love as the common good of everything. The prophet's knowledge equally serves as "sign of hope" that informs the deposit of faith and runs parallel to it by continually drawing attention to it in every age.

Prophetic Light and the Functioning of Light in Habitus

It remains now to explore the prophetic light and how it serves as the key component in Thomas's account of prophetic knowledge; this light also provides the definitive explanation why prophecy itself cannot be a *habitus*. The prophetic mode of knowledge is determined directly by the way the light of prophecy dwells and inheres in a prophet. As already noted, seen in the virtue of faith, light is the preferred metaphor Thomas deploys when speaking about acts of intellection, whether natural or supernatural: "just as a manifestation of bodily vision happens through bodily light, so also a manifestation of intellectual vision occurs through intellectual light."[33] Intellectual light makes something intelligible to a knower, but this does not mean that the light bestows intelligibility on the object known. When sitting in a dark room, for instance, I cannot see the desk that is in front of me. This does not mean that the desk itself is invisible, but only that there is not enough light in the room for me to see it. Visible light enables me to see the desk as a visible object, and while the light bestows visibility on the desk with respect to me as a viewer, it does not bestow on the desk itself the property of visibility. Similarly, intellectual "light" is what enables one "to see" things not purely as images in my imagination, but as universals abstracted from their particular instances.

This general account becomes slightly more complicated because prophecy extends to things that "surpass natural reason," enabling one to know things that are either unknowable or difficult to know under the natural light of reason. To distinguish prophetic light from reason's light, Thomas relies on several outlines that map out the different ways intellectual lights function in the human mind. He observes that these intellectual lights function similarly in the mind, and this similarity reflects a common source—the so-called principle of light and its capacity or power. For instance, if I shine a light in a room from the ceiling, I see most things in the room: the desk, the chair, and a bookshelf; anything the light "touches" I can see. This is like the light of reason. There are, however, places in the room that I cannot see even with the ceiling light; it may be too dark underneath the desk to see a lost pen that rolled off it. The light of prophecy would be analogous to using a flashlight to see under the desk to find the lost pen. How I use the flashlight differs from the way I use my ceiling light. While the ceiling light is on, I only need to shine the flashlight briefly to see what is under the desk. In principle, I could point it anywhere in the room where the ceiling light does or does not reach to see what is there. In a similar way, prophetic light can extend to all the things the natural light of reason can or cannot extend to. Referring to the objects of prophetic revelation under this aspect, Thomas calls them *prophetabilia*; and as objects *prophetabilia* are all the things the prophetic light can "touch" to make them visible.

---

33. ST, II-II, q. 171, a. 2, co.

It is at this stage that our flashlight metaphor begins to break down because visible light stops at the senses and goes no further—there being nothing beyond the visible object for the eyes "to see." Intellectual light, in contrast, does not necessarily terminate with the senses or even in the imagination. While Thomas readily acknowledges that all human knowledge must begin and end with something sensible, the channels that go in between extend beyond the senses. With the intellectual light, a person tries to resolve all things to first principles through an act of judgment; this is how someone comes to know. In the natural light of reason, for instance, the intellect attempts to see all things in relation to being as expressed in the principle of non-contradiction. It tries to see what things "are" and what things "are not." It does this by a process of dividing and composing so that what is in the mind corresponds to what is in reality. All that is naturally knowable can be revealed by the light of reason; and what this light reveals especially are the principles of what is naturally knowable—the starting points on which all further human knowledge builds. In the case of prophetic light, the light reveals a principle of knowing whereby everything is knowable; it reveals how all things are supernaturally knowable through a share in a supernatural light given by God. All things are supernaturally knowable insofar as they are known and knowable by God, who is the Creator of everything. The light of prophecy ultimately comes to approximate this divine mode of knowing to a greater degree than the natural light—thus making prophetic knowledge supernatural and more certain. Thomas's approach, which he outlines in the second article's response, is not to focus on the differing principles of knowledge *qua* principles, but rather on introducing distinctions through the metaphor of light. This method enables his distinctions about supernatural knowledge to remain within the framework of human psychology and acts of intellection.

Having established that prophecy requires some kind of supernatural light, Thomas turns to how light can "exist in" (*inesse*) something or someone.[34] Light can inhere in two ways: either "through a permanent form," as when physical light is in the sun or a fire, or "through some kind of passion or transient impression like light being in the air."[35] Prophetic light exists in a prophet in this latter mode—as light exists in air. As a passion or transient impression, prophetic light cannot be united permanently to a person; Thomas bases this assertion on the combined authority of scripture (2 Kgs 3:15) and St. Gregory the Great.

---

34. ST, II-II, q. 171, a. 2, co.: "lumen autem dupliciter alicui inesse potest."
35. ST, II-II, q. 171, a. 2, co.

Both attest to prophets' inability to prophesy at will.[36] While these authorities play a critical role in the article's ultimate determination (*determinatio*)—the magisterial response to the question raised at the article's outset—one observes how Thomas is not satisfied to end his inquiry there. He wants to give a reason why, for example, someone like Elisha says to the Sunamite woman that he cannot "read" her soul and know prophetically the exact cause of her distress, even though he is publicly recognized as a prophet (2 Kgs 4:27). Following this passage concerning Elisha, Thomas immediately adds, "And the reason for this is..." (*Et huius ratio est...*), indicating that he is now going to explain why Elisha confesses to lack any prophetic knowledge about the woman.

The Dynamic of Reading Scripture and the Lights of Prophecy and Faith

It is worth highlighting in this example of Elisha how Thomas's *ratio* is occasioned by the scriptural text itself, not by a curious theoretical speculation, as interesting as such might be. On a deeper level, we can appreciate here in his treatment of biblical and patristic authorities a vital cornerstone of his theological method. Sacred doctrine is determined jointly by reason and by its authorities, which include both scripture—its proper and intrinsic authority—and the Christian doctors—its intrinsic but only probable authorities.[37] What strikes one here in this article is the subtle usage and layering of rational arguments in conjunction with inspired authorities. On the one hand, the authorities of 2 Kgs and St. Gregory remain "most effective" for determining the way the question is answered. On the other, structurally, they offer Thomas very little material to help explain why it is that prophecy does not function like natural intellectual *habitus*, like understanding, that can be employed "at will." Instead of appealing to these two authorities for further explanation, he draws on a Pauline statement (Eph 5:13)—*everything that is manifested is light*—to structure the article's explanation. Yet even this biblical passage is not self-explanatory. Thomas must draw out the implications hidden within the statement, and he does this through his own study and consideration on the issue. By giving a rational explanation of the passage in the light of faith, he is in some way

---

36. See ST, II-II, q. 171, a.2, sc. and co., where Thomas refers directly to 2 Kgs and St. Gregory the Great's *On Ezekiel*, I, 1.

37. See ST, I, q. 1, a. 8, ad 2.

sharing in the knowledge and intention of its author, who in this case—since the passage is biblical—is principally the Holy Spirit and secondarily St. Paul.[38] One sees in this example how sacred doctrine functions as a kind of sharing both in God's knowledge and intention and the knowledge and intention of the saints that is mediated by faith and through concrete canonical texts, whose authors, especially in the case of sacred scripture, Thomas thinks, were prophets and apostles.

On this last point, we can recall that Question One states: "our faith is founded *on a revelation made to apostles and prophets, who wrote the canonical books*, not on a revelation, if there was any, made to other doctors."[39] Thomas indicates here that primacy within faith's foundation rests not on the canonical books, but on *the revelation* made to one set of individuals over another. It is not that canonical scripture is an unimportant or "unnecessary" aspect of Christian faith in Thomas's view; quite the contrary. Even with its diverse senses, he thinks scripture treats under its literal sense everything "necessary for faith."[40] It also is the primary source for Christian symbols and creeds.[41] There is, however, a deeper point that this passage highlights—a point that Thomas himself rarely articulated because it was so foundational to his approach to scripture in general; and that is, what is contained in scripture always depends on some prior revelation to prophets and apostles. While Thomas's own historico-critical analysis of the canonical books would by today's standards be considered primitive, he nevertheless places great importance on the underlying reality that animates scripture's historical and literal sense. He refers to this underlying reality whenever he appeals to the divine "authorship" of canonical scripture or to the apostles and prophets as human authors.

The framework that Thomas relies on to understand God's authorship of the Bible seems to draw heavily from his notion of revelation. Some scholars of the twentieth-century, as we have seen, have even tried to pin-point in Thomas's notion of prophetic revelation certain "principles" that could be developed into broader notions of divine authorship and scriptural inspiration.[42] The work of

---

38. See ST, I, q. 1, a. 10, co.: "auctor sacrae scripturae est Deus."

39. ST, I, q. 1, a. 8, ad 2: "innititur enim fides nostra *revelationi apostolis et prophetis factae, qui canonicos libros scripserunt*, non autem revelationi, si qua fuit aliis doctoribus facta" (emphasis mine).

40. ST, I, q. 1, a. 10, ad 1.

41. ST, II-II, q. 1, a. 9, obj. 1 and ad 1.

42. See Synave and Benoit, *Prophecy and Inspiration*; Benoit, *Inspiration and the Bible*.

these mainly Roman Catholic scholars cannot be evaluated fully in the context of this discussion, but it was a characteristic of many of them to introduce Thomas's treatment of prophetic revelation into late nineteenth- and early twentieth-century debates surrounding the theology of scriptural inspiration and revelation in general.[43] Prominent within these debates was a tendency to approach the notions of scripture and tradition dialectically, as if juxtaposed rather than as mutually interdependent. This framing of the interpretation of Thomas's questions on prophecy inevitably led to tensions between biblical inspiration and tradition, on the one hand, and between biblical inspiration and prophetic inspiration, on the other. These tensions proved difficult to resolve. In contrast to these later developments, Thomas himself never places scripture in tension with the notion of tradition—as embryonic as the latter may have been for him. For him, there is only one divine revelation that undergirds faith. The unity and primacy of faith serve as the most basic reality that underpins scripture, any notion of tradition, or prophetic revelation. Thus, the above statement from Question One illustrates how Thomas identifies the revelation made to the apostles and prophets and received as a sharing in divine knowledge—a knowledge that is ultimately reliant on the gift of faith—as the framework more "necessary" in sacred doctrine than any other framework that juxtaposes the canonical books and tradition. In stressing the primacy of "revelation" in the context of the virtue of faith, Thomas is identifying something that is not the equivalent to scripture. This "revelation" refers principally to the person and evangelical message of Jesus Christ in its entirety as given to his apostles and prophets and confirmed by the Holy Spirit.

A scholar like Per Erik Persson, however, who meticulously catalogued Thomas's pairings of *sacra doctrina* and *sacra scriptura* to argue persuasively for their near synonymity,[44] has given the impression that Thomas thought that "the

---

Benoit's attempt to discover such principles—if they existed at all—was animated largely by a desire to answer some of the challenges raised by nineteenth- and twentieth-century historical-critical biblical exegesis as it had a bearing on dogmatic theology.

43. For an overview, see Burtchaell, *Catholic Theories of Biblical Inspiration.*

44. Per Erik Persson, *Sacra doctrina: Reason and Revelation in Aquinas*, trans. Ross Mackenzie (Oxford: Basil Blackwell, 1970), 50: "Scripture is not to be identified with revelation." Persson makes it clear that he does not think Thomas ever conflates revelation and scripture. At the same time, he does not always clarify what it means for scripture to share the same formal object as the object of faith: "The content of the whole Bible is identified with the object of man's faith (ST, II-II, q. 2, a. 5)." He must mean here the Bible is a secondary material object of faith, but his sentence is ambiguous.

subject-matter both of theology and of scripture is subsumed under one and the same *objectum formale*, revealed truth," and this is what unifies the two.[45] He maintained that sacred doctrine and scripture for Thomas share a formal connection which relates to their content, writing:

> Scripture is an instruction in the revealed truth which is necessary for man's salvation [according to Thomas], and it was written *ad instructionem omnium futurorum*. This instruction, mediated by prophets and apostles, is transmitted within the church through the *doctrina* which is taught by the *doctores* of the church.... Hence in a formal sense there is a direct connection between revelation as the communication of knowledge and the continuing instruction of the church given by Thomas himself.[46]

The difficulty with Persson's analysis here is that he is somewhat vague about this "formal sense."[47] From his earlier statement, he has led us to think that both scripture and sacred doctrine are united because their subject-matter is revealed truth, even though Persson has not brought into sufficient relief the fact that the recognition of something as "revealed" depends on the virtue of faith for Thomas. His overall analysis at times pivots back-and-forth between, on the one hand, juxtaposing scripture and the theological notion of "tradition"—the dominant conceptual framework of much of the scholarship he is engaging during the 1950s—and, on the other, attempting to bring out Thomas's fundamental framework of sacred doctrine as an impression of the *scientia Dei et beatorum*.[48] This leaves some unresolved tensions in his book, which sometimes gives the impression that sacred doctrine is subordinated to scripture for Thomas, even though Persson appears to explicitly denies this.[49]

---

45. Persson, *Sacra doctrina*, 88.

46. Persson, *Sacra doctrina*, 88.

47. In support of this claim, he cites Jean-François Bonnefoy, *La nature de la théologie selon saint Thomas d'Aquin* (Paris: Vrin, 1939), 429.

48. Persson, *Sacra doctrina*, 89.

49. Persson, *Sacra doctrina*, 89: "Theology is not to be regarded here as an addition to scripture, nor a study which may be pursued independently of scripture: in Thomas's view it is rather the extension of scriptural teaching through the ages, the *traditio* of imparting doctrine which must always be found within the church. Since it is the content of scripture which is being transmitted, *sacra doctrina* and *sacra scriptura* may be used interchangeably as synonyms." This statement comes close to defining *traditio* solely in terms of scripture. Someone who admits to drawing heavily on Persson's study in order to understand Thomas's

The unhelpful framework that Persson repeatedly falls back into (perhaps inadvertently) is one where *sacra doctrina* is defined almost exclusively as "an extension of scriptural teaching." He does not clarify where the emphasis lies in "scriptural teaching," whether on the "scriptural" or on the "teaching." Lurking in the background of his analysis is a conceptual tension between scripture and teaching that is looking for resolution, but when trying to resolve it, Persson tends to stress one notion over the other. Overall, as we have seen, he tends mistakenly to stress the scriptural over the teaching; and he is not able to resolve this tension satisfactorily.

Nevertheless, Persson's study has introduced the critical first side of the coin, so to speak: sacred doctrine and scripture are used at times synonymously by Thomas. Sacred doctrine can be understood in one sense as "an extension of scriptural teaching," but there is yet another side to this coin. In addition to arguing for sacred doctrine's character as "an extension of scriptural teaching," it seems necessary to observe the limits of this conceptual model that seems only to go one way—that is, sacred doctrine is understood in terms of scripture. It may be necessary to acknowledge that Thomas's use of the word *sacra scriptura* is equally open to more flexibility than Persson was comfortable admitting. In his analysis, Persson puts the stress of Thomas's contrast between the revelation entrusted to apostles and prophets and the revelation—if any—given to doctors on the aspect of the former *being written down in the canonical books*. This emphasis on the "canonical books" may be overstressed for the sake of Persson's wider argument that seems at times to have been influenced by his perceived confessional commitments as a Swedish Lutheran. As a result, the impression is given that Thomas subordinated sacred doctrine to scripture as if the former derived its principles *as a science* from the latter. Rather than following Thomas's own distinction between the "authorities" of scripture and the doctors that

notion of revelation is Nicholas M. Healy, introduction to *Aquinas on Scripture*, ed. Weinandy, 1–20, at 14n36. Healy tends to read Thomas through Persson within a framework that juxtaposes scripture and tradition but without noticing the tensions in Persson's own analysis. Thus, Healy contends that "Thomas does not anticipate the later Roman Catholic doctrine of two sources of revelation, Scripture and Church tradition. Though he admits an oral apostolic tradition, this has no authority with regard to doctrine, but applies only to specific practices. Scripture alone is the basis of our faith, and of itself it gives us knowledge sufficient for our salvation, to which nothing new can be or need be added." He ends this by citing Persson, *Sacra doctrina*, 71–90. Healy's analysis neglects to notice how a statement like "Scripture alone is the basis of our faith" fails to adequately address faith's role in the formation of scripture itself and the historical development of the canon.

maps onto different types of inspiration,[50] Persson determines that the true structure of Thomas's thought lies in his understanding of what an inspired text is. His argument suggests that Thomas asserted a clear and firm hierarchy between sacred scripture and the writings of the doctors in sacred doctrine that was rooted in a prior distinction between inspired texts (=sacred scripture) and non-inspired texts (=the writings of the doctors, Fathers, liturgical texts). This reading, however, is determined more by Persson's earlier conceptual framework of scripture and tradition—a juxtaposition he admits he himself is trying to resolve and overcome—than by Thomas's consistent use.

Critically, Thomas's notion of *sacra scriptura* does not exclude the possibility that non-canonical texts can still in some way be "inspired." "Inspiration," as we have seen, for Thomas refers chiefly to a human mind's elevation through grace.[51] Only secondarily does "inspiration" denote the products of the inspired person—for example, a written text. Adriano Oliva in his historical study of Thomas's concept of *sacra doctrina* observes that the word *sacra scriptura* may in fact have had a much more expansive and dynamic meaning when it was employed in contexts dealing with *sacra doctrina*.[52] Allowing for the possibility of "a more dynamic relation" between scripture and sacred doctrine to exist in our understanding of Thomas's account may offer a helpful corrective to Persson's study.[53] Overall, his identification of sacred doctrine as an impression of the *scientia Dei et beatorum* seems to require the following acknowledgement:

---

50. ST, I, q. 1, a. 8, ad 2.

51. See ST, II-II, q. 171, a. 1, ad 4.

52. Adriano Oliva, "'*Doctrina*' et '*sacra doctrina*' chez Thomas d'Aquin," in *Vera doctrina: Zur Begriffsgeschichte der Lehre von Augustinus bis Descartes*, ed. P. Büttgen, R. Imbach, U. J. Schneider, and H. J. Selderhuis (Wiesbaden: Harrassowitz, 2009), 35–62, at 50: "the expression *sacred Scripture* does not designate only the books of the Bible, but embraces also their teaching, their doctrine, and its own foundation: divine revelation. What is fundamental for comprehending this conception of sacred doctrine, or of theology, according to Thomas Aquinas is precisely its own relation with divine revelation and, ultimately, with God Himself."

53. Oliva, "'*Doctrina*' et '*sacra doctrina*,'" 55. It seems that in trying to make the case that *sacra doctrina* and *sacra scriptura* are synonyms for Thomas—an argument that has persuasive elements—Persson limits his attention too much to defining the terms and probing their usage. Even though he asserts the unity of sacred doctrine and scripture at the level of content and even some shared formality, he does not pinpoint satisfactorily their formal differences, which would require a deeper analysis of Thomas's understanding of faith. When it is clear that he must assert that they are different, Persson has the tendency to fall back into considering sacred doctrine under the rubric of scripture—almost as if scripture constituted the principles of sacred doctrine.

that Thomas allows the hermeneutic of faith to shape, form, and underpin any hermeneutic of the biblical text.

The view, pace Persson, that Thomas ascribes primacy to the revelation made to prophets and apostles over any notion of the inspiration of canonical scripture gains added plausibility in the light of what Thomas says elsewhere about the New Law: "the New Law is principally a law inscribed on the heart [*lex indita*]; secondarily it is a written law."[54] The point of this side-discussion has not been to resolve all the problems that relate to Thomas's views on scriptural inspiration and its relationship to prophecy, but rather to suggest a reframing of the issue. Questions about Thomas's purported "scriptural theology" or his usage of authorities (whether scriptural or other Christian writers) should be posed more along the line of a framework of sharing or participation in supernatural knowledge. Human participation in divine knowledge is a central feature not only of Thomas's accounts of faith and sacred doctrine, but also, as we have seen, of prophecy. It is under this rubric of a sharing in divine knowledge that Thomas understands the inspiration and interpretation of scripture: "the interpretation of words can be reduced to the gift of prophecy."[55]

We have seen that by starting from a scriptural authority Thomas's rational explanation of prophetic knowledge itself becomes assimilated to sacred doctrine. In trying to explain prophecy further he is already being led by the intention of the inspired authority. In a certain way, Thomas allows himself here to be instructed by the biblical text, in a way that is analogous to how prophets allow themselves to be taught by God under the light of prophecy. One of the key differences here is that prophets need the transient light; Thomas needs at least the light of faith as a stable *habitus* in him. When any intellectual light inheres in a person as something permanent as in the case of faith's light, it perfects the intellect "chiefly so that the principle [or source] of those things which are manifested through that light may be known."[56] For example, under the natural light of reason, the human intellect comes to know the first principles, which the natural light manifests. Under the supernatural light of prophecy, Thomas says that the intellect sees by virtue of a supernatural first principle which is "God Himself"—*ipse Deus.*

---

54. ST, I-II, q. 106, a. 1, co.: "principaliter nova lex est lex indita, secundario autem est lex scripta."

55. ST, II-II, q. 176, a. 2, ad 4: "interpretatio sermonum potest reduci ad donum prophetiae."

56. ST, II-II, q. 171, a. 2, co.

If prophets are united to this supernatural first principle (even transiently), does it follow that they see God's essence? Thomas thinks not. The vision of God *per essentiam* is reserved for the beatific vision enjoyed already by the saints in heaven, "in whom this same light dwells in the manner of a permanent and perfect form."[57] Were prophecy a *habitus*, prophets would continually have access to the source of their supernatural knowledge as something seen; in other words, they would "see" the divine essence. This, however, he notes, does not seem to fit the accounts of the biblical prophets. Thomas gives this question of prophecy's nonequivalence to the beatific vision a fuller treatment in a later article.[58] In the intervening articles, he reiterates his denial that prophecy raises someone to a vision of God's essence. The fact that this denial arises so early on in his articles on prophecy's essence indicates just how much Thomas relies on the notion of the beatific vision to clarify his understanding of what prophetic knowledge is and is not.

If prophetic light does not exist permanently in prophets, Thomas must offer another explanation for how prophetic light dwells in them. Instead of being something permanent, prophetic light exists in a person in the manner of "a passion or transient impression."[59] Thomas thinks the metaphor of light existing in the air is useful for illustrating this. Air does not retain the light that shines through it; once the light source is extinguished or impeded, the air instantly becomes invisible or dark. Just as air always needs "new illumination" to be visible, so also "a prophet's mind always requires new revelation; similarly, a student, not yet adept at the principles of his art, needs to be instructed about individual things."[60] At this point, Thomas introduces another metaphor we have encounter already: the teacher and the student, which itself echoes a theme of sacred doctrine in Question One. This classroom metaphor draws out how instruction in individual things must be used at the earliest stages of education because students are still unfamiliar with a given discipline and do not yet possess its principles. Thomas likens prophecy to the kind of instruction in individual things that precedes a student's acquisition of the principles of a discipline or science.

The light metaphor emphasizes Thomas's point that while prophecy involves a perfection of the intellect, it is a type of perfection that does not rely on a permanent form being given to a person. From this (human) point of view,

---

57. ST, II-II, q. 171, a. 2, co.

58. ST, II-II, q. 173, a. 1.

59. ST, II-II, q. 171, a. 2, co.

60. ST, II-II, q. 171, a. 2, co.

prophecy is supremely contingent; it cannot be called up at will or predicted but relies solely on the divine will. The second metaphor of the teacher instructing students in singulars helps us see how Thomas models prophecy along the lines of the acquisition of scientific knowledge. In this respect, it highlights especially the function of the teacher whose ultimate aim is to help students acquire the firsts principles of disciplines. The teacher accomplishes this gradually through the medium of individual things that are better known and more familiar to the students. In this way, Thomas sees prophecy as particularly adapted to the natural way of human knowing.

Through this second metaphor, Thomas simultaneously permits us to draw another link between prophecy and the acquisition of the virtue of faith. Just as instruction in individual things is ordered to students' acquiring a more stable and permanent knowledge of higher scientific principles, so also prophecy—as something transient—is ordered to the acquisition of the more stable (but equally supernatural) *habitus* of faith. Prophets, like the students, receive knowledge gradually and piecemeal through singulars. The most important of these singulars become faith's *credenda*. While these singulars are not identical with God, they are ordered toward manifesting the principle of prophecy, God, and are preparatory for the act of faith and for the consummation of this act in the beatific vision, just as being taught individual topics in geometry is preparatory for students acquiring the discrete *scientia* of geometry.

Thomas also uses this image of the teacher instructing in singulars to interpret passages in scripture where God is described as speaking directly with prophets. When scripture says that the "word" or "hand" of the Lord was upon a prophet, this "way of speaking" (*modus loquendi*), he says, is meant to designate someone as a prophet and to assert that "God spoke to such-and-such a prophet."[61] These scriptural passages offer examples of the kind of instruction in singular things that Thomas is speaking about. Expressions like God's "word" and "hand" are not meant to be interpreted literally; they are said to be "upon" a prophet as a way of designating prophecy, accomplishing the same task as other expressions such as "the Lord spoke" to such-and-such a prophet. These biblical images do not teach that God has a body with a mouth and hands, but rather these bodily objects convey some aspect of God's power and presence, just as a teacher's individual example of a circle or triangle is meant to convey to students deeper geometric principles.

---

61. ST, II-II, q. 171, a. 2, co.

Q. 171, a. 3—Prophecy and Future Contingents: Prophecy's Unity Revisited

Having established that prophecy is not a *habitus*, but a transient passion or impression, Thomas begins to address in greater detail what exactly this is a transient impression of in the third article. He does not ask this question directly; instead, he frames his discussion around prophecy's object(s) and whether prophecy is exclusively about future contingents. This framing of the question provides him the occasion to extend his inquiry into what properly determines the category of prophecy: the prophetic light, which unifies all prophetic phenomena.

Thomas calls this light, prophecy's "formal light." Already in his earlier disputed question *De veritate* on prophecy (q. 12), he resists restricting prophecy to future contingents, even though he admits future contingents are still the "most proper" objects of prophetic knowledge due to their remoteness from the ordinary objects of human natural knowledge.[62] In the *Summa theologiae*, his mind does not change. To explain why he thinks prophecy cannot be limited to future contingents, he returns to the light of prophecy. Based on a consideration of the prophetic light alone, he thinks it is already apparent that things other than future contingents can be known prophetically.

Nevertheless, Thomas is well aware of the venerable and authoritative theological tradition that tends to associate prophecy exclusively with future events. Cassiodorus's definition of prophecy looms large here; it came to Thomas most likely through Peter Lombard's *Sentences*: "prophecy is an inspiration or divine revelation announcing the occurrence of things with immovable truth."[63] According to this definition, knowledge of future "occurrences" and of contingent facts is prophecy's proper object. Thomas, wanting to respect the witness of a Christian authority like Cassiodorus, does not reject this definition; instead, he tries to harmonize this traditional definition and interpretation with a broader taxonomy based on light. To bridge the divide between these two taxonomies, Thomas deploys a third, albeit weaker model based on the relative distance of prophecy's material objects from the objects of natural human knowledge. According to this third model, future contingents make up a class of objects that are most remote from our natural knowledge; in fact, he maintains that future contingents in themselves are strictly unknowable to human beings through natural reason because they do not exist:

---

62. *De ver.*, q. 12, a. 1, co.
63. ST, II-II, q. 171, a. 3, obj.1.

> In themselves future contingents are remote from human knowledge.
> They are not knowable because they lack being [*ab esse deficiant*]; they
> neither exist in themselves nor are determined in their causes.[64]

Future contingents are only knowable with certitude by God who knows them
in se and who can reveal them to prophets.[65] Explaining this third taxonomy
based on distance—which he feels comfortable deploying based on St. Isidore
of Seville's (now dubious) etymology of "prophecy" as deriving from *procul*
and *phanos* (meaning "appearing at a distance")—Thomas says that "since
prophecy is about those things which are far from our knowledge [*procul a
nostra cognitione*], the further things stand away from human knowledge the
more they pertain to prophecy."[66] By appealing to this principle of distance for
classification, he tries to reconcile Cassiodorus's definition—with its explicit
singling out of future contingents as the "most proper" (*propriissime*) objects of
prophetic knowledge—and his preferred taxonomy based on prophetic light.[67]

To accomplish this, Thomas must go beyond future contingents and a
simple identification of the material objects of prophecy. He seeks ultimately
to unite the various things called "prophecy" not by their material objects, but
by the mode these objects are prophetically known. He, thus, can qualify the
earlier definition: "the 'occasions of things' are posited in prophecy's definition
as its maximally proper material, but not so that it makes up prophecy's total
material."[68] Doing this brings to the forefront prophecy's formal object—the
prophetic light—which extends well beyond future contingents and is what
unifies the various material objects of prophecy under one category.[69]

---

64. *De ver.*, q. 12, a. 2, co.: "ex parte quidem ipsorum sunt procul futura contingentia,
quae per hoc non cognoscibilia sunt, quod ab esse deficiunt, cum nec in se sint, nec in causis
suis determinentur."

65. See ST, I, q. 14, a. 13, co. Thomas's key point is that God knows future contingents
neither contingently nor temporally, but absolutely "as if in the present [*ut praesens*] ... as
when I see Socrates sitting down."

66. ST, II-II, q. 171, a. 3, co. For Thomas's adaptation of Isidore's etymology, see *De ver.*,
q. 12, a. 1, co.; see *Isidori Hispalensis Episcopi Etymologiarum sive Originum Libri XX*, ed. W.
M. Lindsay (Oxford: Clarendon Press, 1911), VII, c. 8, 1–40. Compare ST, II-II, q. 171, a. 1,
co. See also Torrell, *Question XII: La prophétie*, 30n2.

67. ST, II-II, q. 171, a. 3, co.

68. *De ver.*, q. 12, a. 2, ad 1.

69. ST, II-II, q. 171, a. 2, ad 3: "The formal element in prophetic knowledge is the divine
light. From the unity of this light, prophecy has its specific unity, even though there are various
things that are manifested prophetically through the divine light."

The centrality of light in this taxonomy introduces yet another avenue by which we can see how Thomas considers prophecy, faith, and human natural knowledge along a type of continuum. In all three cases, some intellectual light is the formal object. The image of light thus allows him to move back-and-forth between the natural light of reason and the supernatural lights of prophecy, faith, and glory with some conceptual clarity. This analogically based back-and-forth between natural and supernatural lights also structures his understanding of sacred doctrine. Because prophetic light has God as its proximate and principal cause and God knows everything through His own divine light, Thomas concludes that by the light of prophecy "everything can be known: both divine and human things, both spiritual and corporeal things."[70] The diversity of material objects does not determine the scope of prophecy; instead, the formal object is determinative. Because prophecy's formal object can extend to everything, prophetic revelation can also potentially extend to everything. Analogously, Thomas thinks sacred doctrine can share in this universal scope through its own formal object: "sacred doctrine, being one, can consider things that are treated in the different philosophical sciences under one aspect, namely, insofar as they are divinely revealable [*divinitus revelabilia*]."[71]

In sum, while Thomas still affirms the traditional, restricted definition of prophecy as relating to future contingents, he at no point ever limits prophetic revelation exclusively to these. The more operative sense of prophecy is for him one that refers not to the material objects of prophetic knowledge but to its formal object: the light of prophecy. He defends the view that there is one sense of "prophecy" that fits for all things that fall under the description of something visible under the prophetic light—a *prophetabilium*. This formal-object-oriented sense makes it clear that prophecy refers chiefly not to the material objects prophets know, but more to the light of prophecy, which holds the category together.

Thomas's Prophetic Taxonomy: A Consideration of His Method

Had Thomas limited prophecy's object to future events alone, he could have defined prophecy exclusively along the lines of its content. While this categorization is conceptually very neat and tidy, Thomas observes that both scripture

---

70. ST, II-II, q. 171, a. 2, co.
71. ST, I, q. 1, a. 3, ad 2.

and authorities like St. Gregory the Great attest to prophets knowing things other than future contingents: Genesis gives an account of the creation of the world (a past event); Isaiah (Is 6:1) reports having a theophanic vision (an event that cannot be called "future"); he also (Is 58:7) advises to break bread with the hungry (an admonition concerning present moral conduct). From the witness of scripture alone, Thomas knows he cannot limit his taxonomy of prophecy to future contingents, or even focus too much on them. Many different objects are prophetically knowable; in fact, when pressed, he concludes that everything is prophetically knowable in principle.

This conclusion immediately raises some difficulties. In opening up prophecy's object to things other than future contingents, Thomas must now show how these diverse objects can be understood to belong to a single category or phenomenon called "prophecy." This methodological dilemma is noteworthy, since, elsewhere in the *Summa theologiae*, Thomas chooses to distinguish human acts chiefly by their objects. The fact that prophecy can extend to any knowable object means that this method is no longer a viable option for identifying prophecy's essence. If he were to follow the classification scheme of defining prophecy by its different objects, then any claim that prophecy is unified would be doubtful. The different objects of prophetic knowledge would imply that for each new set of objects there would be a different type of prophecy altogether: one prophecy about future events, another about present events, another about past events, and so forth. The result would be a proliferation of prophetic genera, while still falling short of a generic definition of prophecy—the aim of inquiring into something's "essence." More critically, Thomas realizes he cannot employ this material-object-based taxonomy if he wants to maintain the unity of divine revelation—that is, the claim that there is one unified reality understood to be divine revelation, which in turn underpins the unity of the theological virtue of faith.[72] Motivated more by a desire to preserve the unity of faith than by any rationalistic penchant for generic definitions or distinctions, Thomas distinguishes the object or content of prophecy by the way revealed objects come to be received in a prophet's mind via the formal object of "prophetic light." It is in the *lumen propheticum* that Thomas pinpoints the reality that unifies all prophetic knowledge and determines the essence of prophecy.[73] The remaining articles of Question 171 all revolve around this central insight.

---

72. On the unity of the faith through the course of history, see especially ST, II-II, q. 2, a. 7; q. 4, a. 6.

73. ST, II-II, q. 171, a. 3, ad 3.

Q. 171, a. 4—Do Prophets Know Everything That Can Be Prophesied?

With the centrality of its formal light established, Thomas next asks whether someone, upon receiving prophetic light, knows all the material objects of prophecy—that is, everything that can be prophetically known (*prophetabilia*). The article's first objection allows him to address the question of why God reveals only a limited amount of knowledge to prophets and not the fullness of divine knowledge. Firstly, God does not reveal all His knowledge because this would mean the prophet sees the divine essence. God's knowledge is identical with His essence, and to possess fully God's knowledge would be comparable to seeing the divine essence. But this does not happen with prophets.[74] Excluding this possibility in the response, Thomas looks at why God chooses to reveal only "parts" of His knowledge to prophets:

> The Lord reveals to prophets all the things that are necessary for the instruction of the faithful people.[75]

Here we witness again how deeply the exigencies of salvation structure Thomas's thinking about the content of prophecy's instruction; this structuring was seen in his notion of sacred doctrine as well. To bring about salvation, God does not give prophetic knowledge to all. God gives some of it to one, some of it to another. As was suggested earlier, this piecemeal bestowing of knowledge onto prophets is best understood as an exercise of divine government that has a care for the salvation of all human beings and that adapts divine revelation to the natural mode of human knowing, which is equally piecemeal and rooted in history.

Earlier in his *De veritate* question, Thomas explicitly connects the "limitation" (*arctatio*) of prophetic knowledge with divine wisdom:

> This limiting does not come from an impotency in the giver, but *from the order of [God's] wisdom*, which distributes to individuals as He wills.[76]

---

74. See ST, II-II, q. 173, a. 1, where Thomas treats this directly.

75. ST, II-II, q. 171, a. 4, ad 1.

76. *De ver.*, q. 12, a. 1, ad 5: "haec autem arctatio non provenit ex impotentia largientis, sed *ex ordine sapientiae ipsius*, qui dividit singulis prout vult" (emphasis mine).

God guides his people in everything that they require for salvation. This exhibits His sapiential nature, which is participated in by prophecy and sacred doctrine. Nevertheless, prophets receive everything necessary to teach the people about the gift of faith. God shows forth or "proves" this promise in the very act of choosing prophets whose gifts are meant to edify the Church:

> In everything that acts for an end [*propter finem*], the matter is determined by the exigency of the end [*exigentiam finis*], as shown in *Physics* II,15. The gift of prophecy is given for the utility of the Church, as is clear from 1 Cor 12.... Thus, everything, the knowledge of which can be useful for salvation, is matter for prophecy, whether it be of the past, present, or future or eternal, necessary or contingent. Those things which cannot pertain to our salvation fall outside the matter of prophecy.[77]

Here Thomas asserts a strong connection between prophets and those individuals who teach the things necessary for saving faith. At the same time, he reminds us just how robust the controlling force of the final end—as determined in faith—is for prophecy. For intellectual creatures—"things that act *propter finem*"—the matter is determined by the end or final cause. In this case, Thomas identifies "the good of the Church" as the end of prophecy. This end is identical with the ordering of the theological virtues, given that faith is what draws and incorporates one into the Church and charity moves one to seek its good. Prophecy's material objects are in fact determined essentially by the needs of the Church as historically constituted. From this observation, a further connection to sacred doctrine becomes visible. In treating things that relate to the Christian religion founded on faith, sacred doctrine determines its "matter" by the final end as it is divinely revealed in faith. This means that sacred doctrine's very existence is determined and shaped by the exigencies of salvation and especially the need to instruct the faithful of the Church.

Thomas has the added occasion in this article to compare the relative perfections and defects found in prophets. It seems that limiting prophetic knowledge to only a particular set of things could be perceived as an imperfection compared to the perfection of the divine mind. Because Thomas's notion of prophecy is oriented by its end (*propter finem*), this imperfection is not truly an imperfection in prophecy's functioning. What is more important is that

---

77. *De ver.*, q. 12, a. 2, co.

prophecy does not fail with respect to what it is specifically ordered to, and that is to instruct the faithful people of God. Prophecy, in fact, is said to be "perfect" or "imperfect" relative to how well it serves the needs of the Church; and the most pressing need of the faithful, Thomas thinks, is to be instructed in things as they relate to eternal salvation—the final end. These things include everything that we saw enumerated by Thomas earlier in the prologue to the questions on prophecy: things to be believed in faith, the mysteries of faith (a specification of what faith is ordered to), the discernment of spirits, and the direction of human actions and morals. Thus, it is prophecy's orientation to the final end and more specifically its orientation to faith that is structurally reiterated here in prophetic knowledge's "limitation." This helps us to see more clearly how Thomas's understanding of prophecy is primarily *functional*; it is governed principally by what it is ordered to: supernatural knowledge of God that is conducive to inducing others to faith and incorporation into the Church, which will assist them on their pilgrim journey to the common good of all creation, eternal salvation.

This article's third objection leads us back to reflect on the relationship between principles known by reason and the principle of prophecy. The objection tries to draw on a comparison between prophetic light and the light of reason. In raising this objection, Thomas wants to distinguish the different relationships *scientia* and prophecy have relative to their respective principles. Someone who has a *scientia* knows everything that pertains to that science. The grammarian, for instance, knows everything that pertains to grammar (*omnia grammaticalia*). Thomas agrees, but he also sees the need for a distinction. To say that a person "possesses a *scientia*" entails, he thinks, that one knows the principles of that *scientia*. Everything in the *scientia* depends on these principles. Thus, to say that someone has "the *habitus* of a certain *scientia*" means precisely that that person knows the principles of that *scientia* and thereby "knows all the things that pertain to that *scientia*." Prophecy, however, cannot be said to relate to its principle in exactly the same way. Prophets do not know "in itself the principle of the things that can be known prophetically," the divine light; and so the comparison breaks down, given that prophets do not see the fullness of divine light.[78]

Here we see how Thomas's understanding of *scientia* helps to clarify the difference between natural and supernatural modes of knowing. What makes something a *prophetablium* is its direct connection to one thing—the principle

---

78. ST, II-II, q. 171, a. 4, ad 3.

of prophetic knowledge. To illustrate this point further, he gives the example of how the different virtues all depend on prudence (for the moral virtues) and charity to function. Each of the virtues is connected and depends on one virtue as the keystone. For the intellectual virtues, all the things that are known through some principle are connected to that principle. A helpful image here is that of the central axle of a wheel and the spokes coming out of the axle to make the wheel's frame. The central axle is the basis for all the connections at the disparate points on the wheel's frame. In a similar way, everything that a person knows in a given *scientia* (the various points on the wheel's frame) depends on a single principle (the axle). Someone who knows the principle "perfectly according to its total power" (*secundum totam eius virtutem*) knows simultaneously all the things that are known through that principle. Someone who perfectly knows the principles of geometry can be said to know simultaneously everything that is treated in geometry—all the conclusions that follow from those principles. Thomas thinks that principles contain virtually all the conclusions that rely on those principles.

With this model in mind, Thomas shifts to the case where the common principle of knowledge is either unknown or only "perceived generally" (*communiter apprehenso*). In the latter case where there is only a general knowledge of the common principle of knowing, "there is no need to know everything at once." With the principle itself not completely comprehended and known, there is strictly speaking "no need," because the conclusions cannot follow necessarily. Instead of knowing everything that follows from the common principle, "each one of these things [that is, the things following from the common principle] must be made manifest" individually. The example of the teacher and the student again illustrates this point. While Thomas does not directly invoke it here (his argument is moving too quickly), it appears to be in the background. The teacher is the one who perfectly possesses the common principle of the subject being taught. The student only knows the common principle of the subject generally. At the beginning of a given course of study, students do not know the whole subject; they gradually come to know it, at first vaguely and then in a fuller sense as the teacher begins to introduce the different parts of the subject individually. The teacher does not immediately present the students with the common principle of the subject; this would be ineffective. The students need to be lead piecemeal to allow them to build up a cognitive *habitus* that relates all the different parts of a subject back to a common principle. All the while, the specific aim of the teacher is not to instill the individual parts of the subject (this is incidental to the educative aim), but to foster the inherence of the common principle of the subject in the student. Only when the students have the common principle *in themselves*, will they be able to know and judge *for themselves* a subject's truths. Without the principle inhering in them, students can only take things on the authority of their teacher; for natural knowledge, this is not truly knowing, but opinion. Similarly, since prophets do not possess habitually the principle of their prophetic knowledge (God as First Truth), their prophetic knowledge remains limited and dependent entirely on divine authority. This limitation points to prophecy's completion in the lights of faith and glory.

Thomas denies that even those enjoying the beatific vision already—the saints and good angels in heaven—see and know *everything* that can be known through God in the light of glory.[79] The saints fully possess God as the common principle of their knowledge, and everything they know they know through Him. Nevertheless, they still do not comprehend God's essence, not understanding it in the same way God understands Himself. Since God's power is infinite, the blessed cannot comprehend completely His power (*virtus*) to know. Seen in comparison to the light of glory, this limitation of prophetic knowledge—of the *prophetabilia*—can be rooted in the basic metaphysical structure that is inscribed in all created intellects. In the final analysis, the distinction between knowing a limited amount of things and knowing everything that can be known is rooted in the prior distinction between the created and the divine nature; it reflects God's absolute incomprehensibility expressed in terms of a creaturely limitation.[80]

Conclusion

Prophecy's formal object—the light of prophecy—is the key reality for Thomas that distinguishes prophetic knowledge from other types of knowledge, whether natural or supernatural. Among the types of supernatural knowing, it is precisely at the level of the formal object that prophecy shares a common principle with faith and an indirect principle with sacred doctrine. Prophecy and faith share the same formal object: God as First Truth. Sacred doctrine strictly speaking does not have this identical formal object; nevertheless, it does require the light

---

79. ST, I, q. 12, a. 8, sc.: "Non ergo quicumque vident Dei essentiam, vident omnia."
80. See ST, I, q. 12, a. 7.

of faith to be operative in a person for its scientific structure to exist. In all three types of supernatural knowing, the formal object is each held differently: in prophecy, transiently; in faith, habitually; and in sacred doctrine, habitually through an interaction between the natural light of reason and the light of faith.

While three formal objects exist differently in the human person, they all share a common ordering to the beatific vision. Juxtaposing the relative imperfection of prophecy with "the perfection of divine revelation" that exists in the blessed in heaven, Thomas sees divine revelation existing along a single continuum.[81] On this continuum, prophecy exists "as something imperfect in the genus of divine revelation."[82] The giving of the light of prophecy does not entail the complete reception of the principle of knowledge that stands behind divine revelation, but rather the reception of a new kind of light that establishes a new type of relationship with God's knowledge and, thus, with God Himself. Part of this new relationship from the prophet's perspective is a fuller partaking in God's own knowledge and intentions, if only transiently.

An essential aspect of God's intentional knowledge is that it is ordered to the good of creation. By partaking in this aspect of divine knowledge, prophets are oriented toward the good of creation and are called to communicate the knowledge God has given them to others and use it for the good of the Church. By sharing this knowledge, the prophet is not simply bestowing knowledge, but sharing knowledge in order to share with others a new relationship with God. When we say that prophets "share" their knowledge with others, it is perhaps more accurate to say that they "attempt to share." Prophets only act as instrumental causes when transmitting their knowledge to others; they cannot cause the light of prophecy or faith to exist in those they meet and speak to. They can only speak external words and perform external actions in the hope that God illuminates interiorly the minds of their listeners. Incidentally, Thomas thinks this story is exactly the same for the human teacher who attempts to share natural knowledge, with the exception that the natural light need not be supernaturally given seeing that it already exists in the student.[83]

The inner illumination given by God to those who hear the testimony of prophets and grasp it as something divinely revealed is *not* the light of prophecy. It is still a supernatural light, but it exists in a listener under a different mode—

---

81. ST, II-II, q. 171, a. 4, ad 2.

82. ST, II-II, q. 171, a. 4, ad 2.

83. ST, I, q. 117, a. 1; *De ver.*, q. 11.

the light of faith. In this way, the content of prophecy functions as a material cause in the act of faith—providing believers with the testimonial content that guides them to assent to other propositions concerning their ultimate end. In a restricted sense, prophets also function as an *exemplary cause* insofar as they can cause (instrumentally) something similar to the type of relationship they have with God in those who listen to them and accept the light of faith.[84] Thomas often characterizes this relationship between the prophet and God as a kind of "teaching" (*doctrina*): "prophecy is a kind of knowledge from divine revelation impressed on a prophet's intellect *in the manner of a kind of teaching.*"[85]

In receiving the supernatural light of prophecy, prophets come to receive it as a kind of "impression" (*impressio*) or "passion" (*passio*).[86] In comparing prophecy to a passion, Thomas indicates that prophets are the ones being acted upon in the first instance. This does not, however, leave them to become mere puppets of the divine will. Even before the gift of prophecy is given, God is already causing the human person to exist, to live, and to know. With the gift of prophecy, God strengthens and intensifies a person's already existing natural light of reason by adding a new supernatural light. This new prophetic light strengthens and assists the natural light of reason, allowing the mind of the prophet to see more clearly the truths that God wants to be seen.

In many instances and especially in those recounted in scripture, the reception of the light of prophecy becomes a transformative experience for the individuals who receive it;[87] all the same, it does not change their nature. Prophets still remain morally fallible.[88] This is because the prophetic light does not directly affect the will's orientation to or away from God as final end. While they do not choose to receive prophetic light, prophets can still act freely with respect to how they use the knowledge they have come to gain; they can even use it immorally, or not all.

---

84. In fact, the relationship between God and the believer is superior to that between God and the prophet in the order of love or charity, which is the ultimate measure of merit. In the order of knowledge, however, the prophet knows more than the simple believer. It is in the order of knowledge that we properly describe prophets as "exemplary causes" of belief.

85. ST, II-II, q. 171, a. 6, co.: "prophetia est quaedam cognitio intellectui prophetae impressa ex revelatione divina *per modum cuiusdam doctrinae*" (emphasis mine).

86. ST, II-II, q. 171, a. 2, co.

87. See Abraham Joshua Heschel, *The Prophets* (New York: Harper Collins, 2001), 3–31.

88. ST, II-II, q. 172, a. 4.

Can prophecy's supernatural element now be isolated and identified? When pressed, Thomas points to the prophetic light. And what precisely makes prophetic knowledge supernatural? In calling knowledge "supernatural," we can identify two chief things that are meant to be conveyed. First, "supernatural" refers to the mode of knowing; this means to know something through the light of prophecy rather than through the natural light of reason. Second, "supernatural" can also refer to the object known; a "supernatural" object is an object that cannot be known through natural reason. Thomas considers our knowledge of the mysteries of Christian faith, like God being Trinity, to fall into this category. Prophetic knowing is always supernatural in mode and sometimes supernatural in object.

The supernatural "instruction" that prophets receive contributes to prophecy's certitude.[89] For prophets, certitude is not something confirmed by a further external sign or demonstration; they do not require any confirmation. God has communicated to them personally through angelic messengers.[90] Sometimes the angels announce or make known their presence, sometimes not. In either case, the divine testimony that they communicate is infallible, just as much as divine knowledge and truth are infallible. Thomas thinks this certitude extends in many cases to the prophet's own subjective certitude. He illustrates this through the example of Abraham's obedience to the prophetic message he received to offer his son Isaac as a sacrifice (Gn 22). Upon learning God's command, Abraham does not ask for any further sign. He accepts it in complete certitude, since it comes from God, who cannot lie.[91] The patriarch's obedient example, Thomas thinks, functions as a "sign" for us of prophecy's certitude. We do not experience Abraham's subjective psychological certitude directly ourselves, but we can experience a type of certitude—mediated through the sign of Abraham's actions and the light of faith—that shares in his certitude as it is caused by God's truth and is itself a participation in divine knowledge. In this way, the certitude of prophecy contributes partially to the certitude of faith. If prophecy were not certain, then "faith," Thomas says, "which is founded on the things prophets have said, would not be certain."[92]

---

89. ST, II-II, q. 171, a.5, co. and a. 6.

90. Thomas thinks all prophetic revelation is communicated to humans by angels; see ST, II-II, q. 172, a. 2, co.

91. ST, II-II, q. 171, a. 5, co.: "et signum propheticae certitudinis accipere possumus ex hoc quod Abraham, admonitus in prophetica visione, se praeparavit ad filium unigenitum immolandum, quod nullatenus fecisset nisi de divina revelatione fuisset certissimus."

92. ST, II-II, q. 171, a. 5, co.: "De his ergo quae expresse per spiritum prophetiae

By way of summary, we have encountered four main features of Thomas's notion of prophecy so far:

(1) Others share in the certitude of prophecy through the theological virtue of faith where they assent to the message of prophets as seen under the light of faith.

(2) Prophecy, in its proper sense, has a supernatural cause, which is God as First Truth; its formal object is the light of prophecy, which exists only transiently in prophets.

(3) As a gratuitous grace that relates principally to knowledge, prophecy does not entail necessarily the possession of charity or good morals; it is oriented to the common good of the Church.

(4) Prophecy as a notion is functional; it is governed principally by what it is ordered to. It is supernatural knowledge of God that is conducive to inducing faith and promoting salvation through incorporation in the Church.

---

propheta, cognoscit, maximam certitudinem habet, et pro certo habet quod haec sibi sunt divinitus revelata.... Alioquin, si de hoc ipse certitudinem non haberet, *fides, quae dictis prophetarum innititur, certa non esset*" (emphasis mine).

5

Prophetic Knowledge, Judgment, and Wisdom's Ordering to Salvation

Now that the central importance of prophecy's formal light as its essence and cause in Thomas's account is in view, it remains to explore how this light operates in the prophet's mind. On this score, the prophet's act of judgment is decisive, just as much as it is for his account of natural knowledge. The thrust of his analysis of prophetic judgment takes its starting point from Question 173—on the manner (*de modo*) of prophetic knowledge—"the speculative heart of the treatise" according to Jean-Pierre Torrell, who parses the question's four articles into two equal parts.[1] The first part explores "the medium" of prophetic knowledge. Is prophetic knowledge received in the same way as the vision of the divine essence (a. 1)? Does it require the introduction of new mental representations (*species*), or can it happen through an influx of prophetic light alone (a. 2)? The second half looks at the psychology of prophetic knowledge from the point of view of prophets themselves.[2] Do prophets always experience alienation from their bodily senses in prophetic revelation (a. 3)? Are they always conscious of the full meaning of their prophecies (a. 4)?

Torrell's claim that these four articles make up the "speculative heart" of Thomas's theory of prophecy is based largely on his research into the history of twelfth- and thirteenth-century scholastic debates on prophecy. From the

---

1. Torrell, *Somme théologique, la prophétie*, 60*.

2. See Jean Richard, "Le processus psychologique de la révélation prophétique selon saint Thomas d'Aquin," *Laval théologique et philosophique* 23, no. 1 (1967): 42–75.

historian's point of view, Question 173 touches upon some of the hotly debated and weighty topics of the early thirteenth-century theological schools: the mode of knowing in the beatific vision, the status of divine ideas and whether prophets have access to them, the role of bodily senses in human knowledge (a question of increasing prominence thanks in part to the rediscovery and new Latin translations of portions of the *Corpus Aristotelicum*), and the role of images and judgment in human knowledge. In contrast to Torrell, our aim here is not to present a historical overview of these thirteenth-century debates; there are already a number of specialized studies that adequately do so.[3] My objective in this chapter adheres to our general method of tracing out these topics so as to discern the structural dependencies between sacred doctrine and prophecy in Thomas's thought and their implications.

Pivotally, his brief but seminal treatment of prophetic judgment brings to light an important structural link with Thomas's earlier distinction from Question One where sacred doctrine is said to be able to judge the principles of other sciences "from knowledge" rather than "from inclination." This in turn will enable us to identify prophecy as a kind of knowledge from inclination and sacred doctrine as one from judgment. Rather than starkly contrasting these two types of knowledge and judgment, Thomas sees them as appealing in complimentary ways to the two principles that lie at the heart of all human action: the intellect and will. This distinction will enable us to see the full integration of prophecy within Thomas's moral reflection in sacred doctrine through a comparison between it and judgments made under the influence of wisdom as a gift of the Holy Spirit and as a gratuitous grace.

Thomas and Judgment

Thomas's account of the act of judgment has received substantial scholarly attention in the twentieth century. Benoit Garceau's lexicographical study is particularly helpful in tracing out how the word *iudicium* and similar words relating to judgment were deployed in his *Summa* and other writings.[4] This is helpful, not least of all because his writings on judgment are scattered throughout his corpus.[5] On its own, the subtly of Thomas's notion of judgment

---

3. See our discussion in the Introduction.

4. For the relevant bibliography, see Benoit Garceau, *Judicium: Vocabulaire, sources, doctrine de Saint Thomas d'Aquin* (Montreal: Institut d'Études Médiévales, 1968), 259–64.

5. While the subject of judgment is treated in many places by Thomas, the question on

merits specialist attention, which is why in in our own analysis we feel justified in relying heavily on Garceau's study which prioritizes close attention to texts and their historical circumstances. This feeling is bulwarked by his comprehensive presentation of the relevant secondary scholarship up to 1968, which is voluminous.[6]

From his study, Garceau concludes that one of Thomas's uses of *iudicium*, when applied to the speculative intellect (as opposed to the practical intellect), implies a two-part act. First, there is the *discernment* of a rule, and, then, one *measures* according to this rule the things that ought to be.[7] In its first part, the act of judgment implies the reception of some rule. In its second part, this rule is applied to the realities that one encounters. We will begin our analysis of this first part of the act by examining Thomas's discussion of how the object of prophetic knowledge differs from the object of the beatific vision.

Prophetic Vision versus Beatific Vision

Thomas's analysis of the modes of prophetic knowledge brings into relief the questions about what prophets actually know in particular and how that knowledge relates to the knowledge of God. He reiterates multiple times a contrast between prophetic knowledge and the knowledge had in the beatific vision, where the divine essence is seen perfectly and immediately by a creature. Prophecy should never be confused with the beatific vision, Thomas insists.[8] Moreover, the saints in heaven have no need of prophecy.[9] It remains then a terrestrial form of knowing, albeit supernatural, as we have already seen. Having distinguished prophecy from any type of natural knowledge in an earlier

---

judgment (*de iudicio*) found in the *Summa theologiae*'s section on justice (II-II, q. 60) remains particularly important.

6. Since 1968, one can add Ambrose McNicholl, "On Judging," *The Thomist* 38, no. 4 (1974): 768–825; Frederick D. Wilhelmsen, "The Concept of Existence and the Structure of Judgment: A Thomistic Paradox," *The Thomist* 41, no. 3 (1977): 317–49.

7. Garceau, *Judicium*, 234–41, at 234: "l'acte de juger ne signifie pas exclusivement l'*appréciation* d'après une règle de ce que les choses devraient être, mais aussi et surtout le juste *discernement* d'un objet" (emphasis in original). Garceau makes a convincing case that for Thomas this sense of "judgment" derives primarily from his notion of justice; see especially ST, I-II, q. 99, a. 4, ad 2: "iudicium significat executionem iustitiae, quae quidem est secundum applicationem rationis ad aliqua particularia determinate."

8. ST, II-II, q. 173, a. 1.

9. ST, II-II, q. 174, a. 5.

article,[10] the first article of Question 173 attempts principally to distinguish prophetic knowledge from the beatific vision.

Thomas initially locates prophecy as something in-between natural knowledge and the beatific vision. In placing prophecy on a continuum between natural and beatific knowledge, the question arises: What is the basis for this continuum? More precisely, what is the common feature of each thing that falls on such a continuum? Is it based on what is known, the object of knowledge? Or is it based on the mode of knowing? Thomas thinks this last case can be ruled out (based on the mode of knowing); this is confirmed by what he says elsewhere about the beatific vision.

Excluding the Beatific Vision from a Continuum Based on Modes of Knowledge

In an article from the *De veritate* (q. 18, a. 1) on whether Adam enjoyed the vision of the divine essence before the Fall, Thomas sets out two ways acts of understanding can be compared and divided into different, continuous classes, as if existing on a spectrum. They can be divided either by differences in their objects or by differences in their modes of understanding. In the latter division (modes of understanding), what is being distinguished chiefly is how one person understands more or less perfectly than another. This explains why Thomas thinks he can exclude this subdivision when speaking about the beatific vision; when comparing the beatific vision to other types of knowledge, one can only speak meaningfully about differences in the object known.

Without denying the possibility that some rational creatures do in fact see God more or less perfectly in the beatific vision, Thomas insists that when talking about the beatific vision now in this life (and within sacred doctrine), we cannot adequately grasp these cognitive differences experienced by *comprehensores* or classify them meaningfully along a spectrum of a more or less perfect knowledge.[11] Our incapacity to make these distinctions ultimately comes down to the fact that the reference point for all human knowledge lies in material creation as perceived initially by the senses. In the beatific vision, however, the object is uncreated and immaterial; there is no adequate "bridge" for our knowledge to cross to see the divine essence as an object, to cross from created to uncreated. He explains further:

---

10. See ST, II-II, q. 172, a. 1.

11. ST, I-II, q. 5, a. 2.

> Every rational creature finds its beatitude in the fact that it sees the
> essence of God, and not in the fact that it sees it with such a degree
> of clarity, more or less. Consequently, the sight of the blessed is not
> distinguished from the sight of those in this life because the former see
> more perfectly and the latter less perfectly, but because the former see
> and the latter do not see.[12]

When speaking thusly about the beatific vision and comparing it to natural
modes of knowing, we simply cannot situate it on a continuum that is based on
our natural modes of understanding. To attempt to do so would in fact require
us to consider an infinite number of modes of understanding, given that a more
perfect mode could always be posited:

> It is not possible for the final limit of human perfection to be taken
> according to some manner of understanding, for among these modes
> of understanding one can perceive an infinite number of levels, one of
> which understands more perfectly than another. Nor is there anyone
> who understands so perfectly that it is impossible to devise another
> who understands more perfectly, except God, who understands every-
> thing with infinite clarity. Hence, the final term of human perfection
> must lie in the understanding of some most perfect intelligible object,
> which is the divine essence.[13]

While Thomas in this context is more interested in clarifying why the vision
of the divine essence is the final perfection of the human person, what he says
here remains pivotal for our understanding of the key differences between
prophecy and the beatific vision. The only way to compare meaningfully
beatific knowledge and other human acts of understanding (whether natural
or prophetic) is by looking at their respective objects. To try to situate beatific
knowledge on any continuum based on different modes of understanding
would be a mistake, according to Thomas, since this creates an incommensurability problem: One would be trying to compare a limited and finite act to
an unbounded and infinite act. There is no meaningful comparison when one
of the terms is undetermined due to an infinite act.[14] Any basis, therefore, for

---

12. *De ver.*, q. 18, a. 1, co. (trans. McGlynn).

13. *De ver.*, q. 18, a. 1, co. (trans. McGlynn).

14. In the mathematical order, where one treats only essences and not acts (unlike in the
above case where we are dealing with *acts* of understanding), it would be like someone trying
to compare the number fifty to the sum of all the natural numbers.

distinguishing prophetic knowledge from the beatific vision cannot be rooted exclusively in a distinction between modes of knowing; how the blessed in heaven know is simply incommensurable with how prophets know.[15]

This incommensurability also partially explains why Thomas repeatedly turns to the analogy of light in order to distinguish different modes of intellection. Within this analogy, light draws our attention especially to what enables *objects* to be seen. It represents the medium by which knowledge is actualized. The fact that he must rely on analogical language comes as a direct consequence of this problem surrounding the incommensurability between natural, prophetic, and beatific modes of knowing. If it is impossible to give a full account for what distinguishes these modes of knowing *qua* modes of knowing, one still needs to be able to indicate or gesture to the fact that they are different modes of knowing. Thomas's preferred way of overcoming this difficulty, as we have seen, is by associating each mode of knowing with a different type of light: the natural light of reason, the light of grace (which includes both the light of faith and of prophecy), and the light of glory, which only the blessed in heaven possess. All three lights are closely related to each other for Thomas because they all derive from one light—the divine light—and participate in God's own knowledge, sharing it as their source and being measured by it.[16] This idea of participation will be revisited shortly.

A Continuum Based on the Object of Knowledge

Instead of using a continuum based on different modes of knowledge, Thomas relies on the objects of knowledge to distinguish prophetic and beatific knowledge. It will be helpful first to consider what Thomas thinks the proper objects of natural human knowledge are before turning to supernatural objects. Our natural knowledge embraces, but is also limited to, objects knowable through the natural light of reason; and what is naturally knowable by reason also must have some root or beginning in the senses. Beatific knowledge, on the other hand, has the divine essence as its object, and through it the rational creature is united to God and knows everything else through God. In prophetic revelation, knowledge can extend, as we have seen, to all "supernatural things"

---

15. Compare St. Paul's observation, "what no eye has seen, nor ear heard, nor the heart of man conceived, what God has prepared for those who love him" (1 Cor 2:9).

16. See ST, I-II, q. 5, a. 6, ad 2.

(*supernaturalia*), but not to the divine essence itself.[17] This is not to say that prophets *actually* know all "supernatural things," which would imply they are omniscient, an attribute unique to God alone.[18] The range of what prophets can know only *potentially* extends to everything that is supernaturally as well as naturally knowable.[19] In short, its potential object of knowledge is everything short of the divine essence.[20]

God's Knowledge: A Closer Look

Only God's knowledge extends *actually* to everything, both natural and supernatural. In fact, the application of natural and supernatural modalities to God's knowledge is highly misleading; instead, one should say that for God it is simply "natural" to know everything perfectly in Himself.[21] Everything points to the conclusion then that divine knowledge is radically different from human knowledge—a point Thomas repeatedly stresses in his question on divine knowledge

---

17. See ST, II-II, q. 176, a. 2, ad 3: "revelatio prophetica se extendit ad omnia supernaturalia cognoscenda."

18. See ST, I, q. 14.

19. ST, II-II, q. 171, a. 3, co.: "Cognitio autem prophetica est per lumen divinum, quo possunt omnia cognosci, tam divina quam humana, tam spiritualia quam corporalia. Et ideo revelatio prophetica ad omnia huiusmodi se extendit." The prophet can potentially know an infinite number of things as divinely revealed, but even saying this, such a potential infinity would still not add up to the vision of God's essence, who is *actually* infinite.

20. Elsewhere, Thomas speculates that this vast, potential scope of prophetic knowledge is one of the reasons why prophecy can only exist as a transient impression and not habitually in a person. Other gratuitous graces like the gift of tongues, he observes, can be held habitually, as St. Paul reports of himself (1 Cor 14:18); see ST, II-II, q. 176, a. 2, ad 3. Thomas explains that this is appropriate because the gift of tongues extends only "to a particular kind of knowledge, namely that of human voices," and it does not go beyond this limited object. Thomas's reasoning here takes the form of an argument from convenience; he is trying to explain why it is "not repugnant" to reason that some gratuitous graces are held habitually, while others like prophecy are not. The testimony of scripture has already indicated that someone like Paul spoke in tongues habitually. Thomas offers a suggestive but not overly forceful argument from convenience: The determining factor for whether a certain charism can be received and held habitually lies in the proximity of the perfection associated with that charism to the perfection of beatitude. Because prophecy excels so much above "the state of imperfection of this life," or so he reasons, it cannot be held habitually but only "imperfectly as a kind of passion."

21. See I, q. 14, a. 5, co.: "alia autem a se [Deo] videt non in ipsis, sed in seipso, inquantum essentia sua continet similitudinem aliorum ab ipso."

from the First Part (q. 14) and which he thinks is rooted in scripture.[22] While human knowledge is always derived from external things perceived in the senses, divine knowledge is always essential; it is who God is and is in no way derived from any creature that exists. In fact, it is the very cause of a creature coming into existence.

To speak about God's knowledge of things as they exist in the divine essence is to enter the realm of the divine ideas. As with divine knowledge, Thomas has already emphasized in the First Part (q. 15) the radical difference between God's ideas and human ideas. Divine ideas are exemplars for everything that exists; they are also identical with the divine essence. Human ideas, in contrast, are only tokens or types derived from exemplars abstracted out of material substances through the process of intellection; they remain entirely dependent on things that are only likeness of God's ideas.

For this reason, Thomas insists that prophecy cannot properly be called a vision of the divine ideas; to do so would imply that there is also a vision of God's essence. Instead of comparing prophetic knowledge to a vision of God's ideas, Thomas says it "is an impressed likeness or sign of divine foreknowledge."[23] On one level, this definition is reminiscent of his likening sacred doctrine to "an impression of divine knowledge" in Question One.[24] On a deeper level, the expression "impressed likeness" (*similitudo impressa*) signals that Thomas understands prophecy as a kind of participation in divine knowledge. He identifies it more specifically as a participation in God's foreknowledge, based on his earlier discussion of future contingents as prophecy's proper object and in deference to St. Jerome's definition, which he has adapted. This expression appears slightly removed from Jerome's definition in the article, and this clarifies how "the truth of prophetic knowledge and announcement" derives principally from God's knowledge.[25] Thomas's own definition should not be taken to limit prophecy exclusively to divine foreknowledge.

---

22. See especially the *sed contra*'s in q. 14.

23. ST, II-II, q. 171, a. 6, ad 1: "Et ideo etiam *prophetia, quae est divinae praescientiae similitudo impressa vel signum,* sua immobili veritate futurorum contingentiam non excludit" (emphasis mine). Thomas has adapted this definition of prophecy as a "sign of divine foreknowledge" from St. Jerome (*Commentary on Daniel,* c. 2, 10), whom he cites earlier in the article's response: "per hunc etiam modum Hieronymus dicit quod 'prophetia est quoddam signum divinae praescientiae.'"

24. ST, I, q. 1, a. 3, ad 2.

25. See ST, II-II, q. 171, a. 6, co.: "oportet igitur eandem esse *veritatem propheticae cognitionis et enuntiationis quae est cognitionis divinae,* cui impossibile est subesse falsum" (emphasis mine).

In saying that prophecy is a *participation in divine knowledge*, we are attempting to delineate chiefly how prophetic knowledge involves *acts* of human intellection that are caused by God (either directly or indirectly) but yet are not identical with God's own act of understanding. We will try first to clarify this latter idea of non-identity in a participating act of understanding; we will then address how participatory acts imply some kind of causal relation. Admittedly, the topic of creaturely participation in the divine nature or operation could be explored through other notable paths: being, goodness, or beauty. Our present purpose, however, limits us to Thomas's discussions about human participation in truth and knowledge—prophecy's primary domain.

Participation in God's Knowledge as Non-Identity with the Divine Essence

Thomas often adopts the method of identifying what "something is *not*" before trying to define what it is.[26] He applies a similar method at times to prophecy, and appreciating this method will help us to get behind his characterization of prophecy as a special sort of participation in God's knowledge. As already seen, Thomas focuses first on the object of prophetic knowledge and tries to determine what it is not. It is not the divine essence because in prophecy (and, indeed, in any mode of creaturely knowing) the mode of knowledge must be distinct from the object known. Only God's mode of knowledge is identical with the object of His knowledge: His own nature.[27] This helps to highlight how the mode of human knowing always requires some type of bridge or medium, which Thomas describes as an intellectual light. This light is the bridge between the knower and the object known which allows the knower to become in some sense the object known but without the knower becoming identical with it.

Any intellectual light—whether natural (as in the natural light of reason) or supernatural (as in the light of prophecy or glory)—indicates the non-identity of the knower and the object known. For example, in knowing my dog, I do not become my dog—that is, we remain separate and distinct realities. Nevertheless, in knowing my dog, I do in some way become *like* my dog but without

---

26. See ST, I, q. 3, prologue.
27. ST, I, q. 14, a. 2, co.: "Deus se per seipsum intelligit."

him necessarily becoming like me.[28] This likeness between me and my dog while I am thinking about my dog is only a *formal likeness* that depends on the relationship between two terms: the concrete dog and the likeness of the dog in my mind, which is my concept of the dog. My natural intellectual light is what enables an act of understanding to come about, in part, by allowing me to make a judgment that determines my concept to the actual dog. In prophecy, this intellectual light is supernatural and brings about a supernatural act of judgment and understanding. We must now discuss a second aspect of participation: the causal dimension of acts of understanding.

Participation and Causality

To start with, all intellectual light is caused by God, but this does not mean that all acts of human understanding are directly and immediately caused by God alone. Our acts of understanding accomplished under the light of reason rely on the natural light innate in every person, which in part *causes* a person's act of understanding. What does *cause* mean to here? Any act of understanding, Thomas thinks, can be likened to "a motion," broadly speaking. It is like a motion not in a physical sense as in local motion, but in a metaphysical sense as in something being actualized from a potency to act. Now he thinks that just as any motion must be reducible to some first mover, so too must every act of understanding be led back to God as first mover and efficient cause.[29] This does not mean that God directly infuses a new light for every natural act of human understanding, like a sudden beam of light from a torch. The natural light is not the mere occasion for God formally causing knowledge directly in the human mind. The natural light exists as a real and immediate formal cause of human knowledge, and while it is caused by God, the natural light functions through the human person as an innate power.

This means that in causing the natural light, God allows human intellection to function innately by divine design. In addition to being an efficient cause of every intellectual act, God also causes and designs the content of every act of understanding, not only the thing known but also the knower and the natural intellectual light possessed by the knower. Thomas elaborates:

---

28. See ST, I, q. 12, a. 11, ad 4: "visio intellectualis est eorum quae sunt in anima per suam essentiam, sicut intelligibilia in intellectu."

29. See ST, I, q. 2, a. 3, co.

The act of understanding or [the act] of any created being whatsoever depends on God in two ways: first, inasmuch as it is from Him that it has the form whereby it acts; secondly, inasmuch as it is moved by Him to act.[30]

Having already identified this second sense of God as "moving" all things to act (including to know), we can now focus on the first sense of God as the designer of every creature's act. Humans depend on God because He bestows on them a natural light that exists innately as the principle (or "form") of every natural act of human understanding. He explains:

> Now every form bestowed on created things by God has power for a determined act, which it can bring about in proportion to its own proper endowment; and beyond which it is powerless, except by a superadded form, as water can only heat when heated by the fire. And thus the human understanding has a form, viz. intelligible light, which of itself is sufficient for knowing certain intelligible things, viz. those we can come to know through the senses.
>
> . . .
>
> Higher intelligible things the human intellect cannot know, unless it be perfected by a stronger light, viz. the light of faith or prophecy which is called the "light of grace," inasmuch as it is added to nature. Hence we must say that for the knowledge of any truth whatsoever man needs divine help, that the intellect may be moved by God to its act. But he does not need a new light added to his natural light, in order to know the truth in all things, but only in some that surpass his natural knowledge. And yet at times God miraculously instructs some by His grace in things that can be known by natural reason, even as He sometimes brings about miraculously what nature can do.[31]

Thomas explicitly denies that God must formally give natural light anew for each act of human understanding. Only the prophetic light—a type of light of grace—is given suddenly and immediately like the sudden flash of light in a dimly lit room. Like all intellectual light, prophetic light is caused by God

---

30. ST, I-II, q. 109, a. 1, co. (trans. Fathers of the English Dominican Province [hereafter English Dominicans], 3 vols. [New York: Benzinger Brothers, 1948]).

31. ST, I-II, q. 109, a. 1, co. (trans. English Dominicans).

in the soul of a prophet, but unlike the natural intellectual light, prophetic light is not caused continuously, being a sudden flash or "impression" in the prophet's mind. The prophetic light is meant to interact with and strengthen the prophet's already-existing natural intellectual light, so that it can perceive supernatural things that are beyond its reach or that would otherwise be naturally unknowable.[32]

To say then all created acts of understanding, both natural and supernatural, are ways of participating in God's knowledge means the following. First, the creature's knowledge is not identical with God's knowledge. Human acts of understanding always require the bridge of an intellectual light. Even the blessed in heaven see God through the medium of the light of glory (itself divinely given) without becoming identical with divine knowledge. While the saints who share in the light of glory become "godlike" in their very natures, prophets do not; they cannot be said "to see" God's knowledge or ideas directly or see Him face-to-face like the blessed in heaven, lest one admit prophets see the divine essence.

This leads to a second clarification: Participation for Thomas has reference to causation and likeness. While all acts of understanding are caused by God as first mover, they also all depend on God for their structure and for the formal content of what is known. Thus, Thomas can write:

> We are said to see all things in God and to judge all things according to Him inasmuch as we know and judge all things through a participation of His light; for the natural light of reason is also a kind of participation in the divine light, just as we say we see and judge all sensible things in the sun.... Just as in order to see something through the senses it is not necessary that the substance of the sun be seen, so too in order to see something intellectually, it is not necessary that God's essence be seen.[33]

Within this framework of participation, prophecy acts like a sudden flash of light that illuminates something unseen in the natural light of the sun. This new burst of light, the light of prophecy, is caused directly and formally by God and is infused into the prophet's mind in order to know supernatural and sometimes even natural things.

---

32. ST, II-II, q. 171, a. 2, co.
33. ST, I, q. 12, a. 11, ad 3.

Prophecy Does Not Imply a Vision of the Divine Essence

The basic question of the first article of Question 173 can now be reposed in a slightly more helpful way: Does the reception of prophetic light necessarily imply that prophets see the divine essence? All the article's objections revolve around a single argumentative structure that admits initially that a prophet does share in an aspect or genus of divine knowledge.[34] Critically, they all fail to make the decisive distinction between how God knows and how prophets know, applying (mistakenly) the premise that acts of divine knowledge must properly be identical with God's essence—something Thomas had established earlier.[35] They draw relatively similar conclusions (again mistaken): If prophets share the same objects as God's knowledge, it follows that they must have access to some type of "vision" of the divine essence.

In the article's response, Thomas tries to resolve the main thrust of these objections by clarifying exactly what kind of objects of "divine knowledge" are seen by prophets. The type of divine knowledge that prophets receive exists "from afar," he says, somewhat metaphorically; with more metaphysical precision he elaborates that prophetic knowledge is objectively different from the knowledge that the blessed in heaven enjoy;[36] they have different objects. The object of the beatific vision is the divine essence itself mediated to an intellectual creature through the light of glory.[37] Prophetic knowledge does not have the divine essence as its object; otherwise, it would be identical to the beatific vision. As we saw earlier, the potential object of prophecy extends to any created being through the medium of prophetic light, but not to God's being *in se*.

Prophecy and Thomas's Metaphor of Distance

We also see Thomas deploying here in passing a distance metaphor when describing prophecy's object: It is "far off." He often makes use of a distance metaphor when describing prophetic knowledge: Prophecy occurs as if someone is seeing or "existing from afar" (*ut procul existentis*).[38] As far as I can tell, this metaphor tends to be utilized in three main ways.[39] At times, Thomas applies it to

---

34. ST, II-II, q. 173, a. 1.

35. ST, I, q. 14, a. 4.

36. ST, II-II, q. 173, a. 1, co.: "cognitio prophetica alia est a cognitione perfecta, quae erit in patria."

37. ST, I-II, q. 5, a. 6, ad 2.

38. ST, II-II, q. 174, a. 5, co.

39. The source of the metaphor, as seen earlier, very likely stems from Isidore of Seville's

draw attention to the prophet's own cognitive perspective, like someone looking at a house from across a vast field or any seer who sees "from afar." In a second way, he extends the metaphor of "seeing" to the language of "existing," describing the prophet as one who also "exists" far from divine knowledge and supernatural truth.[40] This latter usage allows Thomas to juxtapose prophets with the blessed in heaven who exist "not as being remote" from the perfection of beatitude, but "as being near" to it. He frames this juxtaposition in the language of vision in order to emphasize the order of knowing, but he plainly means it also to extend to the order of being. Prophets "see" supernatural truth at a distance, because they exist "farther" from heaven; in contrast, the blessed in heaven are "nearby."[41] In a third way, the distance metaphor is used to underscore the remoteness of prophetic knowledge from normal human knowledge: "Prophets know things that are at a distance and remote from human knowledge."[42] The prominence of this distance metaphor and its various instantiations in his analysis of prophecy confirms our earlier observation that Thomas understands prophecy as being situated between natural human knowledge and the beatific vision.

These appeals to distance have an added effect in allowing Thomas to introduce discussion of the *degrees of perfection* into prophecy. When compared to natural human knowledge, prophecy is superior, but when compared to the vision of the blessed in heaven, prophetic knowledge is something imperfect and inferior. The beatific vision is the most perfect kind of knowledge, due to the immediate union with God that is implied. Prophecy falls well short of the highest perfection of the beatific vision, given that the two have different objects.

Prophecy and the "Mirror of Eternity"

During the course of this differentiating of degrees of perfection, Thomas devotes a large portion of his response (q. 173, a. 1) to addressing the opinions of "certain persons" (*quidam*) who appeal to a particular image, that of the

---

dubious etymological entry for "prophecy" (*Etymologiae*, VII, c. 8). See also *De ver.*, q. 12, a. 1, co.

    40. ST, II-II, q. 173, a. 1, co. See ST, II-II, q. 174, a. 5, co.

    41. ST, II-II, q. 173, a. 1, co.: "prophetia importat cognitionem divinam ut procul existentem, unde et de prophetis dicitur, Heb. [11:13], quod 'erant a longe aspicientes.' Illi autem qui sunt in patria, in statu beatitudinis existentes, non vident ut a remotis, sed quasi ex propinquo, secundum illud Psalmi [139:14], 'habitabunt recti cum vultu tuo.'"

    42. ST, II-II, q. 171, a. 1, co.

"mirror of eternity" (*speculum aeternitatis*), to differentiate prophecy from the beatific vision. While never naming the individuals he had in mind, research into the history of thirteenth-century scholastic disputations on prophecy reveals that such appeals were quite popular, even if the meaning of the mirror of eternity was variously interpreted.[43] Thomas at first explains why the image was thought useful among certain schoolmen or even necessary: "There were some who, wanting to distinguish prophetic knowledge from the knowledge of the blessed, said that prophets see the divine essence itself, which they called the 'mirror of eternity.'"[44] For such theologians the "mirror of eternity" was not meant to be identical with the object of the beatific vision; instead, they wished to identify the "mirror" as the place within the divine essence where "the reasons for future events" were kept.[45] In this way, the mirror helps to account for how a prophet could see these "reasons" in a prophetic vision without ever seeing the divine essence itself as the object of beatitude. Thomas seems to acknowledge the good instincts of these schoolmen. They were trying to preserve the uniqueness of the divine essence as the object of the beatific vision, while still enabling one to account for the exceptional and superior access to divine knowledge that prophets had. The "mirror of eternity" was their attempt at conceptualizing an object of the human mind that stands in between the divine essence as the object of the beatific vision and the normal objects of human knowledge—no simple task.

What did these schoolmen think prophets exactly saw in the mirror of eternity? Based on the text of Thomas's *Summa* article, it is almost impossible to reconstruct what exactly they taught on this score. It seems that very few theologians of the thirteenth century actually thought the mirror of eternity was identical with the divine essence.[46] Thomas interpreted his contemporaries' appeal to the mirror in the following way. The things seen in the mirror of

---

43. While the expression has biblical roots (Wis 7:26), Torrell thinks it was likely first coined by Godefroid of Poitiers; see Torrell, *Théorie de la prophétie*, 134, 188–207. For its use elsewhere in the thirteenth century (notably by Hugh of Saint-Cher), see Torrell, *Recherches sur la théorie de la prophétie*, 26–27.

44. ST, II-II, q. 173, a. 1, co.

45. ST, II-II, q. 173, a. 1, co.: "rationes futurorum eventuum."

46. In his disputed question on prophecy (a. 2, § 1, solutio), St. Albert the Great held that the mirror of eternity was not God; see Albert the Great, *Quaestio de prophetia: Visione, immaginazione e dono profetico*, ed. Anna Rodolfi (Florence: Edizioni del Galluzzo per la Fondazione Ezio Franceschini, 2009), 42.

eternity are certain concepts given by God directly to prophets. These concepts are ultimately linked to the divine ideas, but cannot be the divine ideas themselves, given that God's ideas are identical with the divine essence.[47] No one can "see" a divine idea outside of the beatific vision. Consequently, there must be some kind of mediation between the divine ideas and the prophet's mind in order to preserve a coherent understanding of the beatific vision, and the mirror attempts to preserve that coherence. Thomas admits that the mirror of eternity could be appropriately employed as a metaphor as long as it is understood that any object seen in the mirror is only a "likeness" (*similitudo*) of a divine idea. At the same time, he himself is not overly attached to mirror-language, presumably because he realizes its potential to cause confusion. As we have already seen, Thomas prefers simply to state that prophetic knowledge corresponds to "a likeness of the truth of divine foreknowledge."[48] The language of "likeness" is front and center in this description, which simultaneously avoids hypostatizing this "likeness" into something existing independent of both God's mind and the prophet's mind—a risk one opens up when using the metaphor of the mirror of eternity.

To sum up the discussion so far, Thomas in this first article upholds the view that the object of any act of human intellection concerning God in this life is only ever a likeness to God's knowledge; it can never be called or confused with the divine nature itself. This view is consistent with Thomas's thought as a whole. Knowledge is a participation in God's knowledge, where the likeness is understood to be caused by God, whether mediately or immediately. This view also harkens back to Thomas's earlier description of sacred doctrine as "an impression" of God's knowledge. His understanding of prophetic knowledge shows something similar is at work; prophecy functions only as an impression or sign of divine knowledge given to select individuals who participate in God's knowledge in a special, intensified way.

Thomas also introduces an important distinction between the divine ideas and the divine essence, on the one hand, and the relationship the divine ideas have with a prophet's mind, on the other. He respectfully dismisses his contemporaries' reliance on the image of the mirror of eternity. Wishing, nevertheless, to take what is helpful in the metaphor, he revises it. The mirror—as used by the schoolmen—suggests (incorrectly) that God's ideas are (1) non-identical with

---

47. See, ST, I, q. 15, a. 1, ad 3.
48. ST, II-II, q. 173, a. 1, co.: "similitudo veritatis divinae praescientiae."

the divine essence and (2) ectypal of reality rather than archetypal. This would entail that there is some already-constituted reality which the divine ideas are derived from—a sort of independent realm of ideas, a view Thomas must reject. He holds that God's ideas are the causes of things that exist, and instead of being already-constituted realities existing quasi-independently of the divine mind, the "likenesses" in the mirror can only result from other real things. The one who perceives a likeness depends on some reality in order to receive that likeness. We can call this likeness *resulting likeness* or *exemplary likeness*, even though Thomas can use one word for it: *exemplatum*.[49] For human beings, exemplary likeness is the common way we come to know things. Humans use ideas in order to know realities, and all human ideas are derived from things that already exist and have some root in sensible reality.

God does not know things in this way; His knowledge is not derived from anything, but rather it causes everything. For God, the "likeness" of something in the divine mind "preexists" the thing in reality. We can call this a *causing likeness* or an *exemplar*. A causing likeness cannot fall under the metaphor of the mirror, Thomas thinks, because there is no reality in the likeness other than as it exists in God virtually. If the metaphor is to be taken properly, the only things that can be said to be seen in the mirror of eternity are resulting likenesses, which are not identical with the divine ideas. At the same, these exemplary likenesses always refer ultimately to the divine ideas, which are their exemplars, but the two are not identical.[50] If one were to say that prophets see the divine ideas as exemplars, this would imply that they are enjoying the beatific vision, which Thomas already thinks is impossible for prophets in this life, it being contrary to scripture. Prophecy relies on resulting likenesses of God's knowledge.

Prophecy and Judgment

Structured at the heart of the act of human knowledge which relies on these exemplary likenesses is the act of judgment. In prophecy it is central, given that the prophetic light works within the natural structuring of human cognition—with grace not supplanting nature, but perfecting it. The second article of Question 173 asks whether prophets require new species in the mind or only the presence of a prophetic light in a prophetic vision. In asking this, Thomas reveals

---

49. See *De ver.*, q. 12, a. 11, co.
50. See ST, II-II, q. 26, a. 4, co.: "exemplar potius est, quam exemplatum."

that his speculations about the inner workings of prophecy have penetrated deep into his account of human psychology, where judgment is decisive for intellection. To sketch it briefly, it is an intellectual light that causes a judgment, and it is only through a judgment that knowledge is made complete. This basic structure will apply equally to prophecy; prophetic light causes prophetic judgments, which are necessary for prophetic knowledge.

In this context, Thomas observes that two things can be considered when talking about knowledge (*cognitio*) in general: (1) "the acceptance or representation of things" and (2) "the judgment of the things represented." Of these two elements, Thomas insists that judgment remains primary, because "judgment is what completes knowledge" (*iudicium est completivum cognitionis*).[51] This is not to say that "acceptance" or "representation" are unimportant in acts of knowledge; they clearly are vital. But given that the essence of prophecy lies in the prophetic light and this light affects principally judging, our attention needs to be primarily on judgment within prophetic knowledge in what follows.

Judgment in General

The act of judgment (*iudicium*), as already alluded to, remains a key aspect of Thomas's theory of knowledge, even if it is somewhat imprecise to say he deliberately sets out to develop one. His task throughout the vast majority of his writings focuses largely on knowing how things relate to God as divinely revealed; this, after all, is the subject of sacred doctrine, to which the *Summa theologiae* is dedicated. One might say that, as a teacher, Thomas rarely strays far from the topic of knowledge. He treats it in several different works, and the centrality of this topic in his thought has evoked great interest among his readers, especially in modern times. At the same time, the concept of judgment has unearthed its fair share of difficulties when readers are faced with the task of trying to reconstruct a general theory of knowledge that could be attributed to Thomas within which to integrate it.[52] With these caveats in mind and

---

51. ST, II-II, q. 173, a. 2, co.: "Per donum autem prophetiae confertur aliquid humanae menti supra id quod pertinet ad naturalem facultatem, quantum ad utrumque, scilicet et quantum ad iudicium, per influxum intellectualis luminis; et quantum ad acceptionem seu repraesentationem rerum, quae fit per aliquas species.... Horum autem duorum primum principalius est in prophetia, quia *iudicium est completivum cognitionis*" (emphasis mine).

52. See Étienne Gilson, *The Christian Philosophy of St. Thomas Aquinas*, trans. Laurence K. Shook (New York: Random House, 1956), 207–35.

despite the scattering of texts and different occasions of writing, there are certain key features of what can fairly be called his theory of knowledge. When these features are taken together, one cannot conclude that for Thomas human knowledge simply means the reception or acceptance of certain images or concepts in the human intellect. Concept formation is certainly a part—indeed, an indispensable part—of his account, but it is not the whole story. For him, the human person only comes to know by making a judgment "according to the power of an intellectual light."[53] If prophecy involves the supernatural giving of an additional intellectual light, the act of judgment must be affected.

Acceptance, Judgment, and the Degrees of Prophecy

Prophecy influences the mind on the level of both judgment and the mental "acceptance or representation" of things.[54] Of these two, Thomas sees judgment as the more important, because one can receive prophetic mental representations without the light of prophecy needed to judge them. Absent this infusion of a prophetic light to illuminate the one judging, a person cannot properly be called a "prophet." To illustrate this he cites the story of Joseph's interpretation of Pharaoh's dream from Gn 41. While Pharaoh is the one who receives the dreams and their respective images (the prophetic mental representations), only Joseph is able to expound their true meaning. For this reason, scripture calls Joseph, not Pharaoh, a "prophet." Individuals like Pharaoh who do not receive a prophetic light but only receive images are not considered prophets, "unless [their] mind is illuminated so as to make a judgment."[55] This is as true for visions received in a dream as it is for visions seen when awake as in the case of Belshazzar who only sees a hand miraculously writing on the wall without understanding the meaning of the letters (Dn 5:5). Thomas calls all such visions that lack prophetic light and, thus, judgment "something imperfect in the genus of prophecy." On the other hand, Joseph, who receives no prophetically infused images or content save what Pharaoh communicates to him, is a genuine prophet. So much emphasis is placed on the prophetic light's power to evoke

---

53. ST, II-II, q. 173, a. 2, co.: "iudicium autem humanae mentis fit secundum vim intellectualis luminis."

54. See R.N. Della Croce, "*Acceptio rerum et Judicium de acceptis* nella Somma 2/2 q. 173, a. 2," *Ephemerides Carmeliticae* 2, no. 2 (1948): 315–32.

55. ST, II-II, q. 173, a. 2, co.

judgments that Thomas considers someone to be a prophet even when the mind alone is illuminated.

Even though judgment remains prophecy's more essential element, Thomas still shows interest in categorizing the different ways prophets can receive images or mental species which their knowledge is based on. He outlines three chief ways prophets can receive them: under sensible form, imaginary form, or intelligible form. Daniel exemplifies the first class when he sees the visible writing on Belshazzar's wall. Imaginary forms, as the name suggests, come to exist initially in the human imagination without necessarily requiring any input from the senses. Thomas describes two possible ways these imaginary forms can be given. Either they are fully impressed by God *de novo* on a person's mind, as when a man blind from birth has infused into his imagination the likeness of colors, or they are images that preexist in a person's memory with God simply rearranging and ordering them. Thomas thinks Jeremiah's vision of a boiling pot exemplifies the latter scenario (Jer 1:13). There Jeremiah, having seen a boiling pot in his everyday experience, would have had a memory of it, a kind of stored image. In the prophetic vision, the image of the boiling pot is not infused supernaturally; rather, God draws it from Jeremiah's memory to rearrange it in his conscious imagination. In the third class (and the one most difficult to grasp), God impresses "intelligible species" on someone's mind directly. Solomon and the apostles, who receive directly "infused knowledge or wisdom" (*scientiam vel sapientiam infusam*), are given as examples.

Following the authority of St. Augustine closely, Thomas determines that the type of prophecy in which both light and an image or species are received is the "highest" kind, where there is a combination of both supernatural judgment and supernatural acceptance.[56] Admittedly, it is somewhat difficult to think one's way back into this hierarchy of visions, which was a prominent feature of Augustinian thought.[57] Thomas is certainly not indifferent to these considerations of hierarchy; several other *Summa* articles treat explicitly the superiority of certain types of prophetic vision over others.[58] The issue of hierarchy is especially prominent in his article about Moses's exalted status as the "greatest" of the Old Testament prophets, where Dt 34:10 is cited.[59] Thomas is here

---

56. ST, II-II, q. 174, a. 2, ad 1.

57. Étienne Gilson, *The Christian Philosophy of Saint Augustine*, trans. L. E. M. Lynch (London: Victor Gollancz, 1961), 77–96, 215.

58. See ST, II-II, q. 174, a. 2 and a. 4.

59. ST, II-II, q. 174, a. 4: "exellentior omnibus prophetis." On Maimonides's influence

carefully engaging a number of traditional questions being raised at the time and respectfully engaging with major Christian authorities on them—St. Augustine, St. Gregory the Great, St. Isidore, and Cassiodorus—as well as Judeo-Arabic philosophical authorities who are less explicitly present due to the *Summa*'s prioritization of Christian doctors. Despite this, the full implication of these considerations of the degrees of prophecy remains difficult to discern, unless we consider how they bring out and elaborate on Thomas's idea of supereminence. His article on Moses being the most excellent prophet lays out most straightforwardly this idea.

At the same time, it could be argued that his hierarchizing of the types of prophetic vision may be too reliant on somewhat dubious traditional distinctions that rely excessively on St. Augustine and especially his ontology.[60] This criticism has merit, but it fails to appreciate the deeper undercurrents of Thomas's method. The hierarchy of vision functions in his thought not so much on the level of the content of revelation—the *type* of vision and what is revealed—but on the degree to which such content manifests the truth. In this sense, the language of hierarchical visions points to an attempt by Thomas to appropriate the traditional hierarchy of Augustine based around visionary *types* into a more functional and dynamic model of prophecy. Admittedly, the result is not completely satisfactory, which is why the criticism of someone like von Balthasar remains valid. Thomas cannot fully integrate the Augustinian hierarchy of types of visions into a more functional hierarchy based around degrees of manifesting the truth. In this latter hierarchy, the degree to which something manifests the truth determines how closely a type of vision approximates the beatific vision.

---

for this view, see Torrell, *Question XII: La prophétie*, 236–38.

60. Von Balthasar, *Thomas und die Charismatik*, 225, which raises this criticism. See also his later discussion in *Explorations in Theology*, vol. IV, *Spirit and Institution*, trans. Edward T. Oakes (San Francisco: Ignatius Press, 1995), 309–51; not specifically focusing on Thomas, von Balthasar reflects on prophecy and the gratuitous graces in relation to Christian mysticism and the discernment of spirits, voicing his criticism of Thomas's account of prophetic visions again. His criticism of Thomas on this particular issue, however, is misplaced; see the corrective studies on prophetic images by Serge-Thomas Bonino, "Le rôle de l'image dans la connaissance prophétique d'après saint Thomas d'Aquin," *Revue Thomiste* 89, no. 4 (1989): 533–68; Serge-Thomas Bonino, "'Les voiles sacrés': À propos d'une citation de Denys," *Studi Tomistici* 45 (1992): 158–71. Less helpful on this specific issue than Bonino, but still useful is the general discussion of Pamela J. Reeve, "The Metaphysics of Higher Cognitive States in Thomas Aquinas," in *Essays in Medieval Philosophy and Theology in Memory of Walter H. Principe, CSB: Fortresses and Launching Pads*, ed. James R. Ginther and Carl N. Still (Aldershot: Ashgate, 2005), 105–19.

It is not surprising then that we find immediately following these articles on the hierarchy or degrees of prophecy an article that directly asks whether there will be "any grade of prophecy among the blessed" in heaven.[61] This article reveals the trajectory of Thomas's attempt to complete the Augustinian hierarchy of visionary types with a functional one that classifies prophecy along the lines of its orientation to the final end while still maintaining a firm distinction of the respective objects of prophecy and of the beatific vision. In the rough outline of this functional model, the closer a prophetic vision imitates the beatific vision, the higher it is. Supereminence within prophecy for Thomas, therefore, has as its ultimate and decisive reference the superabundant manifestation of truth that is the beatific vision.

Judgments under the Prophetic Light

With the first representational aspect of prophetic knowledge classified ultimately by the degree to which it manifests the truth, the question still remains how this truth is determined within the prophet's own act of knowing. Here the act of judgments is determinative and again indicates why representations—the cognitive content of prophecy—are dependent on judgment in Thomas's account. Initially, he outlines several ways prophetic light can be given by itself and without accompanying images or mental representations so as to focus our attention on the preeminence of the act of judging.[62] First, prophetic light can be impressed on the minds of people who do not see or receive things themselves but who come to judge things seen by others. The first example is already familiar: Joseph receives only a prophetic light so as to judge the things Pharaoh dreamed. The second example is more intriguing and significant: the scene of the two disciples on the road to Emmaus (Lk 24:13–35). The risen Jesus, hidden from their recognition, opens their minds so that they might understand the scriptures (cf. Lk 24:45). This is a type of illumination of their minds that Thomas describes as pertaining to "the interpretation of speech" (*interpretatio sermonum*)—a kind of prophecy.[63] From this example, we see that

---

61. ST, II-II, q. 174, a. 5.

62. Instances where God impresses prophetic light alone also raise the question about whether this account of prophecy could be used as the basis for a comparison with judgments made under the light of faith.

63. ST, II-II, q. 173, a. 2, co.

any act that interprets speech and, by extension, texts potentially falls under the gift of prophecy, should the light of prophecy be present to affect judgments. Scriptural exegesis, thus, can (and in some sense should, according to Thomas) have a prophetic dimension.

If the interpretation and expounding of a given text can be considered a manifestation of the gift of prophecy, this may shed additional light on the final two articles of Part One, Question One (9–10), where Thomas addresses the use of scripture in sacred doctrine. Considering that our central concern remains the act of judgment, our inquiry here must be limited; nevertheless, it seems that prophecy provides a vital link for helping to integrate these last two articles of Question One on scripture with the earlier ones on the nature of sacred doctrine. From this link, one begins to discern Thomas's view that the teaching of sacred doctrine and the interpretation of sacred scripture are two sides of the same coin, given that both can be prophetically inspired.[64]

If scripture is a written testimony of particular things seen and experienced by others, what does it mean for someone to make a judgment about these things? More generally, what does it mean for someone to make a judgment about things seen by others? If "judgment is," as Thomas says, "that which completes knowledge," what is exactly happening in prophetic judgments, and what role does the light of prophecy have in them? Before addressing the question of "how" the prophetic light works in a judgment, still another question seems more pressing. Why does Thomas insist that prophecy includes a judgment at all? The answer to this question goes to the very heart of his notion of divine revelation and its relationship to the divine nature.

Judgment must be included in his discussion of prophecy because Thomas thinks prophecy ultimately relates to truth. The rooting of prophecy in a judgment enables him to root prophecy in his account of truth. This, in turn, roots all divine revelation in truth. This point is more clearly seen in Thomas's *De veritate*, q. 12, a. 2 than in the *Summa theologiae*, although it is certainly

---

64. I explore this topic in "Prophecy and the Moral Life in Thomas Aquinas's *Commentary on 1 Corinthians*," in *Towards a Biblical Thomism: Thomas Aquinas and the Renewal of Biblical Theology*, ed. Piotr Roszak and Jörgen Vijgen (Pamplona: Ediciones Universidad de Navarra, 2018), 197–217. See also Mark F. Johnson, "Another Look at St. Thomas and the Plurality of the Literal Sense of Scripture," *Medieval Philosophy and Theology* 2 (1992): 118–42; Christopher T. Baglow, "Sacred Scripture and Sacred Doctrine in Saint Thomas Aquinas," in *Aquinas on Doctrine: A Critical Introduction*, ed. Thomas G. Weinandy, Daniel A. Keating, and John P. Yocum (London: T & T Clark, 2004), 1–25.

present in his mature thought, albeit more diffusedly.[65] As we look briefly at this earlier disputed question, it will be important for our purpose to keep in mind Thomas's emphatic identification of the object of faith with God as First Truth.[66] Prophecy's connection to truth and its accompanying certitude is fully appreciated only in this context of faith.

Prophetic Certitude

Thomas does not want to isolate prophetic truth into an abstract sphere of knowledge that comes from on high but remains unintegrated and entirely inscrutable. While acknowledging that a prophet's certitude ultimately derives from God, knowledge of whom is ultimately inscrutable, Thomas nevertheless relies on a method that we have encountered before: He tries to draw structural parallels between how human knowledge achieves certitude in its natural mode and compares it to how this is achieved in a prophetic mode. The result is not that prophetic certitude is reduced to the certitude that comes through natural reason; reason's light remains insufficient for fully establishing prophecy's certitude, even if it can point to its fittingness. For Thomas, prophecy is certain in a way analogous to how faith is absolutely certain. In both faith and prophecy, this certitude is caused by God. When discussing this certitude in the act of faith, Thomas explicitly says that believers adhere more firmly to the things prophets announce than to demonstrations of science, because the messages of prophets are more certain.[67] Prophetic testimonies are more certain because of their cause, and their truth is the primary aspect which Thomas thinks prophets point to. The truth of what a prophet testifies to is caused by God as Truth, who is the basis for the credibility of prophetic messages and of the articles of faith as well.

Thomas holds that the more firmly one adheres to prophetic testimonies in faith the more one encourages others to believe. Why is this so? The firmness of one's faith, he says, enables the truths of faith to be the primary objects signified, not the believer as such. Hence, firmness of faith highlights the truth as what is primarily received in faith and allows it to be concretely perceived and, in turn, desired by others. From this, faith has the potential to spread to others, and by

---

65. See ST, II-II, q. 171, a. 6: "Can something false fall under prophecy?"; q. 172, a. 6: "Do prophets who are demonically inspired say true things?"

66. ST, II-II, q. 1.

67. *De ver.*, q. 12, a. 2, ad 3.

spreading beyond the believer, the efficacy of God's will to save everyone widens and becomes more perceivable or manifest. This allows prophets and believers to become cooperators in redemption, and it becomes clear that the believer's general call to apostolate (to share the faith) itself becomes more visible and, thus, more realizable when seen in the light of individual prophets testifying to God.

Another important aspect relates to how Thomas sees adherence to the truth of prophetic testimonies in faith as a manifestation of divine perfection. Fidelity to these testimonies manifests God's perfection only imperfectly; nevertheless, he asserts that any firm adherence to prophetic testimony especially "showcases the grace of God and manifests His perfect knowledge."[68] Thomas is signaling here how the certitude of prophets, which helps root the certitude of faith, is the outpouring of divine goodness, seen in this case under the aspects of divine grace and knowledge. "God's grace" is an explicit reference here to God's universal will for salvation which grace brings about.[69]

Prophecy, Judgment, and Sacred Doctrine

Having seen how judgments are essential for prophesies to be true according to Thomas, this next section aims to compare at a structural level his account of judgment under the light of prophecy and his earlier claim from Question One that sacred doctrine "judges" the principles of other philosophical disciplines.[70] To recall briefly, the central background of Thomas's claim is that the principles of any science are either known *per se* or are discoverable through the use of reason to be parts of another science, as is the case in all subalternate sciences. Sacred doctrine's principles are neither known *per se* nor provable by reason, but are received through divine revelation. The task of judging principles belongs to the virtue of wisdom (*sapientia*), and sacred doctrine is a wisdom that is rooted in divine revelation. In this way, it differs markedly from the wisdom of philosophy, which has the task of proving or assuring through reason the soundness of the first principles of metaphysics and of all the other naturally

---

68. *De ver.*, q. 12, a. 2, ad 3: "et in hoc etiam Dei gratia commendatur, et ipsius perfecta scientia ostenditur."

69. The juxtaposition of grace and God's perfect knowledge in this reply bears a structural resemblance to 1 Tm 2:4, "God desires all to be saved and come to the knowledge of the truth."

70. See ST, I, q. 1, a. 6, ad 2.

knowable sciences as well. Philosophical wisdom is necessary for identifying, understanding, and defending the scientific nature of any inquiry or discipline. Sacred doctrine, in contrast, can neither prove its own principles through reason nor prove the principles of other sciences. This is due to the unique object of sacred doctrine which is known only "through revelation." This is also in contrast with philosophical wisdom or first philosophy—which judges, orders, and governs the principles of all human knowledge by reason. With respect to first philosophy, sacred doctrine functions as a wisdom from the fact that it can judge the principles of the other human sciences to be either true or false, but it cannot fully show (either apodictically or through any other mode of rational argumentation) how and why something is true or false. Anyone who teaches something that goes against a truth taught by faith must be teaching something false; Thomas is certain of this. Determining where the error fully lies, however, falls beyond the strict competence and intention of sacred doctrine. What has been divinely revealed in faith to be true will not sufficiently explain why something is false.

For something to be proven false, an argument has to be provided for why some conclusion fails to be rooted in something more basically known—a first principle. It remains the task of reason to construct such an argument that leads a person from the conclusion back to first principles, or, in this case, to show how a given proposition or conclusion fails to lead back to first principles. It will be helpful here to clarify: When something is judged to be false, what exactly is being judged? Is judgment only a conclusion expressed propositionally and composed of logical entities or concepts that are necessarily related, that is, a mental synthesis that can be symbolized as "S is P," where S and P are previously formed concepts? Or does judgment involve something beyond the grasping and subsequent synthesis of concepts and the discovery of their necessary and logical relations?[71] On this intricate question of the act of judging in normal human knowing, Thomas maintains that in addition to a conceptual comparison and synthesis there is also a negative consideration of whether the terms of the conclusion when expressed propositionally actually exist—a consideration that is built into our usage of the copula "is" in propositions. He can recognize, then,

---

71. On the state of the question on judgment among a limited survey of European philosophers of the last 400 years and among readers of Thomas, see McNicholl, "On Judging," 768–88, 789–825, respectively.

a distinction between the proposition as conceived in the mind—the mental concept—and the unconceptualized act of existing of some extramental reality.[72] This latter recognition or assertion which occurs in judgment has the function of taking into account the concrete reality which the first concept signifies but is incapable of adequately representing *qua* concept.

At this point, it becomes clearer that sacred doctrine, when it functions as wisdom and judges other principles, is making a distinction analogous to the one above by asking *an sit verum*, "is this true?" In other words, is there a correspondence with reality? When judging the principles of other sciences, sacred doctrine remains restricted to this domain of inquiring into the truth or falsity of a given principle or proposition. It does not contribute its own divinely revealed principles to enable a person to understand or develop a given human science further. It functions as a judge only when a given science starts asserting as true something that is contrary to the faith or to something that follows directly from the faith as shown in sacred doctrine. This is sacred doctrine's limited and "negative control" over the human sciences, and here Thomas views this negative control as being restricted to judgments about the principles of a given science; sacred doctrine makes no direct judgment about a science's method or object of inquiry.

Judgments from Knowledge versus Judgments from Inclination

In Part One, Question One, Thomas also makes a distinction between judgments from inclination and judgments from knowledge that now needs to be revisited.[73] While these two types of judgment can be analyzed from a number of perspectives, Question One stresses the relationship between the person judging and the object judged. In a judgment from inclination, there is a kind of connaturality between the judge and the object judged. In a judgment of knowledge, no such connaturality is presumed; instead, knowledge acquired by study is central.[74] Knowledge by itself, he observes, does not

---

72. See Wilhelmsen, "The Concept of Existence and the Structure of Judgment," 319–20.

73. ST, I, q. 1, a. 6, ad 3; see also ST, II-II, q. 45, a. 2.

74. Incidentally, inclinations can also be acquired either naturally or supernaturally.

necessarily incline a person to act in a particular way. Someone knowledgeable about chastity, for instance, is not thereby made chaste. While it remains true that such a person can judge whether certain generic types of acts are chaste and whether such acts are characteristic of a chaste person, this by itself does not make the person chaste, nor does it make the virtue of chastity present. It equally does not entail that the person will necessarily act chastely. Thomas thinks this is so because people's knowledge of what pertains to the virtue of chastity (or to any moral virtue) does not necessarily become a principle of their own actions—that is, unless their wills are ordered to chastity. The will must become like the will of a chaste person. Anyone who possesses only knowledge about chastity can only make judgments of knowledge. There is no similarity implied between the knower and the object known, here the things that pertain to the chastity. In contrast, the chaste person who already exercises a will rightly ordered by chastity judges appropriately the things that pertain to this virtue through inclination without needing to study them. If chaste people make the effort to acquire knowledge of the virtue by study, they will be able to judge things by knowledge as well. Through study, they would also come to know more fully why their judgments from inclinations are reliable guides for happiness.

Prophecy displays characteristics that could be identified as leading either to judgments of inclination or to judgments of knowledge. The way Thomas distinguishes prophetic judgments derives in part from the different degrees of perfection in prophecy, as he lays out in his article on whether prophets are aware of their prophetic knowledge as prophetic.[75] He observes that, in Genesis, Joseph is fully self-conscious when he prophesies that God is the source of the message. An even less ambiguous case is the prophet Jeremiah, who uses distinctive signaling phrases, like "Now the word of the Lord came to me saying" (Jer 1:4) and "the Lord said to me" (Jer 1:12–14), to indicate unambiguously where his prophesying comes from. It seems that Jeremiah's prophetic knowledge functions connaturally in his own intellect.[76] The supernatural light functions alongside his natural knowledge, and he is able to distinguish between what he knows by the natural light of reason and what he knows by the prophecy given to him by God. Thomas considers self-conscious prophecies to be more perfect than ones that are not self-conscious:

---

75. ST, II-II, q. 173, a. 4.

76. See Paul Synave, "La causalité de l'intelligence humaine dans la révélation prophétique," *Revue des sciences philosophiques et théologiques* 8 (1914): 218–35, at 225–26.

> When someone knows that he is being moved by the Holy Spirit to judge something or to signify a word or deed, this properly pertains to prophecy. However, when someone is moved but does not know, this is not perfect prophecy, but some prophetic instinct.[77]

Prophets, properly so called, are aware that their knowledge comes from the Holy Spirit. Subjectively unaware prophets are moved more by a "prophetic instinct" that they cannot detect or are only vaguely aware of.

When analyzed next to the distinction outlined above between the two types of judgments, this awareness in perfect prophecy seems to stem from a judgment by inclination that operates through connaturality because it is natural for human beings to be aware of an external source for their knowledge. Prophetic instincts, in contrast, occur when individuals cannot distinguish between their own knowledge and what is divinely revealed knowledge. "Instinct" here conveys the sense of some ambiguity with regards to the source of the act of knowing and judgment. In such a case, the person's prophecy resembles more closely the way God guides and governs animals through instincts. Instinctual behavior is, of course, a feature of human life, but it falls below a properly human act since instinctual acts are not truly voluntary. This less perfect type of prophecy functions less connaturally than the more perfect type.

At the same time, the fact that the term "instinct" is applied to this less perfect type of prophecy indicates that Thomas already thinks a kind of connaturality is involved. In animals, instincts are nothing but connatural: They are forces innate to a creature that depend on mutual affinity between innate desires (or needs) and the external objects of those desires.[78] Animal instincts manifest themselves in the spontaneous seeking and attainment of ends appropriate to animal life.

A prophetic instinct, however, differs from animal instincts because it involves the supernatural work of the Holy Spirit on the prophet's mind as an external agent. Through prophetic instincts prophets become inclined to act in a certain way: to know and testify to certain things without realizing that they are being moved and inspired by the Holy Spirit. Crucially, prophetic instincts also do not appear to directly involve judgments. Thomas highlights the peculiar case of Caiaphas's prophecy (Jn 11:51) to illustrate this, given that the high priest

---

77. ST, II-II, q. 173, a. 4, co.

78. See Max Seckler, *Instinkt und Glaubenswille nach Thomas von Aquin* (Mainz: Matthias-Grünewald-Verlag, 1961), 51–53.

did not realize that he was prophesying.[79] He was unable to distinguish between his own natural knowledge and the prophetic inspiration. Thomas describes Caiaphas as being "moved" passively to express certain words but without understanding "what the Holy Spirit intended by these words."[80] Without receiving or understanding the "intention" of the Holy Spirit's message, those who are moved by prophetic instincts appear to have prophetic knowledge and make prophetic judgments, but in reality they do not. Grasping the "intention" of the Holy Spirit (at least partially) is what is critical for prophecy properly understood, and prophetic instincts are "something imperfect in the genus of prophecy."[81] For this reason, Caiaphas does not really count as a prophet.[82] Still, the Johannine example points again to the centrality of judgment in prophetic knowledge and to the fact that Thomas thinks these judgments are from inclination.

The Process of Judgment

In the natural act of judgment, the mind traces conclusions back to better known starting points or principles. If we take Caiaphas's prophecy again, we can see that in making his judgment about Jesus, he is only conscious that he knows Jesus as human. It is to Jesus as a human that his intended statement refers (Jn 11:49–52). His mind is led back from the singular nature of Jesus and comes to a particular judgment about this individual nature in relation to the common good of the Jewish people. In this case, Caiaphas judges in error, not because he has the wrong first principle in relation to the common good of the people; he errs because he lacks (or has rejected) faith which would move one to assert the supernaturally revealed divine identity of the person of Jesus. In rejecting faith, Caiaphas rejects who Jesus truly is (Mk 14:60–65).

Thomas sometimes compares the act of judgment to the act of tracing some conclusion back to something previously known—to the act of resolving conclusions into first principles.[83] It is only in judgments that knowledge is

---

79. ST, II-II, q. 173, a. 4, sc.

80. ST, II-II, q. 173, a. 4, co.: "quandoque autem ille cuius mens movetur ad aliqua verba depromenda, non intelligit quid spiritus sanctus per haec verba intendat, sicut patet de Caipha."

81. ST, II-II, q. 171, a. 5, co.

82. ST, II-II, q. 173, a. 4, co.

83. See *De ver.*, q. 12, a. 3, ad 2: "iudicium non dependet tantum a receptione speciei, sed ex hoc quod ea de quibus iudicatur, examinantur ad aliquod principium cognitionis, sicut de conclusionibus iudicamus eas in principia resolvendo."

complete, because it is only in judgments that things are resolved back into first principles. We can revisit the example of Joseph and Pharaoh to illustrate this (Gn 41). Thomas observes initially that we should distinguish between the dream received by Pharaoh and the judgment of Joseph concerning the dream. Pharaoh receives in his dream the vision of the fat and thin cows, yet he cannot understand their significance. He reports the content of the dream to Joseph, who upon hearing it now has the images that Pharaoh had of the cows. They have now received roughly the same imaginative vision, but possessing the same vision or image does not amount to an act of judgment in Thomas's account. After Joseph hears the content of the dream, he is able to judge the images because he receives an influx of prophetic light. This light allows Joseph to make a prophetic judgment, so that everything that he knows prophetically depends on it. Thomas relates prophetic light to prophetic judgment as cause to effect. Without the light, there could be no judgment. This prophetic judgment has structural similarities to Joseph's natural act of judging. The images conceived in the mind come to be seen to signify something beyond themselves; Joseph is able to see beyond the images of the fat and thin cows and realizes that they point to a truth he knows in a higher mode received from God. He judges that these dream-images point simultaneously to a higher source (their cause) and an additional meaning. Pharoah's cows, thus, are realized to be signs of something God foreknows that He wishes to communicate through Joseph.

In more general terms, Joseph is able "to divide and compose" the different elements of the dream and resolve them in the light of prophecy, wherein he is able to judge their true meaning as intended by God. The number of cows, for instance, is led back through the prophetic light to something known only to the divine mind: The cows correspond to the number of concrete years of feast and famine. (The number seven becomes associated with a count of years: seven years of plenty followed by seven of famine.) Joseph expresses a judgment by asserting the truth that Pharaoh's vision communicates: the cows mean that Egypt will experience seven years of plenty followed by seven of famine. This meaning is traceable back to the principle of prophecy—God as First Truth. The relationship between the meaning and the First Truth revealing it in the light of prophecy enables Joseph to be absolutely certain about the truth of the prophecy.

This relationship can be described as a kind of correspondence between Joseph's mind and a representation of divine foreknowledge. One might say that an immediate identity is established between the prophet's mind and God's knowledge, but not (obviously) a complete identity. A complete identity, after all, could mean a few things. In the first instance, it could mean a prophet's mind is supplanted by God's. In this case it would no longer be correct to say "Joseph interpreted the dream" or "Joseph answered Pharaoh"; instead, one should really say "God answered Pharaoh." This meaning is ruled out by what the biblical text actually says; Thomas also thinks it metaphysically incoherent.[84] Joseph is a true agent, and he plays a role—albeit one subordinate to God's—in prophetic knowledge. This phrase could also mean that the prophet receives the beatific vision. This again, Thomas thinks, is impossible. A third possibility is that it could mean a prophet temporarily sees the divine essence, but this characterization, Thomas explains, pertains only to the special case of rapture, which can be understood, in the final analysis, to be a kind of elevated form of prophecy.[85] Nowhere is it suggested that Joseph experiences a kind of rapture, so this can also be ruled out. Since Joseph neither receives the beatific vision nor is raptured, we must find another way of describing the relationship between the prophet's mind and God's foreknowledge. To do such, we can observe that Joseph's judgment must hit upon the likeness of some kind of divine idea. The metaphor of light is here useful again. It is as if a beam from a flashlight is shined in the corner of a dark room, allowing things once unseen to become seen, even if only temporarily. In the case of prophecy, Thomas notes that God can directly infuse into a person both the objects and the light that enables the objects to be seen.

Now, Thomas maintains that any intellectual light bears some kind of likeness to the uncreated divine light. Intellectual light describes that which allows a rational creature to imitate God's knowledge and, thus, to have a share in it. Moreover, the prophetic light is what gives structure to the prophet's knowledge by allowing there to be a judgment; the light acts as a mediate connection between the prophet's mind and the divine mind. Whatever this prophetic light "touches" the prophet is able to see in a mode similar to the way God knows His divine ideas. From this, we can observe that, when Joseph sees the seven fat cows, he also judges them to be symbolic of God's foreknowledge. As images, the cows function as signs. The prophetic light allows Joseph to

---

84. This characterization of God supplanting (or absorbing) a prophet's mind has some parallels with the target of Thomas's criticism in his treatise *On the Unity of the Intellect against the Averroists (De Unitate Intellectus contra Averroistas)*, trans. Beatrice H. Zedler (Milwaukee: Marquette University Press, 1968).

85. See ST, II-II, q. 175.

see and judge to be true *the hidden significance* of these cows that exists only in the divine mind. His judgment cannot appeal beyond this; and according to Thomas it need not, because his knowledge has been completed and fully resolved. Joseph knows with certainty what God has revealed and simply sees it.

Comparing Prophecy to Wisdom as a Gift of the Holy Spirit

The mode in which Joseph intuitively knows the meaning of Pharaoh's dream appears comparable to that in which the gifts of the Holy Spirit act in a believer united to charity. The gifts of the Holy Spirit prepare someone to be moved directly by the Spirit indwelling through sanctifying grace. According to the presentation in the *Summa theologiae*, each of these gifts corresponds to a particular theological or cardinal virtue. The gift of wisdom corresponds to the virtue of charity and bestows an inclination to judge all things in the light of God as First Principle. One who possesses wisdom as a gift can be led to a "right judgment," and for Thomas a judgment is "right" when "the thinking power apprehends some reality *as it really is*."[86] Rather than being some remote, esoteric outlook that is accessible only to a select few, this wisdom enables any charity-filled person to see the world as it really is—free from error or self-deception. In the gift of wisdom, we thus find an important parallel to prophecy *in the mode of knowing*. Their key difference lies in the fact that the gift of wisdom is caused primarily in the subject's will by charity and exists secondarily in the intellect.[87] Charity is the common cause of all the gifts of the Holy Spirit.[88] While being caused primarily in the human will, the gift's "essence" is still found in the intellect, and its proper act remains right judgment.[89]

More specifically, it belongs to the gift of wisdom to judge things "according to the divine ideas."[90] As a gift, wisdom functions more on the level of intellection

---

86. ST, II-II, q. 51, a. 3, ad 1: "rectum iudicium in hoc consistit quod vis cognoscitiva apprehendat rem aliquam *secundum quod in se est*" (emphasis mine).

87. ST, II-II, q. 45, a. 2, co: "sapientia quae est donum causam quidem habet in voluntate, scilicet caritatem, sed essentiam habet in intellectu, cuius actus est recte iudicare."

88. See ST, I-II, q. 68, a. 5.

89. See ST, I, q. 79, a. 9, ad 4: "diiudicare vero, vel mensurare, est actus intellectus applicantis principia certa ad examinationem propositorum."

90. ST, II-II, q. 45, a. 2, co.: "sapientia importat quandam rectitudinem iudicii *secundum rationes divinas*" (emphasis mine). See also ST, II-II, q. 45, a. 2, ad 3; compare ST, II-II, q. 173,

than on the level of reasoning, allowing its recipients to contemplate and judge "about divine things" (*circa res divinas*), while also disposing them to make right judgments about human affairs from a God's-eye point-of-view. Thomas singles out wisdom's ability "to direct human acts through divine rules."[91] The gift, thus, directs a person not only speculatively in contemplation about "divine things," but also practically "in action." This means that wisdom applies not only to what is necessary and eternal, but also to rules as they govern contingent affairs, which human acts and morals fall under.[92]

A person with the gift of wisdom comes close to a vision of the principle (*visio principii*)[93] that comes about through a kind of "sympathy" (*compassio*) or "connaturality" (*connaturalitas*).[94] This "vision" comes before any reasoning or deliberation about a course of action, and it enables one to direct deliberation and ultimately the acts themselves in the light of that principle. Human acts that emerge from deliberation can only flow from principles known, even if they are only imperfectly known. Under the gift of wisdom, human acts are guided "by divine ideas."[95] The "divine ideas" here are representative of God's *practical* ideas, which is why Thomas uses the word *rationes* here and not *ideae*.[96] A better translation would perhaps be "according to divine *rules*," in order to convey the sense that God's *rationes* "measure" human practical reason. This reading is supported by a fuller definition Thomas gives in his question on wisdom as a gift. Here, the term *divinas rationes* is almost seamlessly replaced by *divinas regulas*, "divine rules": The gift of wisdom "establishes rectitude of judgment about divine things or about other things *by means of divine rules [per regulas divinas]*; [it does this] from a certain connaturality or union to divine things [*ex quadam connaturalitate sive unione ad divina*], which is through charity."[97]

---

a. 1, co: where Thomas sees prophecy as "representing" God's foreknowledge.

91. ST, II-II, q. 45, a. 3, co.: "per divinas regulas dirigens actus humanos."

92. See ST, II-II, q. 45, a. 3, ad 2.

93. ST, II-II, q. 45, a. 3, ad 3: "ad sapientiam per prius pertinet contemplatio divinorum, quae est visio principii; et posterius dirigere actus humanos secundum rationes divinas."

94. ST, II-II, q. 45, a. 2, co.: "Rectum iudicium habere de eis secundum quandam connaturalitatem ad ipsa pertinet ad sapientiam secundum quod donum est spiritus sancti.... Huiusmodi autem compassio sive connaturalitas ad res divinas fit per caritatem, quae quidem unit nos Deo."

95. ST, II-II, q. 45, a. 2, ad 3: "secundum rationes divinas."

96. When Thomas uses the term *idea*, he seems often to be referring to an object of knowledge that is not immediately related to an action or operation.

97. ST, II-II, q. 45, a. 4, co. (emphasis mine).

Having outlined the essential aspects of what Thomas thinks wisdom as a gift of the Holy Spirit consists in, we can now turn to what he says about the *use* of wisdom and the other gifts of the Holy Spirit and compare this to what he says about the use and purpose of prophecy. Wisdom along with all the gifts of the Holy Spirit is something "necessary for salvation" (*necessarium ad salutem*).[98] Thomas explains in his general treatment of the gifts:

> In [the human] ordination to the final, supernatural end—to which reason moves insofar as it is in some way formed, albeit imperfectly, by the theological virtues—the movement of reason is not sufficient, unless an instinct or motion of the Holy Spirit is present from above.... No one can arrive at the inheritance of the land of the blessed unless moved and led by the Holy Spirit; therefore, to arrive at that end, it is necessary for humans to have the gift of the Holy Spirit.[99]

The necessity of the gifts of the Holy Spirit does not come from the fact that they ordain humans to their final end; the theological virtues already do this. Their necessity is rather from the fact that the theological virtues are insufficient with respect to their "mode of operating" in believers.[100] Theological virtues act as potential principles of human action, but the gifts help believers to realize these potentials in concrete moments through the direct inspiration of the Holy Spirit working through charity. Thomas deploys his oft-used metaphor of the teacher and student to illustrate this needed functioning of the gifts: "A physician who knows perfectly the art of medicine, can work alone [*per se*], but the physician's student who is not yet fully instructed cannot work alone, unless instructed by [the physician]."[101] In this way, the gifts act as the continual, personalized instruction of the Holy Spirit for the believer.[102]

Regarding the gift of wisdom, Thomas observes that there may be some individuals who receive higher degrees of wisdom than others and that this superior wisdom is not meant to assist their own salvation, but rather is meant "to ordain others" to salvation.[103] To "ordain others" to salvation involves moving or encouraging others toward the contemplation of divine things and helping

---

98. ST, I-II, q. 68, a. 2, sc.

99. ST, I-II, q. 68, a. 2, co.

100. ST, I-II, q. 68, a. 2, ad 1.

101. ST, I-II, q. 68, a. 2, co.

102. See Torrell, *Maître spirituel*, 275–98 (*Spiritual Master*, 211–24).

103. ST, II-II, q. 45, a. 5, co.

them to direct their actions so that they accord with divine rules. He explains: "this [higher] degree of wisdom is not common to everyone who has sanctifying grace, but rather pertains to the gratuitous graces, which the Holy Spirit distributes as He wills."[104] Drawing on his earlier treatise on grace, he recalls in this passage the distinction between sanctifying and gratuitous grace.[105] This gratuitous degree of wisdom is nothing but the very gift of prophecy. Thomas likely feels no need to mention this link explicitly in the article, given that his focus here is wisdom as a gift of the Holy Spirit, but the allusion to the Pauline language of the Spirit's "distribution" of gifts at will is clear enough (1 Cor 12). Nevertheless, the distinction lays the needed groundwork for what he knows he will fully treat later in his questions on prophecy.

In an earlier article about whether the gifts of Holy Spirit are virtues (*habitus*), Thomas also directly juxtaposes prophecy and the gift of wisdom (not as a gratuitous grace), which serves to further accentuate the differences between them. Since prophecy consists in a "divine inspiration" and the gifts of the Holy Spirit are also "divine inspirations," an objector argues that there is no real distinction between them.[106] Thomas, however, singles out prophecy's functioning not as something strictly necessary for salvation, but as something meant to display the glory and the work of the Holy Spirit: "Prophecy concerns gifts that are for the manifestation of the Spirit, not for the necessity of salvation."[107] The exact Pauline statement at 1 Cor 12:7 to prophecy's character as a "manifestation" of the Spirit includes the added specification that such manifestations are meant to be of service to others and to the common good. Prophecy does this by attracting others through a type of indication or reflexive reference to God's testimony; in this way, the prophet draws others to believe in this divine testimony by accepting the gift of faith—faith which is precisely "necessary for salvation."[108]

To recall the prologue to the *Summa* questions on prophecy, in its ability to manifest the Spirit, prophecy can extend even "to the higher mysteries . . .

---

104. ST, II-II, q. 45, a. 5, co.: "iste gradus sapientiae non est communis omnibus habentibus gratiam gratum facientem, sed magis pertinet ad gratias gratis datas, quas spiritus sanctus distribuit prout vult."

105. See ST, I-II, q. 111, a. 1.

106. ST, I-II, q. 68, a. 3, obj. 3.

107. ST, I-II, q. 68, a. 3, ad 3: "prophetia est de donis quae sunt ad manifestationem spiritus, non autem ad necessitatem salutis."

108. See ST, II-II, q. 2, aa. 3–8; see Heb 11:6.

that pertain to *wisdom*."[109] In Thomas's mind, this prophetic wisdom helps lead others to faith in the mysteries of salvation: "the higher mysteries" of the Incarnation and Trinity. Here, Thomas puts on display his integrated understanding of how the missions of the divine persons of the Trinity relate to his accounts of prophecy and wisdom. More specifically, we now see through our discussion above how it is through a gratuitous gift of wisdom given to certain individuals that others come to know the divine person of the incarnate Son as Wisdom. This gratuitous wisdom, which is equivalent to prophecy, directs others to the mission of the Son, who serves as the root and fountain of all our knowledge of God and leads us to the Father. In doing this, both gratuitous wisdom and prophecy simultaneously make "manifest" the particular mission of the Holy Spirit, to whom Thomas specifically appropriates this act of revealing the fullness of the Trinitarian mystery to people.[110] They do this especially by inviting and attracting those who hear the testimony of prophets and apostles into a deeper relationship with the Trinity. Prophetic testimony, when heard by those who have not yet received or confessed faith, can prepare others to seek and receive the theological virtues and gifts of the Holy Spirit through which the life of the Trinity is born in a person by sanctifying grace. For those who already believe, it can call to mind the saving love and work of the Trinity, who already dwells in their souls. Prophecy does this above all by helping to order a person's judgments through a type of divine enticement or persuasion—by calling to mind the good promised to those who entrust their judgment to the light of faith and seek to judge all things in accord with God's own judgments: in short, by calling one to love divine wisdom.

The Distinction of Graces and Its Relationship to Prophecy and Wisdom

Some notable tensions within Thomas's account of the divisions of grace also arise when prophecy and the gifts of the Holy Spirit are juxtaposed. This division is initially introduced in the pivotal Question 111 on grace from the *Prima secundae*, where we have already encountered the important distinction between sanctifying grace and gratuitous grace. Unlike the former, gratuitous grace is directly ordained not to the sanctification or good of the individual

---

109. ST, II-II, q. 171, prologue.

110. See Emery, *Trinitarian Theology of St. Thomas*, 260–61.

recipient, but to a common good. A difficulty, however, arises from this division: Could any person living a charity-filled life fail to ordain others to the contemplation of divine things or fail to encourage others to live according to God's rules? In knowing and confessing the Trinitarian mystery through supernatural faith, can someone who is already united to God through sanctifying grace fail to manifest this mystery to others? Could it not be said that simply by existing within their community those charity-filled believers already bear witness to what faith teaches about God? Do they not already provide good example for others by simply going about their daily lives without any extraordinary acts or gratuitous graces? The answer to this last question seems to be "yes." And if they do, does this not make the gratuitous graces possible distractions to the ordinary living out of Christian faith by believers?

Here one perceives a structural tension in Thomas's thought between those friends of God who simply "by existing" have a potentially positive effect on their neighbors, on the one hand, and, on the other, certain things said in the New Testament about the need to consciously manifest the life of faith at times more ostentatiously (as in the way teachers point out examples); such New Testament passages may require us to qualify this "yes" to some extent. At times in the Gospels, Jesus vividly reminds his disciples not to put a lamp in a cellar or under a bushel, but rather they should allow their actions to manifest and shine out as a lamp on a lampstand so that others may see the light.[111] He calls his friends to be salt of the earth; as salt, they are meant to season the world without losing their own flavor. Salt, of course, transforms something tasteless into something palatable, just as the friends of God are meant to transform the ordinary, everyday things of the earth through their concrete lives of faith. These and other passages seem to suggest that "simply existing" is not enough for the Christian, but that there is a higher calling by charity to go beyond oneself—to be oriented toward others and the world. To express this tension in Thomistic language, if one were to press this distinction between sanctifying grace and gratuitous grace too hard, one could easily end up, it seems, distorting a structural feature of sanctifying grace—its already superabundant and socially diffusive character. On top of the superabundance of sanctifying grace, the even greater superabundance of the gratuitous graces allows certain individuals to help others to be open to sanctifying grace by means of instruction, correction, and example. The gratuitous graces are really that more gratuitous, "grace upon

---

111. Lk 8:16, 11:33; Mt 5:13–14; Mk 4:21–23.

grace," *et gratiam pro gratia* (Jn 1:16). More specifically, by means of a gratu-itous gift of wisdom, those who have been given deeper knowledge of the divine mysteries can more effectively lead others to faith or can help strengthen those who already believe by reminding them what they are to believe (the *credenda*) and the basis for this credibility (God's own testimony). Gratuitous wisdom functions collectively with all the other gratuitous graces, and as a whole they help to build up and order the common good of the Church. Their common use is rooted in their common origin in the same Spirit who causes them.

One might suppose that it is "more logical" for all gratuitous graces to flow from sanctifying grace, like heat flowing from a fire; but Thomas does not follow this logic.[112] He insists that prophecy and the other gratuitous graces can be had without charity. On this, he thinks he is simply following scripture, which includes St. Paul's teaching regarding the primacy of charity:

> Prophecy can be without charity; and this is clear for two reasons. First, on account of their respective acts: For prophecy pertains to the intellect, whose act precedes the act of the will, which is perfected by charity. Hence, the Apostle [1 Cor 13] numbers prophecy along with the other things pertaining to the intellect that can be had without charity. Secondly, on account of their respective ends; for prophecy like the other gratuitous graces is given for the good of the Church, according to 1 Cor 12:7, *The manifestation of the Spirit is given to every man unto profit.* [Prophecy] is not directly meant to unite a prophet's own affection [*affectus*] to God, which is the purpose of charity. Therefore, prophecy can exist without a good life, as regards the very root of this goodness.[113]

The "very root" of the good life is for Thomas sanctifying grace, which he juxta-poses with the gratuitous grace of prophecy in this passage. Because of this, it remains difficult to define what Thomas means by "gratuitous grace" without some ultimate reference to sanctifying grace. Although he juxtaposes the two, he does not think in the final analysis that the gratuitous graces are caused by sanctifying grace, since not everyone who has gratuitous graces has sanctifying grace. This decision to classify gratuitous grace differently from sanctifying grace also seems to be justifiable from what he says about how they relate differently to the final end. Gratuitous grace points toward the promised good of sanctifying

---

112. See ST, I-II, q. 111, a. 5, ad 2.
113. ST, II-II, q. 172, a. 4, co.

grace without actually bestowing it. A complete analysis of Thomas's doctrine of grace would be necessary to clarify this classification, which goes well beyond our scope here. What this brief discussion reveals is how interdependent the two types of graces are, one shedding light on the other.

From this, the following possibility is worth exploring: Could Thomas's conceptual reliance on sanctifying grace to help clarify gratuitous grace be expressed differently? Could one say that on the personal level individuals have sanctifying grace, but on the social or interpersonal level there are these additional gratuitous graces? Expressing the distinction in this way, however, sounds odd based on what Thomas says elsewhere. He, for instance, explicitly denies that grace exists as an independent substance outside of human subjects—as if grace were a thing floating around in the air; grace always exists and inheres in persons.[114] Since it does not exist outside people, Thomas also calls grace an accidental "quality" in the soul.[115] On this account, it is impossible to talk in any strict sense about a type of grace held collectively or socially outside of individuals; this is why he emphasizes the common origin of these personal graces in the Holy Spirit and their social orientation or function as they are ordered to a common end. It is the origin and end of the various gratuitous graces that unify them according to Thomas, and the same Spirit is the bond of charity that constitutes the Church.

How helpful, then, was our earlier attempt to compare prophecy and the gifts of the Holy Spirit? In light of our discussion of the divisions of grace, it now seems to be somewhat inappropriate. The gifts, after all, exist only in someone who is united to God through sanctifying grace and, thus, entail charity as their cause. Prophecy is a gratuitous grace and does not require charity. Another contrast to the gifts is that the gifts are only given in proportion to what the recipient needs for salvation. Thomas explains:

> Wisdom [as a gift] … implies a certain rectitude of judgment about divine things both to be seen and consulted; with regard to each [of these], people are appointed wisdom according to different grades from their union to divine things. Some people are given only as much right judgment *as is necessary for salvation*—both in the contemplation of divine things and in the ordination of human things according to

---

114. ST, I-II, q. 110, a. 4.
115. ST, I-II, q. 110, a. 2.

divine rules. And this [gift] is not absent in anyone living without mortal sin through sanctifying grace, since if nature does not fail in necessities, much less does grace.[116]

Here he echoes what he said early in his general question on the gifts of the Holy Spirit: All the gifts are necessary for salvation, but only to a certain degree.[117] Structurally, the gifts function on a different level than the gratuitous graces, which are only inducements toward a necessary end. When expressed in this way, the gratuitous graces can be said to go beyond what is strictly necessary for the salvation of the individual recipient.

As a gratuitous grace, prophecy is strictly speaking not necessary for the salvation of the individual recipient, being given principally then "for the manifestation of the Spirit."[118] It now makes sense to try to unpack this Pauline phrase "manifestation of the Spirit" some more. 1 Cor 12:7 explains that to each person is given a particular manifestation of the Spirit "for the utility" or "advantage" of a common good (*ad utilitatem* or *pros to sympheron*); in this context, the common good in question is the good of the local ecclesial community of Corinth. A "manifestation" is a showing or revealing of something that was once unseen or hidden. As spiritual realities suddenly made apparent and visible in certain individuals, gratuitous graces are visible channels through which Christian faith "is confirmed and propagated" for the common good and especially for the common good "of the Church."[119] These graces, thus, act as signs, pointing to deeper realities at work in the persons who receive them. They simultaneously point to the deeper reality of the Church, for it is only through ecclesial incorporation that one is able to share in the goods that these gifts provide. The Church becomes a sign itself that points to the ultimate good of salvation; in this way, it confirms faith and witnesses to the truth of divine testimony, cooperating in God's saving mission. We can see this parallel between the Church as a cooperator in salvation and prophecy more clearly in the following passage as Thomas tries to pinpoint exactly what is "gratuitous" about a gratuitous grace:

---

116. ST, II-II, q. 45, a. 5, co. (emphasis mine).

117. See ST, I-II, q. 68, a. 2.

118. See ST, I-II, q. 68, a. 3, ad 3.

119. ST, I, q. 43, a. 7, ad 6: "Manifestatio spiritus datur alicui ad utilitatem, scilicet ecclesiae. Quae quidem utilitas est, ut per huiusmodi visibilia signa fides confirmetur et propagetur."

> It is given to someone as something above the faculty of nature and
> above personal merit; it is not given so that the very human person is
> justified, but rather so that he may cooperate [*cooperetur*] in the justi-
> fication of another. Thus, it is not called sanctifying grace. From this,
> the apostle also says (1 Cor 12:7) *to each is given a manifestation of the
> Spirit for the utility*, namely, of others [*scilicet aliorum*].[120]

As a gratuitous manifestation of the Spirit, prophecy functions as a witness to
and confirmation of God's power and especially of His care for human salvation
through supernatural divine revelation.[121] This care extends so far as to invite
other humans to be "cooperators" in God's saving work by bestowing upon them
certain gifts that function personally but are oriented to a collective good: the
ecclesial good. These gifts allow them to perform actions that normally are only
proper to God. Thomas thinks that after the Incarnation, prophecy and all the
gratuitous gifts reveal the work and mission of the Holy Spirit in a special way.[122]
To the Holy Spirit is appropriated any work that has its particular focus on the
building up of the common good, and more specifically the common good of
the Church.

While Thomas thinks the common good is superior to the private good of
an individual, he also considers that the end of the Church as a whole is ordered
to the attainment of God as a proper or personal good commonly shared. This
helps to illustrate our earlier claim that, for Thomas, personal salvation through
faith is communally structured and socially mediated at its very core, because
faith's object as a good is a common good and end.[123] This has significant reper-
cussions for how one understands the notion of "personal salvation." Based
on Thomas's threefold structuring of grace, faith, and prophecy, it seems that
it is only in the giving of one's self for the many that one finds the fulfilment
of life and hits upon its deepest meaning and purpose (cf. Jn 15:13). In God's
superabundant giving to human beings, a similar superabundant self-donation
is elicited as a response in the life of faith; this elicitation or evocation is brought
into particular focus and emphasis by the gratuitous graces. In this way, graces,
like prophecy, simultaneously point back to God's superabundant care for the

---

120. ST, I-II, q. 111, a. 1, co.

121. See ST, I-II, q. 111, a. 4, co.: "in his autem quae sunt supra rationem divinitus
revelata, confirmatio est per ea quae sunt divinae virtuti propria."

122. See ST, I, q. 43, a. 7, ad 6

123. See ST, I-II, q. 111, a. 5, ad 1, 3.

human race and point forward to a human response to God in faith—where one becomes not just a person "saved" by God, but a person who knows that God calls human creatures to give of themselves in a similar superabundance as coworkers in redemption.

Prophecy's Mirroring of Wisdom

Our comparison between prophecy and wisdom as a gift of the Holy Spirit now permits the following conclusions about prophetic judgment to be drawn. With regards to their functioning in human persons, prophetic judgments have some parallels to judgments from inclination caused by the gift of wisdom. Under the gift of wisdom, people make judgments with reference to God's own judgments—the knowledge He has of His own divine ideas—through a kind of connaturality. Prophetic judgments often look like judgments from inclination, since they do not depend on things previously known and acquired through study. As long as the prophetic light is given, a prophet can make connatural judgments about things according to God's own self-knowledge. These prophetic judgments complete prophetic knowledge and are more certain than natural human knowledge, since the prophet participates in divine knowledge to a higher degree.

In briefly considering God's own knowledge as social in the unity of the Trinity, we found a parallel between judgments through the gift of wisdom and prophetic judgments in their distinctive social orientation. In our earlier chapters, this social character of prophecy was seen to be rooted in Thomas's understanding of the final good and the virtue of faith, which orients believers to their final good as supernaturally revealed. The gift of wisdom as a gratuitous grace orients the believer to something beyond what is strictly necessary for one's own salvation. In this way it closely resembles prophecy in that it functions analogously to God's own Wisdom in ordering principally the good of a whole; indeed, wisdom as a gratuitous grace is in the final analysis indistinguishable from prophecy.

If we reintroduce at this stage Thomas's description of sacred doctrine as a wisdom, we see now how sacred doctrine has the potential to overlap with this gratuitous kind of wisdom. While sacred doctrine relies principally on study for its knowledge (making judgments from knowing), it presupposes the capacity to make manifest the truth about God. Its principal focus consists in making more manifest the truth necessary for salvation, but this does not stop the teacher of sacred doctrine from making the truth more fully know, allowing it to be enjoyed as a communal good of the Church. This seems to be a possibility within Thomas's account: the possibility that the teacher receives a gratuitous gift of wisdom, a prophetic gift. In a different but analogous sense, the teacher of sacred doctrine seems to exhibit a distinctive prophetic character for Thomas. This character is expressed most vividly by the way sacred doctrine is orderable to the salvation of others. It is orderable to the salvation of others, he thinks, in the first instance through its speculative or contemplative character, which is focused on knowledge of divine things; it become orderable for the action of others (for human action or morals) in the way this truth shows forth in the person of the teacher who becomes a model to imitate. Considering sacred doctrine's prophetic character in this context helps us appreciate Thomas's vision of the unity of speculative and practical dimensions of sacred doctrine, all the while preserving the priority of the speculative.[124] It is likely due to this prioritization of sacred doctrine's speculative character that Thomas decides not to highlight its prophetic character in Question One to any great extent beyond asserting that it remains secondarily "practical"—for orienting operation and moral action for one's final end.

Where perhaps we see sacred doctrine's prophetic character most clearly on display is in the way it shares aspects of prophecy's orientation toward an ecclesial good; thus, its prophetic character and practical character are closely link. Sacred doctrine's very existence as a science and as the highest human wisdom is an effect of God's superabundant goodness. As an effect of uncreated goodness, sacred doctrine must itself be oriented to a single common good which is simultaneously its cause: God. In juxtaposing the sapiential and practical characters of sacred doctrine and prophecy, Thomas makes manifest that sacred doctrine's certitude is rooted in a superior certitude, that of God's own knowledge, which is the source of all certitude and in which it is a participation through the medium of prophetic testimony. This certitude comes about through judgments that are made under a supernatural light, the light of faith, with the assistance of study. In Thomas's analysis of prophetic judgment, we come to see just how determinative the supernatural light of prophecy is for the prophet's knowledge, which enables us to catch a glimpse of a parallel between prophetic judgment and the judgments made in sacred doctrine. In particular,

---

124. ST, I, q. 1, a. 4.

it illuminates how it is Thomas thinks sacred doctrine has the capacity to judge other human sciences and why this capacity functions in judgments alone.

By examining the deeper links between prophecy as a gratuitous grace and sacred doctrine, one begins to see how sacred doctrine comes to exhibit characteristics of a manifestation of the Spirit that is meant to serve the Church by bearing witness to God's truth and superabundant goodness. Sacred doctrine remains a locus for how the Church participates more fully in this character of superabundant goodness in which God has established her so that she may attract all humans to Him. In fact, sacred doctrine, like prophetic knowledge, is ordered primarily to the good of the Church and especially toward manifesting its goodness.

This insight reveals a final parallel in Thomas's thought between the prior givenness of revelation and the prior givenness of the Church in sacred doctrine. The Church is required for integrating prophetic testimony into ecclesial life (for making sense of it)—a strongly Pauline point; in so doing, it enables prophetic gifts to be profitable for others. Prior revelation to prophets is required for sacred doctrine, but it also needs the Church to whom this prior revelation has been entrusted or deposited. Thereafter, sacred doctrine can continue to assist the Church in integrating prophetic testimony into her life (in the manner of a St. Paul or a St. Thomas Aquinas) to allow it to be profitable to others. This integrative function seen in both the Church and sacred doctrine mirrors wisdom. Thomas's account of prophecy, thus, helps us appreciate this shared sapiential character between the Church and sacred doctrine within his thought. When read at a structural level in the *Summa*, it points to a link between the two seen in an analogous gift of wisdom working at an ecclesial level. The teacher of sacred doctrine can also receive a sapiential impetus through a gift of wisdom as a gratuitous grace, which is nothing other than a gift of prophecy. This specific gift of wisdom as a gratuitous grace helps to make manifest sacred doctrine's general prophetic character, which in turn makes the Church's goodness, beauty, truth, and credibility more manifest. This prophetic character provides the continual impetus to witness to divine Wisdom by integrating all saving (and especially moral) truth in service to the Church.

Conclusion

Examining Thomas's questions on prophecy has accentuated two important features of his notion of sacred doctrine: (1) its character as a participated or shared form of knowledge, whose sharing is the cause of its certitude being superior to things known by human reason, and (2) its orientation toward a social and common good, namely the good of the Church. The tendency in recent scholarship has been to focus on the former cognitive aspect of Thomas's notion of prophecy and its implications for sacred doctrine; this was not without justification, given that his own writings emphasize prophecy's intellectual character as a grace dealing principally with knowledge. At the same time, a structural reading of these questions on prophecy reveals a distinct social and ecclesial orientation for prophecy, which in turn enables one to see how the gift is fully integrated into sacred doctrine and has the potential even to shape the vocation of the teacher-theologian. Prophetic revelation has at its core not only certain knowledge of the truth, but also the correlative purpose of sharing this truth as a good with others. Both correlative aspects structure in turn how the Church understands and witnesses to the truth of the Christian faith in her life.

Our structural reading of a number of key *Summa* texts revealed that Thomas sees prophetic testimonies as being structured so as to point beyond themselves back to the root of their own truth and diffusiveness: God's own diffusive goodness. The knowledge that is imparted to prophets, because it is itself a kind of participation in God's own knowledge, is also diffusive of this goodness.[1] In this way, the social orientations of prophecy and sacred doctrine

---

1. From this, one sees the way in which divine revelation can be described as a sort of recapitulation of God's diffusive creation. We can see revelation as relating to God's initial outpouring of goodness—rooting the doctrines of divine providence and government firmly in the original intention of God's creative operation.

reveal how both are ordered ultimately by truth and love, even though charity is not strictly required for the prophet to prophesy or for the teacher of sacred doctrine to teach.

Following closely St. Paul, Thomas views prophecy and all the gratuitous graces as being ordered principally to the building up of an earthly order: the "ecclesiastical order" (*ordo ecclesiasticus*) or terrestrial Church.[2] In his questions on prophecy and the gratuitous graces one encounters something close to a Thomistic ecclesiology.[3] It is important to recall how these insights about the ordering of the Church are never separated from the larger plan of the *Summa* and most especially from his treatise on grace and the animating principle of every grace, the Holy Spirit. Prophecy as a gratuitous grace makes the Church continually attractive; it helps to purify her of sin through correction, guide her in sanctification through instruction, and console her in times of distress and desolation. Prophecy especially helps to remind the Church of the source of her credibility, which lies not in human reason, but in God's very testimony communicated to specific individuals in history.

Recalling that the Church's credibility resides in history permits one to see how prophecy is also structured in Thomas's thought by his doctrine of creation, another aspect of God's operation that is diffusive of divine goodness. Given to prophets and apostles as an outpouring of divine goodness meant for all but paradoxically entrusted to a few, revelation maintains a constant point of reference in creation—the more basic and original, freely-willed outpouring of divine being and goodness. One is, of course, reminded how Thomas views creation as a structural reference point for the entirety of sacred doctrine in his famous axiom from Question One: "since grace does not destroy nature but perfects it, natural reason ought to serve faith, just as the natural inclination of the will yields to charity."[4] Within the nature-grace superstructure, prophetic revelation falls most straightforwardly in the reason-faith schema.

The historical situatedness of prophetic revelation also suggests that sacred doctrine too is embedded in the created order; this aspect of sacred doctrine

---

2. ST, I-II, q. 111, a. 5, ad 1.

3. On the Second and Third Parts as a theology of the Church, see Max Seckler, *Le salut et l'histoire: Le pensée de saint Thomas d'Aquin sur la théologie de l'histoire* (Paris: Cerf, 1967), 205–11; first published as *Das Heil in der Geschichte: Geschichtstheologisches Denken bei Thomas von Aquin* (Munich: Kösel, 1964). On the specific issue of situating gratuitous graces in a theology of the Church, see Emero Stiegman, "Charism and Institution in Aquinas," *The Thomist* 38, no. 4 (1974): 723–33.

4. ST, I, q. 1, a. 8, ad 2.

simultaneously serves as a reminder to humans to live in the here and now for the kingdom of God as their ultimate happiness and salvation. Thomas shows this principally through the Second Part and the primacy of the final end and beatitude within the moral part. In the discussion of faith in chapter three, we saw how faith is described by Thomas as the beginning of this beatitude or eternal life in the believer; this life is fully embedded in the world through its grafting onto the Church. Set within this larger framework, sacred doctrine's own impetus to discern the particular needs of the world at a given time in relation to salvation can be seen to be in fact an extension of prophetic revelation's essential ordination to the care of a common good—an impetus that ultimately imitates God's providence. This aspect of caring for a common, ecclesial good is at the heart of what was identified as sacred doctrine's prophetic character.

This care for the Church links sacred doctrine also with Thomas's notion of the gratuitous graces and especially the gratuitous gift of wisdom. Adopting the Pauline language of "manifestations of the Spirit" (1 Cor 12) to describe these graces enables him to depict them as simultaneously showing forth God's truth and goodness. On a very basic level, a manifestation is a showing forth or revealing of something that was previously unseen or hidden. Any manifestation of the Spirit is according to Thomas structurally related to the manifestation or revelation of divine glory as something imperfect to something perfect.[5] Seen as manifestations, gratuitous graces, like prophecy, are meant to induce others to be united with God, which only happens through sanctifying grace. Prophecy, thus, exhibits a special character of divine inducement and persuasion, which utilizes the knowledge and external actions of certain people to draw others to God. Sacred doctrine through its teachers also participates in this task of persuasion when they are animated by the theological virtue of faith. As wisdom, sacred doctrine can be animated by the gift of wisdom and, in certain individuals, by a gratuitous grace of wisdom.

Within the *Summa*, faith remains foundational for sacred doctrine's divine pedagogy and persuasiveness. But neither faith nor sacred doctrine is a full disclosure. The life of grace is not immediately consummated for humans on earth, and faith remains a calling to become increasingly like a divine child whose model of filiation is the incarnate Son. The incomplete nature of faith marks it out as a pilgrim journey, and while those justified by faith can possess inchoately the principle of divine life within them as long as they are united to

---

5. Compare ST, II-II, q. 171, a. 4, ad 2: "Prophetia est sicut quiddam imperfectum in genere divinae revelationis.... Perfectio autem divinae revelationis erit in patria."

charity, there still remains a transition period, a need for continued guidance for believers. In his final article on prophecy, Thomas refers to this explicitly as an historical period: the "time of grace" or "state under grace."[6] In this intermediate epoch before the Second Coming, prophecy exists and is ordered to theological faith; it serves as a visible reminder of the promise of incarnate Wisdom to continually renew the Church through the Holy Spirit.

As manifestations of the same Spirit, prophecy and sacred doctrine remain integral sources for renewal in the Church according to Thomas. This insight helps to make sense finally of his rationale for placing the treatise on prophecy at the end of the Second Part of the *Summa*, its moral part: Prophecy and sacred doctrine are especially marked out for the renewal of moral truth. The gift of prophecy continually gives to the Church much needed moral guidance, understood in the broad sense of manifesting the need to live in accord with the truths of faith and to integrate truth and charity in all aspects of life. This enables us also to see how the prophetic character of sacred doctrine reinforces and adds a new incentive to its sapiential character, that is, its integrative impetus.

In their own contemplation and study of the gift of prophecy, teachers of catholic truth are also reminded that sacred doctrine, which relies so heavily on prophetic testimony and revelation, is itself a part of divine providence; prophets become quasi-models for teachers of sacred doctrine at least insofar as they both strive to make manifest, in their proper ways, the wisdom of God at work in the world. After the end of the incarnate Son's earthly mission, prophecy's unique way of manifesting God's wisdom serves as a continual reminder to the Church that the path to salvation is Christ: his life and teaching and the sacraments he has given—all topics of the *Summa*'s unfinished Third Part.

Looking beyond the scope of this study and its need to stay relatively close to Thomas's own *Summa* text, we can say, an integrated account of prophecy and sacred doctrine has the potential in the future to be fruitfully deployed in a fuller theology of the discernment of spirits. Of course, Thomas already explicitly links prophecy with the gift of discernment, but this important theological subject, which can still at times be treated in a somewhat isolated fashion in spiritual or pastoral theology, would very likely benefit from coming into fuller contact with the integration Thomas outlines for it under prophecy in his moral part. The need in today's Church and world to read and understand "the signs of the times" has notably received an added impetus in Catholic theology since the

---

6. ST, II-II, q. 174, a. 6, co.

Second Vatican Council. Here, Thomas's thoroughgoing situating of prophecy within sacred doctrine and especially within Christian moral reflection may prove a helpful guide and inspiration to contemporary theologians. At the very least, his account provides stimulating theological accompaniment for theologians who wrestle with the issues faced by the Church of today. This accompaniment and a special focus on his integrative vision of sacred doctrine would be useful in the areas of both general discernment of spirits or the practice of personal spiritual guidance and the more specialized cases of the discernment of public prophetic phenomena in the Church.

It is no exaggeration to say that Thomas's approach reminds Christians of the crucial truth that any desire to read "the signs of the times"—whether in the Church, the world, one's family, one's work, or one's personal prayer—can never be an excuse for setting aside the other aspects of sacred doctrine and the teachings of the faith. The Thomistic approach to this issue as outlined here takes its starting point from a historically rooted call for renewed engagement with all aspects of God's pedagogy as shaped by the integrative function of wisdom. To express this in admittedly unconventional terms, the prophetic dimension of the Thomistic spirit lies in its continual impetus and attempt to integrate all truth, with a special focus on integrating and defending truths that serve as moral guidance within the preached and (hopefully) lived life of the Church.

This continual need to integrate moral truth in the Church's life calls to mind once again the incomplete character of both sacred doctrine and prophecy. God is the ultimate initiator of both, and trust in the divine initiative remains the essential starting point for both. Such incompleteness of knowledge does not imply an imperfection on God's part but is structural and serves as a continual invitation to ask for more faith and divine guidance, whether from prophets or teachers. The incompleteness stems in part from the virtue of faith which is itself destined to fall away in the beatific vision. Heaven has no need for faith or prophecy, because there will be the vision of God face-to-face.[7] Prophecy thus is meant exclusively for those on a pilgrimage of faith, for *viatores*. Sacred doctrine in heaven too will be transformed and give way to vision, but such a vision as St. Paul himself stammered to articulate (1 Cor 2:9) is nearly impossible to describe. Due to its pilgrim use, the gift of prophecy cannot be interpreted as an arrival of any sort, neither for the prophet nor for the individuals who heed the message; it certainly cannot be taken as a merited arrival at a permanent,

---

7. ST, II-II, q. 174, a. 5.

high moral state. Any prophecy, no matter how consequential it may seem, will always pale in comparison to the light of glory; and indeed, as was seen, it will pale compared even to the light of faith.

Analogously, knowledge of sacred doctrine does not guarantee personal salvation or even moral virtue for the one who studies theology. What teachers of sacred doctrine, however, can take solace in is that they are invited to serve as incomplete and imperfect channels for God to continually nurture the Church. They can do this by reminding her of the promises of incarnate Wisdom and by making manifest to her this saving truth. They have the special capacity, if faithful, to make wisdom concrete and accessible in every age and in every place, potentially aiding all to encounter Wisdom itself.

Bibliography

Works of Thomas Aquinas

Compendium theologiae seu Brevis compilatio theologiae ad fratrem Raynaldum.
Leonine Edition, vol. 42. Rome: Editori di San Tommaso, 1979.

Expositio libri Posteriorum. Edited by R.-A. Gauthier. Leonine Edition, vol.
1*/2. Rome: Commissio Leonina, 1989.

Lectura romana in primum Sententiarum Petri Lombardi. Edited by Leonard
E. Boyle and John F. Boyle. Toronto: Pontifical Institute of Mediaeval
Studies, 2006.

Quaestiones disputatae de veritate. Edited by A. Dondaine. Leonine Edition, vol.
22. Rome: Editori di San Tommaso, 1970–76.

Scriptum super libros Sententiarum magistri Petri Lombardi episcopi Parisiensis.
Edited by Pierre Mandonnet and M. F. Moos. Paris: P. Lethielleux,
1929–47.

Summa contra Gentiles. Edited by P. Marc, C. Pera, and P. Carmello. 3 vols.
Turin: Marietti, 1961–67.

Summa theologiae. Edita, cura et studio fratrum praedicatorum. Leonine
Edition, vols. 4–12. Rome: Ex Typographia Polyglotta S. C. de Propaganda Fide, 1888–1906.

Super Boetium de Trinitate. Edited by P.-M. Gils. Leonine Edition, vol. 50.
Rome: Commissio Leonina, 1992.

Super Epistolas S. Pauli lectura. Edited by R. Cai. 8th ed. 2 vols. Turin: Marietti,
1953.

Super Evangelium S. Ioannis lectura. Edited by R. Cai. 6th ed. Turin: Marietti,
1972.

English Editions of Thomas Aquinas's Works

Albert and Thomas: Select Writings. Translated, edited, and introduced by Simon Tugwell with a preface by Leonard E. Boyle. New York: Paulist Press, 1988.

Commentary on St. Paul's Epistle to the Ephesians by St. Thomas Aquinas. Translation and introduction by Matthew L. Lamb. Albany, NY: Magi Books, 1966.

Commentary on the Gospel of John. Translated by Fabian Larcher and James A. Weisheipl, with introduction and notes by Daniel Keating and Matthew Levering. 3 vols. Washington, DC: The Catholic University of America Press, 2010.

Compendium of Theology. Translated by Richard J. Regan. Oxford: Oxford University Press, 2009.

On the Unity of the Intellect against the Averroists (De Unitate Intellectus Contra Averroistas). Translated from the Latin with an introduction by Beatrice H. Zedler. Milwaukee: Marquette University Press, 1968.

Select Writings: Thomas Aquinas. Edited and translated with an introduction and notes by Ralph McInerny. London: Penguin, 1998.

Summa contra Gentiles. Translated with introductions and notes by Anton C. Pegis, James F. Anderson, Vernon J. Bourke, and Charles J. O'Neil. 5 vols. Notre Dame: University of Notre Dame Press, 1975.

Summa theologiæ. Vol. 45, *Prophecy and Other Charisms (2a2ae. 171–8).* Latin text and English translation, introduction, notes, appendices and glossary by Roland Potter. London: Blackfriars in conjunction with Eyre & Spottiswoode, 1970. Reprint, Cambridge: Cambridge University Press, 2006.

Summa theologica. Translated by Fathers of the English Dominican Province. 3 vols. New York: Benzinger Brothers, 1948.

Super Boetium de Trinitate. In 2 vols. *Faith, Reason and Theology: Questions I–IV of his Commentary on the* De Trinitate *of Boethius.* Translated with introduction and notes by Armand Maurer. Toronto: Pontifical Institute of Mediaeval Studies, 1987; *The Division and Methods of the Sciences: Questions V and VI of his Commentary on the* De Trinitate *of Boethius.* Translated with introduction and notes by Armand Maurer. 4th rev. ed. Toronto: Pontifical Institute of Mediaeval Studies, 1986.

Truth. Translated by Robert W. Mulligan, James V. McGlynn, and Robert W. Schmidt. 3 vols. Indianapolis: Hackett, 1994.

Other Primary Sources

Albert the Great. *Quaestio de prophetia: Visione, immaginazione e dono profetico.* Edited by Anna Rodolfi. Florence: Edizioni del Galluzzo per la Fondazione Ezio Franceschini, 2009.

Aristotle. *The Complete Works of Aristotle.* Edited by Jonathan Barnes. 2 vols. Princeton, NJ: Princeton University Press, 1984.

Augustine of Hippo. *De Trinitate libri XV.* Edited by W. J. Mountain and F. Glorie. Corpus Christianorum, Series Latina 50. Turnhout: Brepols, 1968.

———. *On Genesis: A Refutation of the Manichees, Unfinished Literal Commentary on Genesis, The Literal Meaning of Genesis.* Translated by Edmund Hill. The Works of Saint Augustine 1:3. Hyde Park, NY: New City Press, 2002.

———. *Sermones de Novo Testamento (157–183): In epistulas apostolicas II.* Edited by Shari Boodts. Corpus Christianorum, Series Latina 41Bb. Turnhout: Brepols, 2016.

———. *The Trinity.* Translated by Edmund Hill. The Works of Saint Augustine 1:5. Brooklyn: New City Press, 1991.

Isidore of Seville. *Isidori Hispalensis Episcopi Etymologiarum sive Originum Libri XX.* Edited by W. M. Lindsay. Oxford: Clarendon Press, 1911.

Moses Maimonides. *The Guide of the Perplexed.* Translated and with an introduction and notes by Shlomo Pines. 2 vols. Chicago: University of Chicago Press, 1963.

Secondary Literature

Altmann, Alexander. "Maimonides and Thomas Aquinas: Natural or Divine Prophecy?" *Association for Jewish Studies Review* 3 (1978): 1–19.

Baglow, Christopher T. "Sacred Scripture and Sacred Doctrine in Saint Thomas Aquinas." In *Aquinas on Doctrine: A Critical Introduction*, edited by Thomas G. Weinandy, Daniel A. Keating, and John P. Yocum, 1–25. London: T & T Clark, 2004.

Benoit, Pierre. *Inspiration and the Bible.* Translated by J. Murphy-O'Connor and M. Keverne. London: Sheed and Ward, 1965.

———. "Saint Thomas et l'inspiration des écritures." In *Atti del Congresso internazionale (Roma–Napoli, 17–24 aprile 1974): Tommaso d'Aquino nel suo settimo centenario.* Vol. 3, *Dio e l'economia della salvezza*, 19–30. Naples: Edizioni domenicane italiane, 1976.

Bonino, Serge-Thomas. "Le rôle de l'image dans la connaissance prophétique d'après saint Thomas d'Aquin." *Revue Thomiste* 89, no. 4 (1989): 533–68.

———. "'Les voiles sacrés': À propos d'une citation de Denys." *Studi Tomistici* 45 (1992): 158–71.

———. "Charisms, Forms, and States of Life (*IIa IIae*, qq. 171–189)." Translated by Mary Thomas Noble. In *The Ethics of Aquinas,* edited by Stephen J. Pope, 340–52. Washington, DC: Georgetown University Press, 2002.

———. "The Role of the Apostles in the Communication of Revelation according to the *Lectura super Ioannem* of St. Thomas Aquinas." In Dauphinais and Levering, *Reading John with St. Thomas Aquinas*, 318–46. Washington, DC: The Catholic University of America Press, 2005.

———. "'*Propheta et dominus prophetarum*': Prophétologie et christologie dans la *Lectura super Ioannem*." In *Études thomasiennes*, 157–86. Paris: Parole et Silence, 2018.

Bonnefoy, Jean-François. *La nature de la théologie selon saint Thomas d'Aquin.* Paris: Vrin, 1939.

Boyle, Leonard E. "The Setting of the *Summa theologiae* of St. Thomas—Revisited." In *The Ethics of Aquinas*, edited by Stephen J. Pope, 1–16. Washington, DC: Georgetown University Press, 2002.

Burrell, David. *Knowing the Unknowable God: Ibn-Sina, Maimonides, Aquinas.* Notre Dame: University of Notre Dame Press, 1986.

Burtchaell, James Tunstead. *Catholic Theories of Biblical Inspiration since 1810: A Review and Critique.* Cambridge: Cambridge University Press, 1969.

Casciaro, José María. *El diálogo teológico de santo Tomás con musulmanes y judíos: El tema de la profecía y la revelación.* Madrid: Consejo Superior de Investigaciones Científicas, 1969.

———. "Santo Tomás ante sus fuentes (Estudio sobre la II-II, q. 173, a. 3)." *Scripta Theologica* 6 (1974): 11–65.

Cessario, Romanus. "Toward Understanding Aquinas' Theological Method: The Early Twelfth-Century Experience." In *Studies in Thomistic Theology*, edited by Paul Lockey, 17–89. Houston: Center for Thomistic Studies, 1995.

Chenu, Marie-Dominique. *Toward Understanding Saint Thomas.* Translated by A.-M. Landry and D. Hughes. Chicago: Regnery, 1964.

———. *La Parole de Dieu, 1: La foi dans l'intelligence.* Paris: Cerf, 1964.

———. *La théologie comme science au XIIIe siècle.* 3rd ed. Paris: Vrin, 1969.

Congar, Yves M.-J. "Le sens de l'économie salutaire dans la 'theologie' de saint Thomas d'Aquin." In *Glaube und Geschichte*, edited by Erwin Iserloh and Peter Manns, 73–122. Vol. 2 of *Festgabe Joseph Lortz*. Baden-Baden: Bruno Grimm, 1958.

———. "Tradition et *sacra doctrina* chez saint Thomas D'Aquin." In *Église et Tradition*, edited by Johannes Betz and Heinrich Fries, 157–94. Le Puy: Xavier Mappus, 1963.

———. "Le moment 'économique' et le moment 'ontologique' dans la sacra doctrina (Révélation, théologie, Somme théologique)." In *Mélanges offres à M.-D. Chenu, maître en théologie*, 135–87. Paris: Vrin, 1967.

———. *A History of Theology*. Translated and edited by Hunter Guthrie. Garden City, NY: Doubleday, 1968.

Dauphinais, Michael, and Matthew Levering, eds. *Reading John with St. Thomas Aquinas: Theological Exegesis and Speculative Theology*. Washington, DC: The Catholic University of America Press, 2005.

Davies, Brian. "Is *Sacra doctrina* theology?" *New Blackfriars* 71, no. 836 (1990): 141–47.

Decker, Bruno. "Die Analyse des Offenbarungsvorganges beim hl. Thomas im Lichte vorthomistischer Prophetietraktate: Ein historischer Kommentar zu *S. theol.* II-II q. 173 a. 2 (*De ver.*, q. 12 a. 7)." *Angelicum* 16 (1939): 195–244.

———. *Die Entwicklung der Lehre von der prophetischen Offenbarung von Wilhelm von Auxerre bis zum Thomas von Aquin*. Breslau: Müller & Seiffert, 1940.

Della Croce, R. N. "*Acceptio rerum et Judicium de acceptis* nella Somma 2/2 q. 173, a. 2." *Ephemerides Carmeliticae* 2, no. 2 (1948): 315–32.

Donneaud, Henry. "Histoire d'une histoire: M.-D. Chenu et *La théologie comme science au XIIIe siècle*." *Mémoire Dominicaine* 4 (1994): 139–75.

———. "Note sur le *revelabile* selon Étienne Gilson." *Revue Thomiste* 96, no. 4 (1996): 633–52.

———. "M.-D. Chenu et l'exégèse de *sacra doctrina*." *Revue des sciences philosophiques et théologiques* 81 (1997): 415–37.

———. *Théologie et intelligence de la foi au XIIIème siècle*. Paris: Parole et Silence, 2006.

Elders, Leo. "Les rapports entre la doctrine de la prophétie de saint Thomas et "le Guide des égarés" de Maïmonide." *Divus Thomas* 78 (1975): 449–56.

———, ed. *La doctrine de la révélation divine de saint Thomas d'Aquin: Actes du Symposium sur la pensée de saint Thomas d'Aquin tenu à Rolduc, les 4 et 5 novembre 1989*. Studi Tomistici 37. Vatican City: Libreria Editrice Vaticana, 1990.

———. "St. Thomas Aquinas on Education and Instruction." *Nova et Vetera* 7, no. 1 (2009): 107–24.

Emery, Gilles. *The Trinitarian Theology of St. Thomas Aquinas*. Translated by Francesca A. Murphy. Oxford: Oxford University Press, 2007.

Farkasfalvy, Denis. *Inspiration and Interpretation: A Theological Introduction to Sacred Scripture*. Washington, DC: The Catholic University of America Press, 2010.

———. *A Theology of the Christian Bible: Revelation, Inspiration, Canon*. Washington, DC: The Catholic University of America Press, 2018.

FitzGerald, Brian. *Inspiration and Authority in the Middle Ages: Prophets and Their Critics from Scholasticism to Humanism*. Oxford: Oxford University Press, 2017.

Garceau, Benoit. *Judicium: Vocabulaire, sources, doctrine de Saint Thomas d'Aquin*. Montreal: Institut d'Études Médiévales, 1968.

Gilson, Étienne. *The Spirit of Mediaeval Philosophy*. Translated by A. H. C. Downes. New York: Scribner, 1936.

———. *The Christian Philosophy of St. Thomas Aquinas*. Translated by Laurence K. Shook. New York: Random House, 1956.

———. *The Christian Philosophy of Saint Augustine*. Translated by L. E. M. Lynch. London: Victor Gollancz, 1961.

Healy, Nicholas M. Introduction to Weinandy, *Aquinas on Scripture: An Introduction to his Biblical Commentaries*, 1–20.

Heck, Erich. *Der Begriff* religio *bei Thomas von Aquin: Seine Bedeutung für unser heutiges Verständnis von Religion*. Paderborn: Ferdinand Schöningh, 1971.

Heschel, Abraham Joshua. *The Prophets*. New York: Harper Collins, 2001.

Hvidt, Niels Christian. *Christian Prophecy: The Post-Biblical Tradition*. Oxford: Oxford University Press, 2007.

Jenkins, John I. *Knowledge and Faith in Thomas Aquinas*. Cambridge: Cambridge University Press, 1997.

Johnson, Mark F. "The Sapiential Character of the First Article of the *Summa theologiae*." In *Philosophy and the God of Abraham: Essays in Memory of James A. Weisheipl, OP*, edited by R. J. Long, 85–98. Toronto: Pontifical Institute of Mediaeval Studies, 1991.

———. "Another Look at St. Thomas and the Plurality of the Literal Sense of Scripture." *Medieval Philosophy and Theology* 2 (1992): 118–42.

———. "Apophatic Theology's Cataphatic Dependencies." *The Thomist* 62, no. 4 (1998): 519–31.

———. "Aquinas's *Summa theologiae* as Pedagogy." In *Medieval Education*, edited by Ronald B. Begley and Joseph W. Koterski, 133–42. New York: Fordham University Press, 2005.

Jordan, Mark D. *On Faith:* Summa theologiae, *2-2, qq. 1–16 of St. Thomas Aquinas.* Notre Dame: University of Notre Dame Press, 1990.

———. *Rewritten Theology: Aquinas after His Readers.* Oxford: Blackwell, 2006.

Keaty, Anthony. "The Demands of Sacred Doctrine on 'Beginners.'" *New Blackfriars* 84 (2003): 500–509.

Labourdette, M.-M. "Théologie morale." *Revue Thomiste* 50, no. 1 (1950): 396–421.

Levering, Matthew, and Michael Dauphinais, eds. *Reading Romans with St. Thomas Aquinas.* Washington, DC: The Catholic University of America Press, 2012.

Mansini, Guy. "Are the Principles of *Sacra doctrina Per Se Nota?*" *The Thomist* 74, no. 3 (2010): 407–35.

Maurer, Armand A. *St. Thomas and Historicity.* Milwaukee: Marquette University Press, 1979.

Mausbach, Joseph. "Die Stellung des hl. Thomas von Aquin zu Maimonides in der Lehre von der Prophetie." *Theologische Quartalschrift* 81 (1899): 533–79.

McCarthy, Brian. "El modo del conocimiento profético y escriturístico según Santo Tomás de Aquino." *Scripta Theologica* 9 (1977): 425–84.

McNicholl, Ambrose. "On Judging." *The Thomist* 38, no. 4 (1974): 768–825.

Merx, Adalbert. *Die Prophetie des Joel und ihre Ausleger von den ältesten Zeiten bis zu den Reformatoren: Eine exegetisch-kritische und hermeneutisch-dogmengeschichtliche Studie.* Halle: Verlag der Buchhandlung des Waisenhauses, 1879.

Michelet, Thomas. *Sacra doctrina: Mystère et sacramentalité de la parole dans la Somme de théologie de S. Thomas d'Aquin.* Paris: Parole et Silence, 2019.

Moreland, Anna Bonta. *Muhammad Reconsidered. A Christian Perspective on Islamic Prophecy.* Notre Dame: University of Notre Dame Press, 2020.

Narcisse, Gilbert. *Les raisons de Dieu: Argument de convenance et esthétique théologique selon saint Thomas d'Aquin et Hans Urs von Balthasar.* Studia Friburgensia 83. Fribourg: Éditions universitaires, 1997.

Nichols, Aidan. *Balthasar for Thomists*. San Francisco: Ignatius Press, 2020.

O'Brien, T. C. "'Sacra doctrina' Revisited: The Context of Medieval Education." *The Thomist* 41, no. 4 (1977): 475–509.

Oliva, Adriano. *Les débuts de l'enseignement de Thomas d'Aquin et sa conception de la* sacra doctrina. Paris: Vrin, 2006.

———. "'*Doctrina*' et '*sacra doctrina*' chez Thomas d'Aquin." In *Vera doctrina: Zur Begriffsgeschichte der Lehre von Augustinus bis Descartes*, edited by P. Büttgen, R. Imbach, U. J. Schneider, and H. J. Selderhuis, 35–62. Wiesbaden: Harrassowitz, 2009.

Persson, Per Erik. *Sacra doctrina: Reason and Revelation in Aquinas*. Translated by Ross Mackenzie. Oxford: Basil Blackwell, 1970.

Pope, Stephen J., ed. *The Ethics of Aquinas*. Washington, DC: Georgetown University Press, 2002.

Preller, Victor. *Divine Science and the Science of God: A Reformulation of Thomas Aquinas*. Princeton, NJ: Princeton University Press, 1967.

Reeve, Pamela J. "The Metaphysics of Higher Cognitive States in Thomas Aquinas." In *Essays in Medieval Philosophy and Theology in Memory of Walter H. Principe, CSB: Fortresses and Launching Pads*, edited by James R. Ginther and Carl N. Still, 105–19. Aldershot: Ashgate, 2005.

Reeves, Marjorie. *The Influence of Prophecy in the Later Middle Ages: A Study in Joachimism*. Oxford: Oxford University Press, 1969.

Richard, Jean. "Le processus psychologique de la révélation prophétique selon saint Thomas d'Aquin." *Laval théologique et philosophique* 23, no. 1 (1967): 42–75.

Rodolfi, Anna. *Cognitio obumbrata: Lo statuto epistemologico della profezia nel secolo XIII*. Florence: SISMEL-Edizioni del Galluzzo, 2016.

Rogers, Paul M. "Pierre Benoit's 'Ecclesial Inspiration': A Thomistic Notion at the Heart of Twentieth-Century Debates on Biblical Inspiration." *The Thomist* 80, no. 4 (2016): 521–62.

———. "Prophecy and the Moral Life in Thomas Aquinas's *Commentary on 1 Corinthians*," in *Towards a Biblical Thomism: Thomas Aquinas and the Renewal of Biblical Theology*, edited by Piotr Roszak and Jörgen Vijgen, 197–217. Pamplona: Ediciones Universidad de Navarra, 2018.

Schlosser, Marianne. *Lucerna in caliginoso loco: Aspekte des Prophetie-Begriffes in der scholastischen Theologie*. Paderborn: Ferdinand Schöningh, 2000.

Seckler, Max. *Instinkt und Glaubenswille nach Thomas von Aquin*. Mainz: Matthias-Grünewald-Verlag, 1961.

———. *Le salut et l'histoire: Le pensée de saint Thomas d'Aquin sur la théologie de l'histoire*. Paris: Cerf, 1967. First published as *Das Heil in der Geschichte: Geschichtstheologisches Denken bei Thomas von Aquin*. Munich: Kösel, 1964.

Stiegman, Emero. "Charism and Institution in Aquinas." *The Thomist* 38, no. 4 (1974): 723–33.

Synave, Paul. "La causalité de l'intelligence humaine dans la révélation prophétique." *Revue des sciences philosophiques et théologiques* 8 (1914): 218–35.

——— and Pierre Benoit. *Saint Thomas d'Aquin: Somme théologique, la prophétie: 2a-2ae, Questions 171–178*. Éditions de la Revue des Jeunes. Paris: Desclée, 1947.

——— and Pierre Benoit. *Prophecy and Inspiration: A Commentary on the Summa Theologica II-II, Questions 171–178*. Translated by Avery R. Dulles and Thomas L. Sheridan. New York: Desclée, 1961.

Te Velde, Rudi. *Aquinas on God: The "Divine Science" of the* Summa theologiae. Farnham: Ashgate, 2006.

Torrell, Jean-Pierre. *Théorie de la prophétie et philosophie de la connaissance aux environs de 1230: La contribution d'Hugues de Saint-Cher (Ms. Douai 434, Question 481)*. Louvain: Spicilegium sacrum Lovaniense, 1977.

———. "Le traité de la prophétie de S. Thomas d'Aquin et la théologie de la Révélation." In Leo Elders, *La doctrine de la révélation divine de saint Thomas d'Aquin*, 171–95. Vatican City: Libreria Editrice Vaticana, 1990.

———. *Recherches sur la théorie de la prophétie au Moyen Âge, XIIe-XIVe siècles: Études et textes*. Fribourg: Éditions universitaires, 1992.

———. "Le savoir théologique chez Saint Thomas." *Revue Thomiste* 96, no. 3 (1996): 355–96.

———. *Recherches thomasiennes*. Paris: Vrin, 2000.

———. *Saint Thomas Aquinas*. Vol. 2, *Spiritual Master*. Translated by Robert Royal. Washington, DC: The Catholic University of America Press, 2003.

———. Introduction to *Somme théologique, la prophétie: 2a-2ae, Questions 171–178*, by Thomas Aquinas, 11*–133*. Paris: Cerf, 2005.

———. "Saint Thomas et l'histoire: État de la question et pistes de recherches." *Revue Thomiste* 105, no. 3 (2005): 355–409.

———. Introduction and notes to *Questions disputées sur la vérité, Question XII: La prophétie (De prophetia)*, by Thomas Aquinas, 1–18, 191–240. Paris: Vrin, 2006.

———. *Nouvelles recherches thomasiennes*. Paris: Vrin, 2008.

———. "Charity as Friendship in St. Thomas Aquinas." In *Christ and Spirituality in St. Thomas Aquinas*, translated by Bernhard Blankenhorn, 45–64. Washington, DC: The Catholic University of America Press, 2011.

———. *Initiation à saint Thomas d'Aquin: Sa personne et son oeuvre*. New ed. Paris: Cerf, 2015.

———. *Saint Thomas d'Aquin: Maître spirituel (Initiation 2)*. New ed. Paris: Cerf, 2017.

———. *Saint Thomas Aquinas*. Vol. 1, *The Person and His Work*. Translated by Matthew K. Minerd and Robert Royal. 3rd ed. Washington, DC: The Catholic University of America Press, 2022.

Van Ackeren, Gerald F. *Sacra doctrina: The Subject of the First Question of the* Summa theologica *of St. Thomas Aquinas*. Rome: Catholic Book Agency, 1952.

Vawter, Bruce. *Biblical Inspiration*. Philadelphia: Westminster, 1972.

Von Balthasar, Hans Urs. *Explorations in Theology*. Vol. IV, *Spirit and Institution*. Translated by Edward T. Oakes. San Francisco: Ignatius Press, 1995.

———. *Thomas und die Charismatik: Thomas von Aquin, Kommentar zu Summa Theologica Quaestiones II-II 171–182, Besondere Gnadengaben und die zwei Wege menschlichen Lebens*. Freiburg: Johannes Verlag Einsiedeln, 1996. First published as vol. 23 of *Die Deutsche Thomas-Ausgabe*, edited by Heinrich M. Christmann. Graz: Anton Pustet, 1954. Citations refer to the Johannes Verlag edition.

Wahlberg, Mats. *Revelation as Testimony: A Philosophical-Theological Study*. Grand Rapids: William B. Eerdmans, 2014.

Walz, Angelus. "De genuino titulo *Summae theologiae*." *Angelicum* 18 (1941): 142–51.

Weinandy, Thomas G., Daniel A. Keating, and John P. Yocum, eds. *Aquinas on Scripture: An Introduction to his Biblical Commentaries*. London: T & T Clark, 2005.

Weisheipl, James A. "The Meaning of Sacred Doctrine in the *Summa theologiae* I, q. 1." *The Thomist* 38, no. 1 (1974): 49–80.

———. *Friar Thomas d'Aquino: His Life, Thought, and Works* (Oxford: Basil Blackwell, 1975).

White, Victor. "St. Thomas's Conception of Revelation." *Dominican Studies* 1 (1948): 1–34.

———. *Holy Teaching: The Idea of Theology According to St. Thomas Aquinas.* Aquinas Papers 33. London: Blackfriars, 1958.

Wilhelmsen, Frederick D. "The Concept of Existence and the Structure of Judgment: A Thomistic Paradox." *The Thomist* 41, no. 3 (1977): 317–49.

Zarb, Serafino M. "Le fonti agostiniane del trattato sulla profezia di S. Tommaso d'Aquino." *Angelicum* 15 (1938): 169–200.

Zerafa, Peter Paul. "The Limits of Biblical Inerrancy." *Angelicum* 39 (1962): 92–119.

Index